The American Counterfeit

The American Counterfeit

Authenticity and Identity
in American Literature and Culture

Mary McAleer Balkun

THE UNIVERSITY OF ALABAMA PRESS

Tuscaloosa

Typeface: Minion

∞

The paper on which this book is printed meets the minimum requirements of American
National Standard for Information Sciences-Permanence of Paper for Printed Library
Materials, ANSI Z39.48-1984.

Library of Congress Cataloging-in-Publication Data

Balkun, Mary McAleer.
The American counterfeit : authenticity and identity in American literature and culture /
Mary McAleer Balkun.
p. cm. — (Studies in American literary realism and naturalism)
Includes bibliographical references and index.
ISBN-13: 978-0-8173-1497-2 (cloth : alk. paper)
ISBN-10: 0-8173-1497-0 (cloth : alk. paper)
1. American literature—20th century—History and criticism. 2. Counterfeits and
counterfeiting in literature. 3. American literature—19th century—History and criticism.
4. Authenticity (Philosophy) in literature. 5. Impostors and imposture in literature.
6. Identity (Psychology) in literature. 7. Passing (Identity) in literature. 8. Self in literature.
I. Title. II. Series.
PS228.C68B35 2006
810.9′353—dc22

2005017750

For John,
who taught me the meaning of authenticity

In society, indeed, a genuine American never dreams of stepping across the inappreciable air-line which separates one class from another.
—Nathaniel Hawthorne, *The Blithedale Romance*

Contents

Acknowledgments

My first debt of gratitude goes to Frederick R. Karl. It was in his American literature doctoral seminar at New York University in 1989 where I first heard about the trope of "counterfeiting" (an image that appears in his study *American Fictions, 1940–1980*). I will remember him always for his generosity and encouragement. I also want to thank the members of the 1994–1995 dissertation study group at NYU organized by Cyrus Patell.

There is a host of people at Seton Hall University I need to thank: James Lindroth and Kate McCoy, my first academic mentors, who taught me how to think about literature; Chrys Grieco, who helped me take the first steps on this path by hiring me as a teaching assistant in the English department so many years ago; Martha Carpentier, friend and colleague, who spent the last four years pushing me in the most loving and collegial way to get the darned book done; John Wargacki, office mate and fellow Americanist, who listened to my rants and complaints without indulging in any of his own; Frank Korn of the classics department for his prayers and encouragement; and Kristina Dzwonczyk, research assistant extraordinaire. I would like to thank the University Research Council at Seton Hall, which awarded me a summer stipend in 1997 that allowed me to begin the first round of revisions.

My family—immediate, extended, and by marriage—has always supported my work, even when they didn't quite understand exactly what

I was doing or why. My parents, in particular, always encouraged me without judging or asking too many questions: Rosemary McAleer, who had the rare gift of making her children feel as if each was the favorite, and my father, Francis Patrick George Aloysius McAleer, who helped me realize that I come by my interest in lovable counterfeits quite honestly. They are gone but not forgotten.

I'd like to thank several people at the University of Alabama Press: both readers of the original manuscript, whose suggestions and comments helped make this a far better piece of scholarship than it otherwise would have been, and Dan Waterman, for seeing the potential in this manuscript and helping me realize it.

Angela Jane Weisl has been an inspiration to me, as both a friend and a scholar, since we first met as new hires at Seton Hall in 1995. I know with certainty that this book would not be here if not for her, and her contributions are obvious throughout. She provided the stick and the carrot, as well as many cups of tea.

Finally, I would like to thank my husband, John A. Balkun. He has patiently tolerated the many hours involved in teaching and scholarship, the infringements on personal time, the piles of books everywhere. More than that, however, he has given me the room to grow as a person and as a scholar. His generosity of spirit and his loving support have made everything possible.

A previous version of the Whitman chapter appeared as "Whitman's *Specimen Days* and the Culture of Authenticity" in the *Walt Whitman Quarterly Review* 17.2 (Fall 1999): 15–24.

The American Counterfeit

The Real, the Self, and Commodity Culture, 1880–1930

"[A]rtificial," like "artefact," and "artful," a characteristic of the spurious, does indeed contain the word "art."

—Susan M. Pearce, *On Collecting*

Published in 1890, Henry James's "The Real Thing" is in many ways a fable for the turn of the twentieth century. It is a tale that addresses issues of class status, consumer culture, the commoditization of people, the re-creation of the self and, as the title suggests, the genuine as opposed to the fake.[1] Major and Mrs. Monarch, "a gentleman" and "a lady" who find themselves in financial difficulty, appear in the studio of the narrator/artist and offer themselves as models for his work. The artist's stock-in-trade is book illustrations, and at first he is intrigued by the idea of having actual members of the social elite posing for illustrations depicting this very type. However, it soon becomes apparent that the Monarchs are completely unsuited to the work, not because they are poseurs but precisely because they *are* "the real thing" (52). Their good birth and breeding are genuine, but this also makes them absolutely incapable of being anything other than what they are. Ironically, it is actual models, such as Miss Churm and Oronte, "a freckled cockney" and "a scrap of a lazzarone," respectively (48, 56), elastic and able to assume various guises, who enable the artist to produce authentic work, at least for the purposes of art. As the narrator observes, the "lesson" here is that "in the *deceptive* atmosphere of art even the highest respectability may fail of being plastic" (63; my emphasis). But questions about the real extend beyond the boundaries of art in this text; the work of art—the thing produced for consumption—is merely an analogue for the authentic self, that elusive figment of the modern imagination.

The Monarchs function under the assumption that the real thing must be somehow superior to the imitation, a judgment fundamental to any discussion of authenticity. Part of their certainty is class based; they cannot believe that their "type" could be represented by anything other than an actual member of the elite. Anything else would subvert their perceived exceptionalism. Class status as a feature of authenticity is addressed even more directly by the narrator's friend Jack Hawley, who describes the Monarchs as "a compendium of everything he most objected to in the social system of his country. Such people as that, all convention and patent-leather, with ejaculations that stopped conversation, had no business in a studio. A studio was a place to learn to see, and how could you see through a pair of feather-beds?" (61). In other words, the authentic—and by extension the inauthentic—is associated with the visual (which is also privileged in this period, as evidenced in the increasing popularity of media such as photography); it can be seen and identified by specific markings, traits, and characteristics.

Even the setting of the story—the art studio, inhabited by an artist who does commercial work to support himself—provides a fitting backdrop for an analysis of the authentic and inauthentic. The artist's studio in late-nineteenth-century America was infamous for being "opulently adorned" and filled with objects and "artifacts" that were intended to suggest "exotic wanderings" (Burns 209). Sarah Burns compares a studio such as William Merritt Chase's, which was renowned for the number of objects it contained and its "atmosphere," to "the contemporary department store, where merchants learned to concoct an atmosphere of rich, evocative displays to tempt the consumer" (210). While the artist in James's story does not seem to be working in such an ornately decorated environment, the association would have already existed in the reader's mind, as would the parallels between the work of art and the commodity that Burns explores and that the commercial artist himself embodied. In addition, with the new potential for the reproduction of artworks, originality, or "authenticity," became an issue of central importance in this period. The artist in James's story does not create copies himself, but the threat of the facsimile always hovers in the background.

In a consumer culture, a copy can itself become a valued commodity, one that can have a direct impact on the value of the original. Not only can the copy call the provenance of the original into question but it can also redirect capital away from the original when people are able to purchase a facsimile. This view of the art object as "product," as a consumable good with a relative value in the market, as well as the place of authenticity in determining the value of the work of art, is borne out by the artist in James's story, who understands that his illustrations are his "pot boilers," distinct from the portraits with which he hopes to win fame. The portraits are his "real art" while the illustrations are shams, albeit well-paying ones, and he is careful to maintain that distinction. His treatment of his illustration work as a profession is evident in his acknowledged "detestation of the amateur" (46), a distinction that also becomes important at the end of the nineteenth century and is evidenced in the obsession with professional licenses, institutional degrees, and family trees. Credentials can be used to validate one's worth, either professionally or socially.

Yet it is not just the work of art that is subject to commoditization. A related concern was that people would themselves become machines. This is certainly borne out in the statement made by Josiah Wedgewood in a letter to a friend about the inconsistencies of production, in which he wrote that he "was 'preparing to make such *Machines* of the *Men* as cannot Err'" (Forty 33).[2] In attempting to re-create themselves as artist models (an interesting term in this context, and one that also suggests the world of things), the Monarchs are consistently associated with objects and, simultaneously, their "genuine" status is called into question. Mrs. Monarch is described as "singularly like a bad illustration" (42), and we learn that as a young woman she was known as "the Beautiful Statue" (44). Similarly, Major Monarch is figured as a mannequin (the narrator decides that a new club would do well to pay the major to stand in a window). The two are described as perfect for advertising (43), a field that becomes closely associated with fraud and the inauthentic in the twentieth century. Continuing the association of persons with objects, the Monarchs are expected to become implements of a sort: having spent a lifetime supplying entertainment and "form" for their friends and acquaintances in return for hospitality (45), they must now become "useful." It is Major Monarch's hope that the narrator might "make something" of them (41), as if they were raw material to be molded into a suitable form (the relationship between content and form being another criterion for authenticity), while Mrs. Monarch's declaration, "Oh, we *never* get tired!" (44), takes the allusion to its most extreme, equating the couple with machinery.

One by-product of the machine age, and the concurrent multiplication of factories and the cities that grew up around them, was the increasing inability to identify those with whom one lived and worked, a concern that had an ever-increasing hold on the late-nineteenth/early-twentieth-century psyche. Young and old flocked to the new industrial centers in ever-greater numbers in order to find work and to escape from what was perceived as the limited opportunities for advancement in rural areas. This was in addition to the vast waves of immigration that left their mark on the composition of urban areas: 10 million immigrants arrived between the Civil War and 1890, and an additional 15 million arrived between 1890 and 1914 (Johnson, *History of the American People* 513–14). One result was the realization that one was surrounded by strangers, perhaps for the first time. No longer surrounded by those who shared a common place and history nor supported by a network of neighbors who could assist them in determining the character of the arriviste, residents of the city were vulnerable to whatever story a stranger chose to tell them.

In one of the pivotal statements in the tale, the narrator/artist says of the Monarchs that "somehow with all their perfections I didn't easily believe in them" (45). The speaker's inability to believe in the Monarchs goes beyond doubting their function as models; it also reverses the focus of the usual questions about personal authenticity, turning it on those who typically ask such questions. It is not clear to the narrator initially just who the Monarchs are, besides being "a gentleman" and "a lady." While the quotation marks that appear around these words in the story are intended to indicate spoken words, they also help to set the phrases apart in a potentially ironic way, raising the first doubt about the couple's authenticity. From their initial appearance the Monarchs become objects of the "speculative" gaze, to use the word in two of its forms: they are objects for the art market as well as a source of doubt. The narrator tries unsuccessfully to "take them in," wondering who they are, what they want, whether they are husband and wife, and whether they are celebrities (39). His confusion is not unwarranted.

The Monarchs claim that they must "*do* something," but "their appurtenances [are] all of the freshest" (41). They have created a life built on denial, and any of the "facts" we learn about them—besides their recent financial setback—comes from the narrator's imagination as he tries to piece together a story for them. While they presumably represent the real thing, they have no experience of reality and the real world, having led sheltered and essentially unreal lives up to this point. Their surname, with its lofty reference to royalty, captures the incongruity of their position. Even as they ask for work, they are concerned that others might learn the truth, so they ask to be used "for the figure" (42), not the face. Such caution is unnecessary with Mrs. Monarch at least, who "[lends] herself especially to positions in which the face [is] somewhat averted or blurred; she abound[s] in ladylike back views and *profils perdus*" (53). Her ability to efface herself, while always giving the impression of remaining what she is, a lady, suggests that there are versions of reality that undermine any attempt to identify the real thing.

This situation is further complicated by Mrs. Monarch's antithesis, Miss Churm, who is a model with a "curious and inexplicable talent for imitation" (53). Although Miss Churm does not have the authenticity of class status, she is the "real thing" by virtue of the mimetic skill that allows her to "represent everything, from a fine lady to a shepherdess" (48). Ironically, her ability to adopt personae, even if only temporarily, is a sign of the authenticity—as a model at least—that the Monarchs lack. Yet James makes clear that the situation is even more complex. As Clifton Fadiman observes in "A Note on 'The Real Thing,'" Miss Churm (and Oronte, a newcomer who eventually displaces Major Monarch) has not only vitality but also an "understanding, crude as it may be, of the sinuous, protean, evasive nature of human character" (217). The stability that one might typically value as a quality of authenticity becomes a detriment when the real thing cannot become anything other than what it is. Thus, there are several related paradoxes in the story: first, the ostensibly real thing may not be "authentic" and the fake may have an authenticity of its own; next, what appears genuine on the surface may be a careful construction; and finally, what appears to be performance or obfuscation may in fact reveal something genuine. The narrator's distinction between the "ideal thing" and the real one (64), the former being preferable, captures a subtlety that the Monarchs are unable to appreciate.

The central issue in the James story is the validity of the real or authentic as an organizing category. Since the real has so much to do with context—what is authentic in one situation may be a sham in another—"realness" becomes a matter of perception rather than a definitive attribute. In "The Work of Art in the Age of Mechanical Reproduction," Walter Benjamin suggests as much when he associates the "authenticity" of a work of art with its place in time and space: only the original object, not the copy, has "its unique existence at the place where it happens to be" (220). He continues, "The authenticity of a thing is the essence of all that is transmissible from its beginning, ranging from its substantive duration to its testimony to the history which it has experienced" (221). James's story contains an example of this dynamic at work when the artist describes Mrs. Monarch as "always a lady, certainly, and into the bargain . . . always the same lady. She was the real thing, but always the same thing" (52). What should have been an authenticity born of consistency results instead in a completely inauthentic likeness; the artist always ends up depicting Mrs. Monarch as if she were seven feet tall. There is a semantic issue at the heart of both the story and the discourse of authenticity; "real" and "authentic" are not necessarily synonymous terms, although they are often used interchangeably. The word "authentic" always begs the question "to and for whom?" in ways the word "real" does not seem to.

James's tale is usually read as an indication of his preference for the work of art and the aesthetic over the real, with the narrator as a representation of the author himself. However, instead of providing answers, "The Real Thing" posits a series of related questions: What *is* the real thing? In relation to what is it real? What is the relationship between the real and the self? What is the relationship between the self and commodity culture? What happens when the self is treated as a thing to be "produced," as an object for consumption? James then proceeds to explore these matters (and he does so in longer works as well, such as *The Golden Bowl*), indicating his interest in an issue that was gaining increasing attention when the story was written: the matter of authenticity, whether in the work of art or the individual, and the connections between authenticity and material culture.

I have posed these same questions of five other texts produced between 1880 and 1930 (the previous year, 1929, having marked the beginning of a new era in American commodity culture): *Specimen Days and Collect* by Walt Whitman, *Adventures of Huckleberry Finn* by Mark Twain, *The House of Mirth* by Edith Wharton, *Passing* by Nella Larsen, and *The Great Gatsby* by F. Scott Fitzgerald. In each case I am interested in seeing how the text addresses these issues, how it reflects a specific type of engagement with material culture and the quest for the authentic, and how this might enrich an understanding of the way contemporary culture informed each. The paradoxes that inevitably arise from any attempt to use authenticity as an organizing category are a recurring feature in these texts.

A number of studies have examined the national obsession with authenticity and its opposite, the fake or "counterfeit," in the late nineteenth and early twentieth centuries, including Miles Orvell's *The Real Thing*, which documents the aesthetic shift from a focus on imitation in the nineteenth century to a desire for the authentic or real in the twentieth, and *Fables of Abundance* by Jackson Lears, which outlines several fields in the search for authenticity: the search for "authentic expression" in the arts (346); "[t]he quest for personal authenticity" that became a touchstone in advertising (347), and the growing tendency to blame advertising for the rise of inauthenticity (349). He identifies James (along with Edith Wharton) as a writer whose work "represent[s] a key intervention in Anglo-American thought about things: a break from the endless opposition of authenticity and artifice, and toward a subtler understanding of how material goods connect people with the world and each other" (387).

A "counterfeit" was not always perceived negatively. In fact, a quick scan of definitions in the *Oxford English Dictionary* (*OED*) shows a gradually shifting sense, from something simply "fashioned, wrought" to something "[r]epresented by a picture or image" to the current sense of the word: "Forged, not genuine, spurious." I use the word quite intentionally throughout this study because it has connotations that the word "impostor" does not. "Counterfeiting" is associated with making and with reproduction, associations that are consistent with a study that looks at the intersection of people and material culture. "Imposture" suggests becoming someone else, while the characters I will be examining are often convinced that the version they have created is the "true" self. In addition, "counterfeit" has associations with monetary systems and consumption, with faith, with the theater, and with art. On the one hand it implies deception and trickery, but on the other it can mean to "resemble, be like (*without* implying deceit)" (*OED*; my emphasis).

What emerges in this period is a widespread discourse of authenticity, part of which was anxiety over the authenticity of objects: the authentic artwork, the authentic artifact, the authentic photograph, the authentic signature, the authentic heirloom. What developed as a result was a language of objects—a way of talking about "things"—that was also then used to describe the created self. This is especially problematic when the emphasis is on the possibility for re-creation/refashioning of the self, as it has been in America since the first settlers arrived. And certainly objects have always been understood, at least in part, in terms of their relation to people, whether symbolically, metaphorically, or literally, but the rise of market capitalism and the subsequent obsession with "things" marked a new relationship between the self and the object world. Yet little if any attention has been given to the question of what happens when the self itself becomes the made (or remade) object, when the self is the thing created for a specific function/purpose. Considered from this perspective, the language of objects can indeed become the language of the self; the traits and properties associated with objects can suddenly become a way to consider the self, especially in relation to other selves that may not be as immediately recognized or acknowledged as constructions. The invented self becomes an object for trade, for collection, and for consumption. It can also provide a standard for the authentic, a purpose "fakes" often serve in other arenas, such as art and archaeology.

This is the basis for the "culture of authenticity" that emerged at the end of the nineteenth century. As explained by the contemporary philosopher Charles Taylor, "authenticity" refers to the philosophical concern with individual self-realization that is typically associated with existentialism. In many ways this philosophical movement—albeit not American in origin—was a result of the same concerns that fascinated and horrified Americans at the time. Existentialism was a response to several nineteenth-century conditions, including the revolutions in science, the shifting attitudes toward organized religion, and what H. J. Blackham describes as "the situation of the person lost in the masses of a progressive society, one among many, isolated and organized" (2). It is a philosophy concerned with reconciling the inner self and the self presented to the world, with a return to the real or essential. In another vein, Marshall Berman defines "the politics of authenticity" as "a dream of an ideal community in which individuality will not be subsumed and sacrificed, but fully developed and expressed." He argues that this "dream" is both modern—because "it presupposes the sort of fluid, highly mobile urban society, and the sort of dynamic, expansive economy, which we experience as distinctively modern"—and "old," because "it has been a leitmotif in Western culture since early in the eighteenth century, when men began to feel modernization as an irreversible historical force, and to think systematically about its human potentialities" (ix).

However, while authenticity has long been associated with the quest for the genuine self (Sartre's concept of "bad faith" comes to mind), the word's provenance, as Lionel Trilling reminds us in *Sincerity and Authenticity*, is the museum (94). Thus, "authenticity" is a way to assess objects as well as persons. The place where the two intersect—where one can speak of the personification of objects and the objectification of persons—is in the realm of material culture, which includes museums (such as the personal natural history museum Whitman creates in *Specimen Days*) but also department store windows, catalogues, world's fairs and expositions, private collections, and even rubbish. Developments in the production of consumer goods, especially the ability to produce and reproduce objects quickly and exactly, were central to concerns about the real and the fake. Yet anxiety about what Orvell calls "the real thing" extended far beyond objects made on the assembly line. The world of art was especially vulnerable, whether the subject was literature, photography, the cinema, the theater, or the renewed popularity of older forms, such as the tableau vivant and trompe l'oeil. The purpose of latter, as Walter Benn Michaels observes, was "to conceal itself as representation" (161), a description that could apply to many "counterfeits." The quest for truth was often seen as the province of the arts in the latter half of the nineteenth century. Paintings, photographs, and literature were a means to the essence of things, but they also pointed to the illusory nature of existence. However, criticism of certain middle-class art forms, particularly a technique like chromolithography, by which works of art could be re-created, suggests the class biases inherent in these discussions of the authentic, especially in art.[3] The connection between class status and culture—which is also a prominent feature of James's story "The Real Thing"—can also be seen in the "antique worship" that developed between 1875 and 1894 as well as the creation of organizations such as the Sons of the Revolution, the Daughters of the American Revolution, and the Colonial Dames of America (Furnas 604).[4]

These issues—the concern for authenticity, the distaste for copies, the unease about shifting class boundaries, the focus on objects as indicators of social change, the anxiety over mass production—converge in the rise of museum culture at the turn of the century. In *Museums and American Intellectual Life, 1876–1926*, Steven Conn points out that museums were especially characteristic of this period, one in which the desire for "order and rationality" figured so prominently (9), while Alan Wallach argues: "The history of the art museum in the United States in the late nineteenth century [is] intertwined with the peculiar histories of urban elites, the rise and fall of different groups within them, and their efforts to achieve cultural hegemony at the local level" (115). Authenticity is at the very heart of the museum enterprise. Not only do museums house the artifacts, the evidence, of a nation's cultural history but they are also valid only insofar as the artifacts themselves are genuine.[5] What museums provide is "a socially agreed-upon reality that exists only as long as confidence in the voice of the exhibition holds" (Crew and Sims 162–63). They manufacture reality, depending for this upon the objects they contain and the context in which they are displayed. Like photographs, museum installations were valued for a verisimilitude that was not always reasonable or justified. However, a museum filled with forgeries is no longer a museum in the classic sense; it is a cabinet of curiosities. Museums are of necessity vigilant about the fake, the reproduction; after all, the identification of a forgery in the mix immediately undermines the validity of the institution, which is to serve as a purveyor of truth and knowledge. As Susan M. Pearce argues, however, faking may be "a subversive activity" but it is only possible because of "the structure of expectations which underpins" both the authenticators and the fakers engaged in the museum enterprise. What she is describing is a complementary situation, one in which the fake and the original play off one another and exist as "the right and left hand sides of the same system" (*Museums, Objects, and Collections* 237). In other words, the fake cannot exist without the original, and the original would not need to declare its status as such without the possibility of the fake.

Museums celebrate the one-of-a-kind or rare as well as the expert who authenticates them, but Trilling's description of the museum—a place "where persons expert in such matters test whether objects of art are what they appear to be or are claimed to be, and therefore worth the price that is asked for them—or, if this has already been paid, worth the admiration they are being given" (93)—raises the specter of consumer culture writ large. Pearce has written about these connections, acknowledging that the simultaneous rise of museum culture and capitalism is far from coincidental: "The hour brought forth the institution, an institution which, most appropriately, concentrated upon objects, physical specimens, wealth and treasure in an age which, increasingly as the Industrial Revolution gathered power, saw its social relations in these terms" (*Museums, Objects, and Collections* 238).[6] This intersection of exceptional objects and consumer culture is also apparent in the more familiar version of the museum, the personal collection.

Collecting emerged at the turn of the twentieth century as a pastime for children and adults alike and continued to grow almost exponentially throughout the century. Whether it took the form of museums, the vast collections of art and objects assembled by giants of industry such as J. P. Morgan and William Randolph Hearst (which often became the basis for museum collections), or the assemblages of ordinary objects such as postcards that were available to the middle class, collecting became a near obsession, one more symptom of the growing consumer culture. Russell W. Belk observes, "At the start of the twentieth century while robber barons like J. P. Morgan were assembling their collections of European paintings and decorative arts, American children were avid collectors of more humble objects," and this trend seemed only to intensify as the century progressed (*Collecting in a Consumer Society* 54). Among the less well-to-do, collecting was a way to imitate the behaviors of the wealthy, a form of pecuniary emulation in which picture post-

cards were the equivalent of oil paintings and ceramic dogs the equivalent of Ming vases. In *Victorian American: Transformations in Everyday
Life, 1876–1915*, Thomas J. Schlereth describes several varieties of middle-
class collecting at the turn of the century. Trading cards bearing pictures of "scantily clad women, baseball players, presidents, and prize-
fighters," used as promotional devices for products such as cigarettes,
were collected and traded (48), as were postcards. Manufacturers encouraged the collecting of the latter by releasing postcards in numbered
series and selling albums to store collections (Schlereth 181). Stereo-
graphs, in which two separate images seen simultaneously with the use
of a stereopticon created a three-dimensional image, were hugely popular into the 1930s.[7] What Schlereth attributes to the middle-class desire
to accumulate (197) is one result of a culture that emphasizes continual
consumption rather than consumption by necessity.

As mentioned above, while it is within the realm of material culture
that people and objects come together, the great fear has always been
that people would themselves become objects. In a fascinating essay on
the process of commoditization, Igor Kopytoff discusses the Western
tendency to place people and objects at different ends of the spectrum,
associating the self with such qualities as "individuation and singularization" while still commoditizing them. What he is referring to specifically here is the practice of slavery, in which persons are treated as objects. While Kopytoff is primarily interested in the "moral economy that
stands behind the objective economy" (64), his theories about objects
and persons are also applicable to the activity engaged in by the self-
made/newly made man or woman (what I will refer to throughout this
study as the "American counterfeit"): the commoditization of the self
through the process of self-creation. The construction of a new self (or
the refusal to accept the self imposed by society) is akin to the creation
of an object, with all that term implies (the self can now be sold, traded,
owned, copied, and even collected).[8] The repeated reaction to the self-
as-product, especially in literature, is aversion, particularly because such
commoditization is antithetical to the Western, Enlightenment emphasis on the individual. The Western binary system of valuation, which,
ironically, also determines which objects end up in museums and which
do not, includes such oppositions as us/them, present/past, authentic/
nonauthentic, art/nonart, real/fake, and cultured/uncultured (Pearce,

On Collecting 286).[9] Interestingly, these binaries can also be used to evaluate the authentic self, and they run as a subtext throughout this study; for example, the us/them comparison is essential to my analysis of *Huck Finn*, while the opposition of cultured/uncultured is one of the bases for authentication in *The Great Gatsby*.

The interest in the real or authentic has a corresponding impulse: the desire to identify those who attempt to create a new self and pass themselves off as genuine. The so-called unmasking trend, which is associated with both psychology and philosophy at the end of the nineteenth century, reflects the modern world's sense that deception—whether of oneself or others (or both)—was the dominant mode of existence.[10] Similarly, "forgery" as it is understood today did not exist as a category in the art world until the late nineteenth century when it was suddenly perceived "as a profound attack upon the cultural system itself"; prior to that the copy had an intrinsic value of its own (Baudrillard, *For a Critique* 103–6). The same can be said of the person who re-creates the self, since the new identity is in almost every case a direct imitation of something considered "real" within a specific context: a member of the social elite, a white person, a female. The discourse of authenticity—bisecting as it does the world of material culture—is an essential element in the construction of the American counterfeit. While not new, and not even specific to literature produced in the late-nineteenth and early-twentieth centuries, the counterfeit trope and figure emerge in their modern incarnations in the years after the Civil War. Previous studies of American literature have identified the confidence man/woman, the painted woman, and the trickster as recurring forms of the impostor, ones that emerged from within specific contexts and responded to particular needs. These analyses often attempt to fit a rather disparate group of characters into a narrow framework or set such wide parameters that almost any character fits the model, while ignoring other types of imposture completely and failing to acknowledge the complex issues that the impostor raises in a consumer culture.[11]

In addition, while early studies engaged in some historicization—Gary Lindberg's *The Confidence Man in American Literature* is a case in point—recent critical developments have led to a greater awareness of the ways in which texts are constructed by and participate in the production of their cultural and historical moment. Studies such as *The*

Ethnography of Manners by Nancy Bentley and *The Social Construction of American Realism* by Amy Kaplan are models for my own work for the way they engage in a culturally informed reading of literary and other texts. In fact, this type of analysis bears out my argument that the afore-mentioned figures—the confidence man/woman, the painted woman, the trickster—are actually varieties of the counterfeit rather than an-tagonistic types. By considering the created self as an object with a spe-cific function within consumer culture, like the work of art in a mu-seum or collection or the object in a department store, I bring into play the complex issues raised by the counterfeit in a society obsessed with authenticity. The resulting analyses provide a new way to understand some familiar character types as well as their relationship to American culture and ideology in the decades before and after the turn of the cen-tury. Counterfeiting actually reveals the *lack* of fluidity in the bound-aries, quite the opposite of Lindberg's claim that the space between "our stated ethics and our tolerated practices" (4)—what I prefer to call "ide-ology and practice"—is "fluid" (9). The counterfeiting trope also reveals the discrepancies between ideology and practice, providing a way to in-terrogate the many tensions in American culture in the period in which the texts I will be discussing first appeared: race issues, gender issues, sexual issues, and class issues as well as the impact of social and cultural changes. The appearance of the counterfeit (or counterfeits) in a text serves as a locus for exploring some of the energies and anxieties that emerged at the turn of the twentieth century.

American culture is heavily invested in issues of identity, in the real vs. the false, in the myth of the new beginning. The counterfeit figure tests the limits of these categories; its subversion takes the form of what Alan Sinfield calls the "entrapment model." According to this model, attempts to challenge any prevailing ideological system only serve to maintain that system's locus of power, perhaps entrenching its power structures even more deeply than before. Sinfield argues that the entrap-ment model "functions as a barrier to dissidence, as a means for the ideology in power to sustain its oppressive constructions of class, race, gender, and sexuality" (629). But while dissidence may be co-opted by existing power structures, it gains a voice: "In the entrapment model, any move seems to have been anticipated by the power system—you only dig yourself in deeper. . . . Dissidence plays into the hands of containment" (629).[12] As a subversive figure, the counterfeit provided the writers I discuss—and readers—with one way to understand the many contradictions between American ideology and practice.

In chapter 2, "Whitman's Natural History: *Specimen Days* and the Culture of Authenticity," I argue that Whitman's autobiographical narrative, reflecting his interest in museums, is itself modeled on the natural history museum with its collections of specimens carefully organized, classified, and labeled. As many scholars have observed, the Victorians were the great museum builders, and some of the finest American museums were founded in the last decades of the nineteenth century and the early years of the twentieth.[13] Whitman, deeply immersed in the culture of his day, engages issues of authenticity, identity, and commoditization and uses a model that allows him to explore the relationship between objects, knowledge, and the authenticity of that knowledge.

Like Whitman, Twain was also engrossed in the events of his day, but particularly in commerce and production. In chapter 3, "'I couldn't see no profit in it': Discourses of Commoditization and Authenticity in *Adventures of Huckleberry Finn*," I consider the way Twain invokes the twin discourses of commoditization and authenticity to examine the potential commoditization of the self, especially through Huck's repeated acts of self-creation.

In chapter 4, "Connoisseurs and Counterfeits: Edith Wharton's *The House of Mirth*," I consider Lily Bart's trajectory through the novel as she passes from valuable object on the marriage market to waste product. Wharton is responding to various cultural forces, including sudden shifts in the composition of the social elite, the disappearance of Old New York, and the Victorian obsession with things of all kinds. These are also the subtext in *The Decoration of Houses,* and I bring those two texts into conversation with one another. (Wharton's text also intersects at several points with *Adventures of Huckleberry Finn.* Surely the Grangerford home is the antithesis of everything Wharton argues for in *The Decoration of Houses.* Also, the idea of a person as "trash" resonates with Jim's criticism of Huck at a key point in that novel.)

Commoditization of the self, the construction of an alternative identity, and the impact of material culture on the self also come together in chapter 5, "Dressing to Kill: Desire, Race, and Authenticity in Nella Larsen's *Passing*." Larsen's text focuses on the role of female desire within commodity culture and the ways this is connected to the construction of race. She engages another area of commodity culture in order to do this: the world of fashion, both fashionable clothing and the fashionable world of the black bourgeoisie. Clothing—especially when only certain people have access to goods—can be a way to construct whiteness for the passing woman. Larsen considers the results of passing, certainly, but she also examines the ways desire and commodity culture influence constructions of and attitudes toward race.

Finally, in chapter 6, "A World of Wonders: Collecting and the Authentic Self in *The Great Gatsby*," I build on previous scholarship that has argued for the influence of early texts such as Columbus's *Journals* on Fitzgerald and discuss the novel as a prose version of the "Cabinet of Wonders" so popular in the sixteenth and seventeenth centuries. *The Great Gatsby* is not only a novel about wonder but also about collecting, with all that implies about authentication, desire, and what that means for the possible reification of the self.

There are certainly any number of other texts I might have chosen to explore these issues: questions about authenticity and "fakes" are raised in Hawthorne's *The Marble Faun* and James's *The American*,[14] while Gilbert Osmond and Ned Rosier in James's *The Portrait of a Lady* are also collectors. There are a number of passing narratives that predate Larsen's and also recognize the social construction of race (Twain's *Pudd'nhead Wilson*, for example), while in "The Wife of His Youth" Charles Chesnutt explores the dynamics of the black bourgeoisie long before Larsen. I chose these particular texts for a variety of reasons, although my first consideration was that the main character be an "impostor" of one kind or another. With this as my starting point, I then looked for texts that approached—and allowed me to approach—material culture (objects and their relationship to the self) from various perspectives. I also wanted to see how some of these ideas played out over the course of time and in different forms. These are primarily novels of the East, which is not surprising given that industrialism—the production of things—was centered in that region, but they represent a variety of genres and literary movements (autobiography, regionalism, realism, passing narrative). Finally, I chose texts I love to read and teach, and which have remained (or become, in Larsen's case) popular in the classroom and with scholars.

In the final irony, the counterfeit turns out to be the standard by which authenticity is determined, the embodiment of American ideology, which is itself marked by contradiction (as in the simultaneous advocacy of liberty, equality, and slavery, to name one example). With these characters, what seems on the surface to be fake or inauthentic can actually have a kind of integrity. A by-product of consumerism at its best and worst, the counterfeit has learned how to package and sell the self, but in the shadows are the dangers associated with a manufactured identity. However, if authentic selfhood is about what is inside rather than outside, about essences rather than surfaces, then the seeming counterfeit can indeed be the one thing (or self) that is truly authentic.

By the conclusion of James's "The Real Thing," the Monarchs have attempted a complete abdication of their original identities, re-creating themselves as servants and offering to "do for" the narrator. However, the reality of having the Monarchs emptying his "slops" clashes with the other reality of their class status. The two realities cannot coexist simultaneously because they create an intolerable tension, one that the narrator ultimately resolves by going along with the pretense for one week before sending the couple away. Forced to recognize the futility of their venture (and after being paid "a sum of money"), the Monarchs simply vanish, leaving nothing more than a memory in their wake. Yet, like a play or any other spectacle, they are a memory for which the narrator is "content to have paid the price" (65). The Monarchs may have indeed been "the real thing"—the narrator consistently grants them that much—but even they must eventually acknowledge "the perverse and cruel law in virtue of which the real thing [can] be so much less precious than the unreal" (64). In a world where "models" are authentic, the real thing can only be a sham.

2

Whitman's Natural History

Specimen Days and the Culture of Authenticity

> In collecting nature, American naturalists collected themselves, either
> through the physical objects they accumulated in their gardens or
> museums or through the words or images they created to reflect on
> what they and others had collected: drawings or paintings, letters, diary
> notes, travel accounts, formal essays, and autobiographies.
> —Christophe Irmscher, *The Poetics of Natural History*

In a brief section of *Specimen Days and Collect* (1892) titled "Patent-Office Hospital," Walt Whitman feels compelled to describe the "fascinating sight" of a temporary hospital for the wounded set up in the patent office in Washington, D.C., during the tumultuous days of the Civil War. The passage would be remarkable for Whitman's vivid description alone, the way he captures not only the incongruity of the spectacle but also its underlying humanity, but what is most striking about this episode is the way the soldiers, as well as the doctors and nurses tending them, have become one with the exhibitions that are typically the main feature of the patent office. The three apartments now seem almost specifically intended for the "sick, badly wounded and dying soldiers" they contain, an appropriate setting for the poignant and terrible tableaux showcasing the consequences of war. The patients lie between glass cases "crowded with models in miniature of every kind of utensil, machine or invention, it ever enter'd into the mind of man to conceive" (717), and the eerie juxtaposition of soldiers and miniature machines is a reminder that inventions of a different and more lethal sort have brought the men here. More significantly, the scene suggests the commoditization of persons in wartime, the way men become cogs in a larger machine not of their own making.

Whitman's references to the lighting, the architectural features ("the gallery above, and the marble pavement under foot" [718], the "forms" that are the soldiers (717), the occasional "glassy eye" and the reference to everything he describes as "sights" (718) are strongly reminiscent of the discourse of the museum or the gallery, where the focus is on the display and the artifact, on material objects as representatives of our ephemeral existence, positioned for observation and reflection. His language also captures the fleeting nature of this experience and, by extension, of all experience. Even more than those sections in which Whitman describes "real" hospital scenes, the patent office episode depicts the cruel ironies of the war and the ways it pervaded every facet of life, even the "noblest of Washington buildings" (717). However, this scene—with the museological quality of its imagery and language—also suggests a new way of thinking about *Specimen Days,* one that aligns the text with the rise of museum culture and the concurrent discourse about authenticity (which has very specific ramifications for the museum enterprise) in the latter part of the nineteenth century. The questions Whitman raises in this passage (and throughout the text), about the nature of the world, the connection between the self and the landscape, and the relationship between the self and objects, were also being raised by museums, especially after the Civil War when Whitman's text was itself being constructed. With its many short segments, its collections of specimens all carefully organized, classified, and labeled, its emphasis on objects as a source of truth, and geared as it is toward the production of history and knowledge, *Specimen Days* is Walt Whitman's prose version of the natural history museum.

Although not a materialist in the sense of needing to own things himself, Whitman was fascinated with objects, as evidenced by the catalogues that fill his poetry, his habit of furnishing his poems and prose works with the ephemera of everyday life (books, articles of clothing, razors, furniture), and his declared interest in exhibits of all types, whether museums, world's fairs, or picture galleries. In the section of *Memoranda* titled "A World's Show," he describes the New York Exposition of 1853, the centerpiece of which was the New York Crystal Palace, a site he visited numerous times: "I went a long time (nearly a year)—days and nights—especially the latter—as it was finely lighted and had a very large and copious exhibition gallery of paintings (shown at best at night, I tho't)—hundreds of pictures from Europe, many master pieces—all an exhaustless study—and scattered thro' the building, sculptures, single figures or groups—among the rest, Thorwaldsen's *Apostles,* colossal in size—and very fine bronzes, pieces of plate from English silversmiths, and curios from everywhere abroad—with woods from all lands of the earth—all sorts of fabrics and products and handiwork from the workers of all nations" (1276).

He also reflects on this episode in "Song of the Exposition," using the occasion to forge connections between the Old World and the New but also privileging the exhibition as a way to give the old a new identity. In this poem the museum is figured as educational, as an antidote to war, and as the personification of the nation itself, representative of everything and everyone in it. In "Old Actors, Singers, Shows, &C, in New York," a later section of *Memoranda,* Whitman describes his intense interest in "[t]he great 'Egyptian Collection'" on Broadway:

> I got quite acquainted with Dr. Abbott, the proprietor—paid many visits there, and had long talks with him, in connection with my readings of many books and reports on Egypt—its antiquities, history, and how things and the scenes really look, and what the old relics stand for, as near as we can now get. . . . As I said, I went to the Egyptian Museum many many times; sometimes had it all to myself—delved at the formidable catalogue—and on several occasions had the invaluable personal talk, correction, illustration and guidance of Dr. A. himself. . . . One of the choice places of New York to me then was the 'Phrenological Cabinet' of Fowler and Wells, Nassau street near Beckman. Here were all the busts, examples, curios and books of that study obtainable. I went there often, and once for myself had a very elaborate and leisurely examination and 'chart of bumps' written out. (1290–91)

Further evidence of Whitman's fascination with exhibits and displays of objects can be found in the section of *Memoranda* titled "My Picture-Gallery," with its descriptions of "the tableaus of life, and here the groupings of death" (524). Finally, Whitman is recorded as having attended the Philadelphia Exposition in 1876: "Relaxing in a rented (60 cents an hour) rolling chair, pushed by a porter, Walt Whitman took in the fair site and its sights" (Schlereth 3). For Whitman, museums and exhibits were places where the past and the geographically distant could be made "present," where they could become knowable and therefore "real"; it was the same goal he had for his poetry: "I raise a voice for far superber themes for poets and for art / To exalt the present and the real" ("Song of the Exposition," section 7, 11.20–21).

Thus, it should come as no surprise that Whitman takes full advantage of the ironic possibilities inherent in the "setting" of the "Patent-Office Hospital" episode. His ever-observant eye captures the incongruity of the scene, but his description of the episode also contains a semantic tension that permeates the entire text. For example, in this particular section the tension is apparent in certain characteristics of the prose as Whitman struggles to both narrate and understand the authenticity of the experience. His use of the word "cases" is emblematic of this struggle. Used to refer to both the glass cabinets housing the original displays ("high and ponderous glass cases") and the soldiers who have become the new, if temporary, "displays" occupying the space ("many of them were very bad cases" [717]), the word conflates the men with the receptacles surrounding them. There is also a verb tense shift within the passage: from the past tense used to indicate historical authority/authenticity to the present tense used to indicate personal authority/authenticity. The passage then concludes with a parenthetical statement (the first part of which reads "the wounded have since been removed from there") that seems intended to provide both reportorial distance and a sense of closure; however, in case there is any doubt, the second part of the statement reinforces the fact that Whitman's primary concern is the men and not the objects ("it is now vacant again" [718]). For the original displays are certainly still in place; it is only the soldiers—the temporary exhibits—who have now vanished. The question of exactly where they have gone, and who (or what) has removed them, remains hanging in the air, adding to the uncertainty and pervasive sense of unreality that Whitman seems unable to dispel despite his best efforts.

As a result, while the stated purpose of *Specimen Days* is to capture the nature of an individual's lived experience, there is an ongoing tension between Whitman's attempt to achieve this and narrative inconsistencies that ultimately reveal his inability to do so. This is similar to the tension inherent in the project of museums, between the desire to recreate a historical moment or narrate a period in history and the realization that even the most supposedly accurate and faithful display can never be more than an artificial construct. The questions inherent in the museum enterprise are all related to authenticity: Are the objects real? Is the context in which they are displayed historically and/or culturally accurate? How does the movement of the viewer from exhibit to exhibit create a larger context that may alter meaning? In what ways do museum exhibits reaffirm privileged stories about the past rather than the actuality of the past (to the extent the latter is possible)? Museums are ways of ordering reality, but the question remains: whose reality? The very choice of what to include, identifying what is of value and what is not, begins a process that is complicated at every turn by uncertainty and subjectivity.[1]

Specimen Days is the structure or "museum" containing Whitman's "collection" of memoranda (his version of war memorabilia), ramblings, and jottings, bloodstains and all, now organized, classified, and labeled into a coherent whole. If the text is a type of collection, with Whitman as the curator, then the titles of both *Specimen Days* and its companion piece, *Collect,* take on interesting connotations. The regular use of words such as "case," "model," and "specimen" also exploit the vocabulary of the museum but refer to persons as well as objects. As did the builders of modern museums, Whitman, too, "strove for a rational, orderly, systematic ideal," "highlighted the representative and the ordinary," and "replaced displays of a world turned upside down with one in which everything had its place." The glass cases that "served as windows onto the world" in the museum (Conn 8) have their counterpart in the various segments of *Specimen Days.* It is helpful to place Whitman's fascination with museums in a broader historical and cultural context.

While Americans have always had a fondness for collecting and for museums in particular, natural history museums have always had a special place, beginning with Charles Wilson Peale's museum in Philadelphia in the late eighteenth century. This may well be because the study of natural history had the reputation, especially in the United States, of being a "democratic" science, one in which both professionals and amateurs could engage with equal energy and success.[2] Collecting "curiosities" soon became a national pastime, one that lasted well into the nineteenth century. The roster of the Academy of Natural Sciences, established in Philadelphia in 1812, reflected this tendency. Membership

included both renowned scientists and working-class men and even
women (Conn 37). In addition, a number of scholars have suggested
connections between the study of natural history and the formation of
national identity in the new republic. Michael Branch, for example, describes natural history as "an expression of America's need to discover
the means by which its national destiny would be enacted" (284), while
Thomas Hallock, writing about William Bartram's *Travels* (a classic of
American natural history), classifies it as "a work that sought to incor-
porate the spatial geography of the new republic, a growing identification with place, and an inclination to be indigenous to the continent"
(130). These impulses, to identify a self with a particular place and even
to become "indigenous," are also central to Whitman's project in *Specimen Days*, where he considers issues of identity, both personal and national, in a fractured, postbellum America.

The rationale behind natural history museums and natural history as
a discipline is "a belief that the world [can] be understood through the
collection, observation, classification, and display of objects; and a certainty that this work serve[s] the higher purpose of illuminating God's
plan for the world and humans' place in it" (Conn 42). The passage describing the patent office hospital is simply one of the more notable examples of Whitman's attempt to achieve the same ends, but in prose.
The overall effect of reading the text is analogous to the experience of
visiting a large and rather diverse exhibition, passing before a series of
dioramas or tableaux, and coming away with (hopefully) a better understanding of what transpired and why. Some critics have described the
effect Whitman achieves in *Specimen Days* as photographic, referring to
another innovation that greatly interested the poet, as evidenced by his
repeated references to this invention and even in the number of photographic portraits—130—the poet had made of himself over the years,
especially in the later years of his life (Meehan 477).[3] While using photography as a lens through which to examine Whitman's writing can be
effective, especially when considering his later work, and while photography has an important place in the discourse of authenticity, I believe
that Whitman had a more complex model in mind when he assembled
the fragments that eventually became *Specimen Days and Collect*, one
that includes photography but does not privilege it exclusively as a metaphor. Photographic analogies alone cannot account for the depth Whit-

man generates in these scenarios and the sense of authentic experience he is able to create. For one thing, the equation of the self with objects—here with machines (soldiers as "models" on display)—or with "specimens" reverberates with the museum rather than the photo album, another late-nineteenth-century form of display. In addition, the museum contains multiple displays, usually following one another chronologically, especially the natural history museum.

Whitman was clearly no stranger to the organizing principles and merits of the museum as a system, ones that he applied just as effectively to the assortment of material to which he needed to give structure and coherence as *Specimen Days*.[4] The materials of which the text is comprised—"diary jottings, war memoranda of 1862–'65, Nature-notes of 1877–'81" (689)—needed to be turned from a mere accumulation into an organized collection. Jean Baudrillard, in his influential study *The System of Objects*, distinguishes between "the concept of collection (Latin *colligere*, to choose and gather together) and the concept of accumulation"; he explains that "collecting proper . . . has a door open onto culture, being concerned with differentiated objects, which often have exchange value, which may also be 'objects' of preservation, trade, social ritual, exhibition—perhaps even generators of profit. Such objects are accompanied by projects. And though they remain interrelated, their interplay involves the social world outside, and embraces human relationships" (103). While a discussion of Whitman's text in terms of exchange value falls outside the realm of this study (although potential profit was certainly one reason he published), *Specimen Days* does indeed contain " 'objects' of preservation, trade, social ritual, exhibition," while also "embrac[ing] human relationships."

Display is central to the educational mission of the natural history museum, and the practice of artistic display intended to highlight specific, representative "specimens" is unmistakable in *Specimen Days*. At the end of the long first footnote to the text, Whitman writes that one reason for publishing the collection was "to perpetuate and preserve which is behind all Nature, authors included," thereby affiliating himself with the larger natural world but also giving the collection a kind of inherency (a word that will come up again later) that makes it seem inevitable. His other reason is "to symbolize two or three *specimen interiors*, personal and other, out of the myriads of my time, the middle

range of the Nineteenth century in the New World: a strange, unloos-
en'd, wondrous time" (690; my emphasis); or, to use the vernacular of
the museum, to create tableaux that not only inform but also capture
specific moments in time, providing a context and linking the present
and the past. His reference to his setting as the "New World," at a time
when this phrase would no longer have had the same kind of resonance
it once did, serves to anchor these "unloosen'd" moments to a larger historical (and cultural) context. It makes them part of a national, and
even more broadly a human, narrative that may possibly bring meaning
to extra-narrative things as well.

The organizational strategy of Whitman's account is reminiscent of
the museum, with each segment functioning much the same way as
the glass cases in which early exhibits were usually housed. Museum
cases "forced the visitor to stare at objects and to consider them first
on their own terms and then in relation to neighboring objects. Museum objects, and the relationships in which they were arranged, were
intended to convey a narrative. The glass cases made sure nothing inter-
fered with that. If museums purported to represent the world metonymically through its objects, then the glass cases served as windows
onto that world" (Conn 6, 8).

Whitman's text is also constructed as a series of relatively brief passages or "cases," many just one or two paragraphs long, each with its
own title. These might well stand alone as isolated moments in time,
although each gains an added resonance as a result of being part of the
larger narrative structure. Like the viewer before the glass at the natural
history museum, the reader of *Specimen Days* must pause at each new
subheading before moving on. And while there is little apparent relationship between sections if one reads the headings alone, what gradually unfolds is an interrelated series of events and experiences following
a loose chronology from Whitman's childhood through his days as a
Civil War nurse up to his years as a semi-invalid in Camden.

Specimen Days is a series of windows onto the world Whitman knew
as a young man, as a Civil War nurse, and later as an invalid in Camden;
most of the sections, especially in the second half, concentrate on a
single object, person, or event, which then serves as a touchstone for
more generalized observations. One example of this is the section "The
Lesson of a Tree," in which Whitman presents the reader with "a fine

yellow poplar, quite straight, perhaps 90 feet high, and four thick at the butt" to draw attention to a modern malaise, one he describes as "a morbid trouble about *seems* . . . and no trouble at all, or hardly any, about the sane, slow-growing, perennial, real parts of character, books, friendship, marriage—humanity's invisible foundations and hold-together" (789, 790). The tree becomes simply a starting point for reflection; it is indeed a case of "representing the world metonymically through its objects." The museum thus provided an ideal and easily recognized model for containing what seems at first glance to be a miscellaneous and fragmented collection of memories but is actually a series of focal points or venues representing the world through Whitman's eyes.

Whitman's other, related goal for his autobiography, one not explicitly stated but evident nonetheless, was to find a form by which he might bring order to apparent disarray. Part of the problem was finding a way to provide cohesion for the amalgam of genres used to relate his experiences—biography, war account, travelogue, to name a few; he had to find a form suited to capturing a shifting and sometimes chaotic reality. This related project is evident from a number of Whitman's comments. He spoke of the book variously as a "prose jumble" (*Correspondence* 301), as potentially "the most wayward, spontaneous, fragmentary book ever printed" (*Prose Works* 1), as "an autobiography after its sort," and as a "gathering up and formulation, and putting in identity of the wayward itemizings, memoranda, and personal notes of fifty years, under modern and American conditions" (*Correspondence* 308). The great project of Whitman's personal "natural history museum" is not simply to exhibit what he has collected over a lifetime but also to provide a context in which these objects might have meaning for others. Form and meaning are therefore inseparable in *Specimen Days.*

Whitman had a high regard for the shape in which experience was presented and contained—the cases in which it was displayed, if you will—and the control of narrative this allowed him. His willingness to experiment with new forms of presentation enabled him also to conceive of prose in new ways, ways that mirrored contemporary experience, such as that of the museum visitor. The labeling of each section, for example, like the labels on museum exhibits, serves to educate the viewer without giving so much information that the author can be accused of blatantly manipulating opinion.[5] Just as the museum and exhibit designers who created spaces focused on specific objects, thereby "encourag[ing] visitors to observe [them] free from too much distracting text and context" (Conn 6), Whitman keeps his own labels minimal in the extreme. Section titles in *Specimen Days,* such as "Sunday with the Insane" and "Denver Impressions," provide only the most essential details, but they are strikingly accurate and incisive. The labels also contribute to the ostensible tone of strict objectivity in the narrative, even though such objectivity can only be a facade, especially when writing one's own life.

Unlike the messiness of an actual life, autobiography allows the author to impose order and meaning on events that may have seemed haphazard and even meaningless at the time. Conn's observation that museums "embodied the Victorian rage for order" (8) might also be applied to a text such as *Specimen Days,* especially in those sections dedicated to the war and its aftermath. The impulse to restore order and put everything right—especially in the form of autobiography (a sort of personal museum or "cabinet of curiosities," a model that will be important in my later discussion of *The Great Gatsby*)—is a common feature of American postbellum literature, represented by such well-known texts as *The Education of Henry Adams, Life on the Mississippi,* and *Life and Times of Frederick Douglass.* In fact, the primary link between the various displays is the narrator—or the "docent," in museum terms—who observes, describes, and explains each exhibit in turn. It is worth pointing out that "exhibit" can be either a noun or a verb, referring either to the thing shown or to the act of showing. It is especially apt in terms of the "Whitman" who narrates *Specimen Days,* the one who actively exhibits himself to others yet also runs the risk of becoming just another object in his own collection.

Like Peale's museum, Whitman's text is a series of fragments bound together by the highly personal rationale of the collector and his assemblage. In *The Poetics of Natural History,* Christoph Irmscher refers to "the image of the naturalist who creates a collection and then puts himself into it, of the collector who is both *apart from* and *a part of* his collection, who is, to quote from Walt Whitman's "Song of Myself," both 'in and out of the game, and watching and wondering at it'" (2). It is not surprising that Irmscher cites Whitman in this context, the poet for whom the self is the raw material that becomes the text. Whitman is an

intriguing figure in this period for a variety of reasons, not least of
which is his active engagement in negotiating the tension between authenticity and artifice that defines the end of the nineteenth century.[6]
While busily constructing the public character known as "Walt Whitman," the author was also occupied in a quest for the real and authentic,
activities he did not see as mutually exclusive. In the process of attempting to come to terms with the paradoxes and ironies inherent in any
search for authenticity, his own in particular, Whitman contributed in
important ways to the national discourse on this subject. His struggle
with the authentic takes place repeatedly in the pages of the various
texts he wrote and revised during these years. Considered from this perspective, *Specimen Days* (as well as other Whitman works) provides
valuable insights into the culture of authenticity and those elements of
fin de siècle America that—each in its own way—contributed to questions about authenticity and identity: these include mass production,
consumerism, public displays of all kinds, and the obsession with objects (the latter in particular an interest the museum epitomizes).

If we understand museums, and *Specimen Days,* as "a way of seeing
the world" (Conn 6), then the endless rows of glass cases that were originally used to house collections, such as those in the patent office and,
metaphorically, the various sections of Whitman's text, take on an added
dimension. Just as curators placed objects under glass, not to turn them
into art objects but in order to create "objects invested with knowledge"
(9), so Whitman's "cases" (both literal and figurative) contain materials
that are intended to edify, not simply entertain. Whitman's encounter
with a hermit is a case in point. One of the briefest passages in the
book—a mere three sentences—it is still rich with potential meaning for
the careful observer. Whitman's surprise at finding "a real hermit" is almost comical, and the man (of Quaker stock, Whitman makes sure to
tell us) resides exactly where one would expect to find a hermit: "a lone-
some spot, hard to get at, rocky, the view fine" (841, 840). This might
be the man Emerson describes in "Self-Reliance," who has been edu-
cated in the States but then must "complete" his education abroad, except that this specimen has also been to California. Whereas he probably
shuns the company of others, the hermit actually invites Whitman to
his hut to rest on their third encounter, and this is one reason for includ-

ing the piece: to establish Whitman as the man with whom even hermits will associate. However, the last sentence holds the real "lesson" of this particular scenario, as Whitman observes that the man "talk'd with ease and moderate freedom, but did not unbosom his life, or story, or tragedy, or whatever it was" (841). Admiration of the man's stoicism is one way of reading this statement, especially given Whitman's own poor health late in life, but it also reveals the author's ambivalence about his own project. A simple experience becomes a window into Whitman's soul, and perhaps our own.

While many of the segments in *Specimen Days* deal with "humanity," Whitman's is really an object-based epistemology, one thoroughly in keeping with the materialist impulses of the late nineteenth century.[7] The connection among industrialism, material culture, and the proliferation of museums has been developed by a number of museum scholars. However, this interdependence has yet to be considered in terms of the ways it is manifested in literary texts of the period. For example, the place of objects in the construction of meaning—and this includes the text as object—is something with which Whitman struggles throughout *Specimen Days*. Objects are tangible evidence of events and even one's existence, but they are static; it is those who participate through the employment of the gaze who give the objects in an exhibit meaning, interacting with them and subsequently giving them a place in memory (which is simply a personal form of history). Just as objects can be arranged in a museum to create a very specific narrative and effect, so Whitman arranges them in his personal museum, whether he is writing about patent models, the bodies of wounded soldiers, or trees. My inclusion of wounded bodies along with the examples of patent models and trees is not arbitrary. Whitman frequently treads a fine line in this regard, occasionally seeming to give as much meaning to the tree as to the wounded man. Conversely, according to Irmscher, an intrinsic problem of museums is that objects pulled from their context and ensconced in a collection can in fact lose their meaning. As a result, "efforts had to be made to reinvent and manipulate new contexts for them" (3). So in addition to designating the items to be displayed, Whitman must create a new context for his collection, one that will have meaning for his readers, not just himself. One way he does this is through the trope of the "specimen," treating each object as a type rather than as something singular or exceptional, and constantly alluding to his own status as Everyman, also a "type" rather than a unique example.

The centerpiece of *Specimen Days*—the part that shapes the sections that precede and follow it—is Whitman's struggle to understand and narrate the reality of an experience without parallel in his lifetime, the Civil War. The very title embodies the pivotal dilemma of the text. The word "specimen" can alternately be used to mean something that stands for the authentic or the thing itself or, although obsolete by Whitman's time, "specimen" has also been used to refer to an experiment or a "brief and incomplete account of something in writing" (*OED*).[8] Either description is appropriate for a work of such indeterminate genre. The section "Some Specimen Cases" is an ideal example of his technique, containing as it does eight scenarios, each dedicated to a different wounded soldier. Like the "specimen cases" in a natural history museum, many of the segments are individually labeled with the subject's name and place of origin: "*W.H.E., Co. F, 2d N.J.*," "J.T.L., of company F, 9th New Hampshire," and "Thomas Lindly, 1st Pennsylvania cavalry." One soldier is simply referred to as "Bed 3, ward E, Armory" (725, 726), situating him even more firmly in the realm of objects on display. This presentation of "types" is a form of exhibition, and the reader passes from one scene to another as if before a series of dioramas. Whitman frequently spotlights the physical in these scenes, commenting on the soldiers' builds, their hair, and their features. In the first scenario he draws our attention to "a regular Irish boy, a fine specimen of youthful physical manliness," but the boy is damaged goods since he has been "shot through the lungs" (724-5). Whitman also draws conclusions about the fates of the men—this one "will surely have to lose three toes," that one "will surely die" (726)—but his larger postulations are about the varieties of suffering caused by the war and the way men face their own mortality. The case studies in this section move steadily, almost inevitably, toward the death of Amer Moore in the final scene, the ultimate lesson of war.

As in an actual museum, Whitman's arrangement of the materials he has collected brings order to the bedlam of war and allows for the construction of meaning. Yet it is meaning and value as determined by Whitman. A collection is an act of interpretation since countless arrangements of a given set of objects are possible, and each can result in a potentially different narrative. One function of the museum is "authenticating and projecting a clear hierarchy of value" (Pearce, *Museums, Objects, and Collections* 237). Whitman accomplishes something very similar here, establishing importance simply by virtue of the way he arranges his materials. The death of a single man may not have been very significant in terms of the general carnage of the Civil War, but like the specimen given pride of place in a museum display, this single death stands for all those who have died; it is both singular and representative. Objects have an "exchange value," but we have seen that even people can become objectified in certain situations, and that this value is "a function of cultural and social determinants" (Baudrillard, *System of Objects* 90). Yet the self is also involved in establishing value simply by the act of possession. The "tautology" Baudrillard describes, the interplay of self with objects and the way objects can reverberate value back to the self, is demonstrated in the exchange of objects between Whitman and those he meets. On the one hand, this can occur at the most prosaic level. One of Whitman's activities during the Civil War was to distribute modest creature comforts and small amounts of money to the soldiers, especially the wounded. This repeated gesture takes the form of ritual as he passes among the men, leaving token objects he hopes will ease their suffering and comfort them: paper and envelopes, tobacco, even "a small bottle of horse-radish" for a young man who has "a great hankering for . . . something pungent" (726). Yet the exchange is mutual, for in return Whitman is given access to the wounded and their stories, often for extended periods of time. These become the raw material of the collection, the bits and pieces he arranges and displays.

On the other hand, the exchange of objects and stories, the latter becoming Whitman's possession by virtue of his recording and then collecting them in *Specimen Days,* has an effect on their collector as well. The singular object is such because I possess it; consequently, "this allows me, in turn, to recognize myself in the object as an absolutely singular being" (Baudrillard, *System of Objects* 90). This singularity of self is something Whitman refers to in the section "Soldiers and Talks" when he observes, "I now doubt whether one can get a fair idea of what this war practically is, or what genuine America is, and her character, without some such experience as this I am having" (735). While *Specimen Days* attempts to provide that experience for the sympathetic reader, who can aspire to the sensation of having "been there" through language that creates vivid tableaux, one senses that even Whitman is unsure about his ability to accomplish this. Re-created experience, however vivid, remains a counterfeit of the real thing. We can come close to the experience, but we can never actually share it without having been there. Whitman reserves the right to determine what constitutes reality, even though his stories often relate events at second hand.

Museums are a form of "visual language," like the tables and charts of anthropologists, the maps and illustrations of geologists (Dias 49). Whitman is likewise creating a visual language in *Specimen Days,* but one in which words substitute for the visual rather than the reverse. Just as the visitor to the natural history museum has the vicarious thrill of observing life in a distant time and place simply through the act of seeing arrangements of objects behind glass, the reader of Whitman's text is invited to enter the scenes being presented. As a result, another form of exchange takes place, this one between reader and text: in return for exposing oneself to the world Whitman depicts, including realistic descriptions of the brutal aftermath of battle—missing limbs, oozing wounds, paralysis, death—the reader can vicariously experience, along with Whitman, the cruelty of the Civil War hospital. Whitman understands that experience is the best and most reliable form of reality, and his narrative consistently reaches out to the reader to participate in the moment being described. He also seems intuitively to understand the relationship between seeing and the creation of meaning; his function as author, then, is to provide the raw material on which our imagination can work.

The role of the viewer of an exhibit is a complex one, and this is true not only of the "viewer" of the tableaux presented in *Specimen Days* but of the original spectator of these scenes, the self who collects the artifacts and arranges the display. This forces the question, of course, of who *is* the "self" identified as "Walt Whitman" in this particular text? For in the course of trying to re-create his own experiences for the reader/viewer, Whitman also engages the complex issue of "authenticity," and in so doing helps to usher in a major shift in American culture, one in which he is joined by such writers and thinkers as Thorstein Veblen, Mark Twain, Frank Norris, William Dean Howells, Edith Wharton, and Henry Adams. It seems paradoxical to associate Whitman with a quest for "the real thing," since he is the American writer who, perhaps more than any other, is the acknowledged adopter of personae, modifier of biographical information, and abettor in constructions such as the "rough" and the "good gray poet." There are countless examples of this sort of counterfeiting in Whitman's life: he had a propensity for writing "reviews" of his own work, such as the two anonymous reviews of the 1855 edition of *Leaves of Grass,* the first beginning famously with the statement "An American Bard at last!"; an 1866 review of *Drum Taps* by John Burroughs (later expanded into *Notes on Walt Whitman, as Poet and Person*) was actually edited and partly ghostwritten by Whitman himself (Reynolds 460); and he even misrepresented his popularity to correspondents abroad. These incidents paint a picture of a man able and willing to become what he thought would "sell" at any given moment. Such metamorphoses also connect Whitman to the trope of the American counterfeit; he was a self-made man who continued to refine that self over the years with the help of friends and supporters.[9] The work of self-creation, establishing the persona who will be our guide to the sights about to unfold before us, is a crucial element of the first section of *Specimen Days;* it is here that Whitman provides a detailed account (for an unnamed correspondent) of his origins and genealogy. He traces the Whitman name back to "one John Whitman, born 1602, in Old England" and makes sure to point out that his Dutch "maternal nativity-stock" was "doubtless the best" (691, 705). He even cites "Savage's 'Genealogical Dictionary' (vol. iv, p. 524)" as a source (691), catering to the interest in genealogy in this period.[10]

If museums are indeed "temples of authenticity" (Belk, *Collecting in a Consumer Society* 107–8), and *Specimen Days* is itself a kind of museum, then any questions about the authority and authenticity of its resident expert would threaten to undermine the entire enterprise. Yet where Whitman is concerned, the concept of the real or authentic is remarkably complex, for not only did he use "authentic" to mean a faithful, surface rendering of reality, he also used it in the sense of capturing the emotional quality of an experience, as understood by the self and as produced by the objects and persons with which the self is engaged. For a demonstration of the "obsession with certainty—specifically certainty as to origin, date, author and signature of a work" that Baudrillard connects to "the demand for authenticity" (*System of Objects* 76), one need

only turn to the opening passages of *Specimen Days,* which provide vali-
dating information and authority for the account that follows: Whitman establishes connections to America's past via his "old pedigree"; he
provides details about his life; and he even cites an outside authority,
John Burrough's *Notes,* as corroborating evidence (692, 694–95). This
material lays the groundwork for Whitman-as-expert, the persona on
which the rest of the text depends for its legitimacy. In the preface to
Leaves of Grass, Whitman claims that what "preserves" the common
people is "faith" and that "they never give up believing and trusting"
(10). This was becoming more difficult in an age of increasing profes-
sionalism and individual expertise where people were forced to trust to
others rather than obtaining knowledge at first hand (Walsh 27). As
Whitman realized, the first step in gaining the public trust was establishing one's authority to speak and, just as it did for the museum, trust
had to be established with facts and other evidence.

There are numerous suggestions throughout *Specimen Days* that Whitman is conscious of manipulating his material, sifting and sorting it in
ways he knows may be construed as inauthentic; but this is a process
both replicated and accepted in the modern museum. In "Answer to
an Insisting Friend," he introduces his concerns quite specifically, with
open recognition of the value of "items" and "details" in the construction of an authentic identity. In a footnote, he refers to the section "A
Happy Hour's Command" as "*nearly* verbatim an off-hand letter of
mine" (689), speaks of the events he will recount as essentially "authentic in date-occurrence and fact," although they will be related in his own
way, and explains that any extracts from previous writings he uses will
be "the best versions" (691), suggesting that authenticity is a process
rather than a fixed state and one not bound by historical accuracy. His
numerous statements about the limitations of prose, especially when
writing about the war—"full details are impossible," "The Real War
Will Never Get in the Books" (721, 778)—at times seem like he is pro-
testing too much. However, such equivocations may actually indicate
Whitman's awareness of the metonymic nature of his text, a trait about
which he needs the reader to be aware as well. This presentation, he reminds us repeatedly, is merely a part of a whole that can never be captured, although capturing some small pieces may give us an idea of the
larger events. He also manages to set the parameters for any future com-

mentators on the war: one must have firsthand experience in order for one's account to be considered authentic, and even then the record will be only partial (although Whitman's only experience was tending to the wounded and not in actual combat).

Despite questions about veracity and accuracy, there is no denying Whitman's equally keen interest in the authentic, in separating the false from the true. It is a theme that runs throughout his work. In "A July Afternoon by the Pond" Whitman describes a sultry summer day; a buzzard sails by overhead while "two large slate-colored dragon-flies, with wings of lace, circling and darting and occasionally balancing themselves quite still, their wings quivering all the time" hover on the surface of the pond. His lyrical description ends with a reflection on the summer sky "with silver swirls like locks of toss'd hair, spreading, expanding—a vast voiceless, formless simulacrum—yet may-be the most real reality and formulator of everything—who knows?" (788). The three separate observations in this sentence—the sky as a simulacrum or semblance of something, the consideration of this as possibly "the most real reality," and the final question, "who knows?"—are a microcosm of Whitman's approach to the subject of authenticity. He is able to recognize the correspondence between things and yet see beyond that to the possible inherent authenticity of individual objects; however, he is also able to acknowledge his own limitations when it comes to knowing what the "real reality" is.

In the penultimate section of *Specimen Days*, "Final Confessions," he justifies any potential errors in his "garrulous notes" by pointing out, "in the deepest veracity of all—in reflections of objects, scenes, Nature's outpourings, to my sense and receptivity, as they seem'd to me—in the work of giving those who care for it, some authentic glints, specimen-days of my life—and in the *bona fide* spirit and relations, from author to reader, on all the subjects design'd, and as far as they go, I feel to make unmitigated claims" (924). Having acknowledged the vagaries of memory, the biases in any attempt to capture reality, Whitman still believes he has captured some of the actuality of his experience for the reader, some "authentic glints." This is not to suggest he was unaware of the alternative; in a section from *Collect*, "Poetry To-Day in America—Shakspere—the Future," he refers to "the human and artificial world we have established in the West" (925), and poems such as "Of the Terrible

Doubt of Appearances" and "Out from Behind the Mask" suggest that something more lurks beneath the surface of things and individuals.[11] This conflict between surface appearances and inner reality arises in *Specimen Days* as well. Describing Abraham Lincoln, Whitman concludes: "None of the artists or pictures has caught the deep, though subtle and indirect expression of this man's face. There is something else there" (733–34). However, it is in the short poem "Shakspere-Bacon's Cipher," written in 1891, that the connection between objects and reality/authenticity is most starkly presented:

> In every object, mountain, tree, and star—in every birth and life,
> As part of each—evolv'd from each—meaning, behind the ostent,
> A mystic cipher waits infolded. (lines 5–9)[12]

The late date of this poem suggests that this is a subject that continued to interest Whitman until the end of his life. The connection between objects and authenticity is certainly more marked in the later sections of *Specimen Days*.

The various tableaux in the third section of the text frequently focus on specific items—"Bumble-Bees," "Cedar-Apples," "Locusts and Katydid," "A Meadow Lark"—and their relation to the self and the real. "A Sun-Bath—Nakedness" is a tableau vivant containing the poet at Timber Creek in Camden, where he spent many hours recuperating from his stroke. His state of nakedness enhances the intersection of self with things, beginning with his own shadow: "As I walk'd slowly over the grass, the sun shone out enough to show the shadow moving with me. Somehow I seem'd to get identity with each and every thing around me, in its condition. Nature was naked, and I was also. . . . Perhaps the inner never lost rapport we hold with earth, light, air, trees, &c., is not to be realized through eyes and mind only, but through the whole corporeal body, which I will not have blinded or bandaged any more than the eyes" (807). Again, in "The Oaks and I," Whitman establishes such a connection, this time between himself and an oak tree on which he pulls for exercise. His goal is to "get into my old sinews some of its elastic fibre and clear sap" (808). His interaction with the tree leads him to "*know* the virtue thereof passes from them into me. (Or maybe we interchange—may-be the trees are more aware of it all than I ever thought)" (808–9). Active association with the things of the natural world results in a more elevated form of experience, but it also leads to the realization that his awareness of the real world, even in such moments of heightened perception, barely scratches the surface: "I often realize a presence here—in clear moods I am certain of it, and neither chemistry nor reasoning nor esthetics will give the least explanation" (809). The old tools—science, philosophy, art—are ineffective in these moments, which seem to have a reality beyond Whitman's powers of description.[13]

In *On Longing: Narratives of the Miniature, the Gigantic, the Souvenir, the Collection*, Susan Stewart considers the connection between the authentic object and authentic experience; she writes, "Within the development of culture under an exchange economy, the search for authentic experience and, correlatively, the search for the authentic object become critical" (133). Whether he is acquiring soldiers, katydids, oak trees, or a "specimen tramp family" (821), Whitman's search for the authentic experience is object driven. Yet the act of setting these things apart in the various sections of *Specimen Days* has the ancillary consequence of objectifying/commoditizing them, however unintentionally. The object-driven nature of the narrative has additional reverberations, for in the process of creating a suitable structure for his authentic experience, what begins as a "discourse on objects" becomes "discourse-as-object."[14] The text itself becomes an object "saturated with meanings that will never be fully revealed to us," its "seriality" a harbinger of inauthenticity, to use more of Stewart's language about objects (*On Longing* 133). Yet the situation is even more complex than this. Since the text and its author are so closely intertwined (not simply because the text is autobiographical but also because Whitman habitually set up this binary of self and book), Whitman runs the risk of becoming an artifact in his own museum, an object on display that has been verified in its own authenticity but that then becomes as elusive as any other form of the authentic. Finally, the authenticity of the text (or lack thereof) also impacts directly on the authenticity of the author with whom it is aligned. Commoditization of the self is a direct result of the self-as-book paradigm, but it is also a result of treating the self as an object that can be manufactured and "sold." This is as true of Whitman as it is of the soldiers he puts on display in the patent office hospital.

Whitman's ongoing questions about authenticity are often projected onto others, but what they ultimately reveal is concern for his own authenticity as well as his growing uncertainty about his ability to render authentic experience in prose. "Some Specimen Cases" again provides numerous examples: there is the soldier who, at first refusing Whitman's money, eventually accepts it and is "evidently very grateful, but [says] little"; the man who reminds Whitman of "that celebrated singed cat, who was better than she look'd"; and the Irish boy, Thomas Haley, who "knew more than he show'd" (726, 725). Yet the sum of the various descriptions always comes back to Whitman himself, as does *Specimen Days*.[15] *Specimen Days* is the epitome of techniques Whitman worked on throughout his career. In "A Backward Glance" he explained that the project of *Leaves of Grass* had been "from first to last, to put a *Person*, a human being (myself, in the latter half of the Nineteenth Century, in America,) freely, fully, and truly on record" (671), a description that is just as applicable to *Specimen Days*. Even his description of the dying Thomas Haley ends with a reference to himself: "Little he knew, poor death-stricken boy, the heart of the stranger that hover'd near" (725).

Whether it is in the war sections or in the later sections about Timber Creek or his trip west, death is the real subject—the central object—of *Specimen Days*, either death as a result of war, the near death of a stroke, or coming to terms with his own unavoidable end as the years pass. Death is also the inevitable subtext of the natural history museum, considering its subject matter and the objects with which it is filled; this is not necessarily the case in other types of museums, which may contain the work of living artists or even living specimens (if one considers the zoo as a type of museum). Baudrillard considers the relationship between objects and death, maintaining that "[t]he person who collects is dead, but he literally survives himself through his collection which (even while he lives) duplicates him infinitely, beyond death, *by integrating death itself into the series, into the cycle*" (*System of Objects* 96–97).[16] The natural history museum, in other words, is the place where death is communally held at bay, where objects are kept in a kind of stasis, neither fully living nor completely dead (since they have received new "life" in the form of the exhibit). Whitman's museum contains dead soldiers and dead heroes (Lincoln, Paine, Bryant), but these are also kept alive by virtue of their inclusion in his pages. The items he has gathered serve a twofold purpose: they commemorate the events of Whitman's life, but they also stave off death. As long as *Specimen Days* lasts, so will its creator.

"Being" as opposed to "seeming," the "inherency" of "earth, rocks, animals," and the "idealistic-real" (789, 790, 826): these are the values set in opposition to death in *Specimen Days*. Finally, since the text is itself an object, it also becomes Whitman's way to counter death, offsetting the reality of death with the authenticity of the object world. "Do you know what *ducks* and *drakes* are?" Whitman once asked William Douglass O'Connor. "Well, SD is a rapid skimming over the pond-surface of my life, thoughts, experiences, that way—the real area altogether untouch'd, but the flat pebble making a few dips as it flies and flits along—enough at least to give some living touches and contact-points—I was quite willing to make an immensely *negative* book" (*Correspondence* 315). As our docent through his experiences, Whitman guides the reader by way of the lessons of life and death/war and peace, by reflecting, providing context, and putting things into perspective.

In "Cedar-Plums Like—Names," Whitman discusses some of the titles he considered for *Specimen Days,* among them the title "Cedar-Plums Like," and then decides that the name shouldn't matter, that neither he nor the reader should be concerned "because certain pages do not present themselves to you or me as coming under their own name with entire fitness or amiability," adding parenthetically, "It is a profound, vexatious, never-explicable matter—this of names. I have been exercised deeply about it my whole life" (885–86). Yet the matter of naming is deeply connected to objects, power, and, ultimately, authenticity. In *Language and Symbolic Power,* Pierre Bourdieu notes that the ability to make concrete and public such things as "people's disquiet, anxiety, expectation, worry—represents a formidable social power. . . . It is easy to understand why one of the elementary forms of political power should have consisted, in many archaic societies, in the almost magical power of *naming* and bringing into existence by virtue of naming" (236). Whitman's text does indeed "name" the anxieties of his day, such as fears about the aftermath of the war, the viability of history, and the encroachment of industrialism; it also posits a solution, which is to seek the authentic whenever and wherever possible, whatever the result. In the final section of *Specimen Days,* he includes the poet among those persons and institutions that "bring people back from their persistent strayings and sickly abstractions, to the costless average, divine, *original concrete*" (926; my emphasis). The poet has the power to create and to re-create, to order and to name, and by doing so to counter the chaos and meaninglessness of life.

By using the museum as a guiding principle in *Specimen Days*, Whitman is able to take the unimaginable—war, social confusion, his stroke—and make it bearable and even edifying. Whitman was organizing and writing *Specimen Days* at a time when both natural history and the modern museum were becoming institutionalized. The trope of the "case" and the authentic item on display therein are essential to the overall organizational structure of *Specimen Days* and its ultimate project: to exhibit authentic experience.

Whitman, while not writing a "natural history" per se, does give the natural history museum a literary form; his version takes seriously the idea of "[c]ollections . . . as narratives" (Irmscher 5), making him the heir apparent to a line of natural historians/collectors extending from John Bartram to William James, marrying their vision of the natural world to his own vision of the authentic self.[17] Certainly the self is central to his collection, although it is the self broadly conceived and with a multifaceted perspective, one with experience on the national stage, and one who speaks for many others, both alive and dead. Whitman's immersion in his cultural milieu, specifically that of the middle to late nineteenth century, is a matter of record, as is his determination to create new literary forms to meet the needs of a nation still heavily influenced by European art and literature. That same impulse to find a new form for his material is evident in the language and imagery of *Specimen Days*. Arranging his materials with an eye toward the museums and exhibits that had so fascinated him, Whitman garners for his experience the same "value and significance" accorded to those displays.[18] His assembled bits and pieces become part of a national collection, even a national history. Using the natural history museum as his model and his touchstone, Whitman constructs for this history a meaningful—and authentic—case.

3

"I couldn't see no profit in it"

Discourses of Commoditization and Authenticity in *Adventures of Huckleberry Finn*

> The accumulation and use of knowledge is a complex form of power in which choices are constantly made about what is worth looking into and what is not.
>
> —Susan M. Pearce, *On Collecting*

In the brief but fascinating "hair-ball" scene from chapter 4 of *Adventures of Huckleberry Finn* (1884) by Mark Twain,[1] Huck tries to determine what the future has in store for him by appealing to a higher authority: a magic hair ball in the possession of Jim, a slave belonging to Miss Watson. These two positions of ownership—Jim's of the hair ball and Miss Watson's of Jim—merely scratch the surface of the complex and convoluted paths of ownership, knowledge, authenticity, and authority at work in this episode and in Twain's novel. Miss Watson owns Jim, who in turn owns the hair ball, which contains a spirit that Jim also "owns." As the owner of the magic hair ball, Jim might also be said to own the key to Huck's future at this particular moment. If Huck wants the secrets of the hair ball revealed, he must do what it/Jim demands. Yet Jim's ownership of the hair ball does not, apparently, come without complications. After all, he must collude with Huck in order to "trick" the hair ball into revealing its secrets. The connection between ownership of objects and knowledge is equivocal: the hair ball "know[s] everything" (19) but seems loath to give up its secrets; however, Jim also "knows" from experience what it will take to make it talk, namely money. In fact, Jim knows more than this—and much more than he lets on. He certainly knows that Huck is rich (as a result of the treasure he and Tom Sawyer found)—it is common knowledge in town—and that he is desperate for information. (Huck is particularly interested in knowing the whereabouts of his violent and malevolent father, who has his eye on Huck's fortune.) Jim also knows, it is reasonable to assume, that the hair ball is not magical at all (unless we believe he is delusional and actually hears voices, not something his overall behavior would suggest). He also knows that the way to make a counterfeit quarter "pass" is to stick it in a potato overnight. In fact, ownership of this supposedly magic object gives Jim authority and power out of all proportion to his status as a slave.

But Huck is not without knowledge of his own: he has a dollar in his pocket that he has received from the Judge in "exchange" for his fortune. This information is withheld while Huck instead offers a counterfeit quarter ("pretty bad money") to the hair ball on the chance that "it wouldn't know the difference" between real money and fake (19). Finally, what appears on the surface to be Huck and Jim working in tandem (the first of many such episodes) is actually a complex game of manipulation and countermanipulation: Jim accepts a fake quarter on behalf of the hair ball because he knows methods for making it appear genuine. The hair ball will be fooled while Huck will get to keep his dollar because Jim can turn "bad money" into good, making it seem authentic enough that "anybody in town would take it in a minute, let alone a hair-ball." Fortunately for Huck, the hair ball seems satisfied with this arrangement; the promise of future money, good or bad, is enough to release its prophecy about Pap. Huck apparently does not notice this discrepancy, caught up as he is in his own predicament and his consternation at having been bettered by Jim in the art of counterfeiting. The transaction ends as it began, with the concept of ownership, although now it is the ownership of knowledge that is at stake, with Huck's hollow-sounding declaration, "Well, I knowed a potato would do that, before, but I had forgot it" (20). Although poorer by a fake twenty-five cents and a bit of his pride, Huck has apparently managed to deceive both Jim and a hair ball, while Jim is a fake twenty-five cents richer.[2]

This early episode establishes a number of tropes that are central to *Huck Finn*—ownership (whether of objects, other people, or knowledge), identity, authenticity (and the primacy of the visual in its verification), and fraud—and that are important for an understanding of the complex relationship between Huck and Jim as well as that between Huck and Tom Sawyer. They are also, not coincidentally, key elements of economic transactions in general. The exchange here, for example, is founded on a trade that is essentially deceptive. This is Huck and Jim's first recorded encounter in the novel and it initiates the power struggle between the two, a struggle that centers on who knows what, when he knows it, and what he does with that knowledge. Knowledge is power, of course, but this is especially true in economic transactions. For example, the phrase most often associated with the buying and selling of goods, "caveat emptor" or "let the buyer beware," implies that a lack of knowledge can work against the unwitting or unwary participant in a transaction. This cautionary tone is established from the outset with Twain's prefatory material, his "Notice" to those who read the book and his "Explanatory" about the dialects that appear in the novel. The tone then continues throughout each encounter Huck and Jim have with others (and even one another). This is a novel in which transactions in one form or another govern almost every situation. In Huck's world, anything can be a commodity for exchange or sale: people, knowledge, time, even "magic."

Twain, like Whitman, was deeply engaged in the culture of his day. Slave narratives, minstrelsy, the Graveyard School of Poetry, Reconstruction: in one form or another each of these makes an appearance in *Huck Finn*. And also like Whitman, Twain was a shrewd businessman who actively promoted himself and his books, activities that are borne out in the correspondence between Twain and his publishers.[3] He was fascinated by the new inventions of the day and objects that reproduced reality in particular, investing in the Paige typesetting machine as well as an engraving company and a publishing company. One of the first writers to use the newly invented typewriter and the dictating machine and one of the first Americans to own a telephone, he also "patented a self-pasting scrapbook and invented a game for improving memory" (Sattelmeyer 89). As Robert Sattelmeyer observes, Twain may have satirized the expansion of industrial capitalism in a book like *The Gilded Age*, but "his own practices constituted an uncritical endorsement of it." For Twain, books were also "commodities to be marketed, and [he] even had his famous pseudonym registered as a trademark" (89). This preoccupation with the world of commerce and entrepreneurship resonates throughout *Huck Finn* in both its language and imagery, but it is an element of the novel that has yet to be fully explored.

While analysis of Twain's masterpiece has frequently turned to its complex language structures—his use of dialect, the origins of Huck's language in African American speech patterns, or the ways in which the various voices that appear in the text, including Twain's, collide and intersect to create meaning[4]—there is another kind of "language" or discourse system that permeates the novel. This is the discourse of commoditization, which is not only concerned with objects and ownership but also with knowledge and power, thus engaging the related discourse of authenticity. Twain's (or Huck's) tale is filled with objects and people that appear to be real but eventually prove to be inauthentic: quarters, hair balls, plaster fruit, kings and dukes, and even slaves who are no longer slaves. The relationship between objects and knowledge—and the authenticity of each—forms the basis of commodity exchange, and commodity exchange is an ongoing activity in the novel. Rooted in the language of things, values, exchange systems, and the authentic, the discourse of commoditization provides new ways to understand *Huck Finn,* especially those aspects of the text that have been most troubling, such as Huck's relationship to Jim, Tom Sawyer's reappearance, and even such seemingly minor incidents as the hair ball episode.

In his introduction to *The Social Life of Things: Commodities in Cultural Perspective,* Appadurai articulates a theory of commodities that is especially useful for a discussion of Twain's novel, focusing as it does on objects and exchange systems. Starting from the premise that a commodity is "*any thing intended for exchange*" (9), Appadurai's main interest is the point at which things can be considered commodities, and this allows us to think in terms of "the commodity phase" of an object (13, 15). From this perspective, almost anything can be a commodity if, at some point in its existence, it can be traded or exchanged. There are, of course, various means by which objects can gain or lose their status as commodities, and the process "can be slow or fast, reversible or terminal, normative or deviant" (13). Objects normally protected from the commodity condition can become commoditized as a result of interactions with strangers (15) or by a process known as "diversion," which is "frequently the recourse of the entrepreneurial individual" (25). This approach to commoditization provides a framework for analyzing several important elements in Twain's novel: Huck's part in the commodity system, his "theft" of Jim and the moral quandary in which he consequently finds himself as an advocate of a commodity system that treats others as objects, and the ways in which Huck's "dealings with strangers" (to use Appadurai's phrase) result in his own commoditization through repeated acts of self-creation.[5]

Huck is obsessed with "things." Whether he is "borrowing," stealing, or finding them, he rarely passes up the opportunity to acquire an object when it becomes available, regardless of how seemingly useless it may be. A good example of this is the hodgepodge of items he and Jim take from the floating house, starting with "two old dirty calico dresses, and a sun-bonnet, and some women's underclothes hanging against the wall, and some men's clothing, too" as well as "a boy's old speckled straw hat." His inventory of what they acquire is impressively detailed. They do pass up a few things: a broken milk bottle, some old playing cards, a chest, and a hair trunk; the latter two "stood open, but there warn't nothing left in them that was any account." There is an almost domestic flavor to the objects they take, and, in fact, when they return to their raft with their haul, Huck says, "We got home all safe." However, Huck is also a shrewd appraiser of value and evaluates items in terms of their potential exchange value, such as the "bran-new Barlow knife worth two bits in any store." His final assessment of the experience is "take it all around, we made a good haul" (45).

Huck is also not above rationalizing when there is something he wants and can't get otherwise; in one instance, when Jim and he are trying to rationalize stealing commodities from people's gardens because "Pap always said it warn't no harm to borrow things if you was meaning to pay them back some time; but the widow said it warn't anything but a soft name for stealing, and no decent body would do it. Jim said he reckoned the widow was partly right and pap was partly right; so the best way would be for us to pick out two or three things from the list and say we wouldn't borrow them any more—then he reckoned it wouldn't be no harm to borrow the others." They ultimately decide, after much discussion, "to drop crabapples and p'simmons. We warn't feeling just right before that, but it was all comfortable now. I was glad the way it come out, too, because crabapples ain't ever good, and the p'simmons wouldn't be ripe for two or three months yet" (56). This is a vivid example of the diversion theory at work, whereby items never intended for trade (but probably for personal consumption) become commodities. Here again, the decision about what to take or not is based on value rather than just desire; items that aren't good to eat aren't worth stealing.

Because the actual value of a given commodity is always uppermost in Huck's mind (and this eventually extends to more abstract things such as friendship and telling the truth, as we shall see), he is interested in real objects rather than illusory ones, unlike his friend Tom Sawyer. This is evident during his brief membership in Tom's gang, when Tom expects the other boys, Huck included, to accept that hogs and turnips are "ingots" and "julery." Typically discussed in terms of Tom's (mis)use of adventure fiction, such as *The Count of Monte Cristo* and *Don Quixote*, this experience is almost a parody of the diversion of commodities. Huck is far more interested in the actual than in the imaginary; his reaction to stealing hogs and turnips is that he "couldn't see no profit in it" (16). Explaining that the objects have been enchanted by magicians, who also have the power of genies at their disposal, Tom tries to explain to Huck how genies—ostensible providers of commodities—operate. "They belong to whoever rubs the lamp or the ring, and they've got to do whatever he says. If he tells them to build a palace forty miles long out of di'monds, and fill it full of chewing-gum, or whatever you want, and fetch an emperor's daughter from China for you to marry, they've got to do it—and they've got to do it before sun-up next morning, too. And more: they've got to waltz that palace around over the country wherever you want it, you understand." To which Huck responds: " 'Well,' says I, 'I think they are a pack of flat-heads for not keeping the palace themselves 'stead of fooling them away like that. And what's more—if I was one of them I would see a man in Jericho before I would drop my business and come to him for the rubbing of an old tin lamp' " (17). Because he has typically been on the losing side in economic exchanges, Huck has developed a knack for holding onto what he does get, and having been at the mercy of others most of his young life, he cannot understand why someone with power would put himself in that position. (He is also, of course, oblivious to the similarities between Tom's description and the life of a slave.) For all that Tom seems like the budding capitalist of the group, Huck is the one who knows the value of things and the importance of "business." What he lacks is the cultural capital—family background, education, reputation—needed to make his knowledge pay off.

Huck's investment in certain objects also indicates his desire (at least in the early part of the novel) to be a member of the community occupied by Tom, the Widow Douglas, the Judge, and even Jim. When Pap does finally show up, as Huck fears he will, he finds a card in Huck's room—a picture of a boy with some cows that Huck had received for learning his lessons—and tears it up. He claims he will give Huck something "better" in exchange: "I'll give you a cow hide" (21). What's interesting here is that Huck, who complains incessantly about being "civilized" and especially about having to go to school, has kept this object, perhaps because it signifies his ability to succeed in the culture it represents (also indicated by Pap's fury that his son knows how to read and write).[6] An absolute materialist and pragmatist, Huck puts all his faith in things, in the concrete object or person rather than the abstract. This also explains why he is willing to "sell" his six-thousand-dollar fortune to the Judge, but he won't give the dollar he actually has in his possession to the hair ball. As Elaine and Harry Mensch observe, "a big sum of money is an abstraction to Huck, but a small one that can easily be converted into things he may want is real" (32). This inability to think beyond the immediate object or person—what Huck calls his "ignorance"—will lead to many of his moral dilemmas; but this tendency also grounds him in reality, as opposed to the dreams and fantasies of Tom Sawyer, whose games of make-believe cause more trouble for others than any of Huck's decisions based on hard reality.

This critical difference between Tom and Huck is captured in a scene near the end of the novel as they work to help Jim escape. Tom, obsessed with following the "rules" of the fictional accounts he has read, has finally agreed to dig him out with picks and pretend they are using case knives. Huck, who simply wants to see Jim free as soon as possible, responds: "'*Now you're talking!*' I says; 'your head gets leveler and leveler all the time, Tom Sawyer,' I says. 'Picks is the thing, moral or no moral; and as for me, I don't care shucks for the morality of it, nohow. When I start in to steal a nigger, or a water-melon, or a Sunday-school book, I ain't no ways particular how it's done so it's done. What I want is my nigger; or what I want is my watermelon; or what I want is my Sunday-school book; and if a pick's the handiest thing, that's the thing I'm a-going to dig that nigger or that watermelon or that Sunday-school book out with; and I don't give a dead rat what the authorities thinks about it nuther'" (194). While some critics have used this moment to criticize Huck for equating Jim with objects,[7] the reference to a watermelon and a Sunday school book also resonates with earlier object-driven episodes, such as the gang's raid on the Sunday school picnic and the foods Huck and Jim decide to "borrow." This is not to suggest that Huck does not objectify Jim throughout most of their time together, but I contend that this attitude—in effect, Huck's entire attitude toward objects—changes by the end of the novel.

Huck's faith in the exchange value of objects and their cultural significance is essential to understanding his relationship with Jim, whose status as slave is fundamental to his identity for Huck. For much of their time together, Huck makes no distinction between the person of Jim and Jim as an object owned by Miss Watson. This is immediately evident in both his early references to Jim, whom he identifies first and foremost as property: "Miss Watson's big nigger" (10) and "Miss Watson's nigger, Jim" (19). As a nonperson, Jim can be the butt of jokes, he can be cheated without remorse, and he can be an absurd example of pride (Huck observes that he "was most ruined, for a servant, because he got so stuck up on account of having seen the devil and been rode by witches" [11]). But all this starts to change once Jim has been "diverted" from his object position, first by himself when he runs away and then by Huck, who helps him; the latter spends the rest of their time together trying to figure out ways to return Jim to the status of commodity. Appadurai describes "theft" as "the humblest form of diversion of commodities from preordained paths" (26). The attempted thefts by Tom's gang, unsuccessful though they are, foreshadow Huck's more serious "theft" of Jim (since even Huck knows that helping Jim is akin to stealing him). The gang's activities hover between mere adventure and actual crime (albeit not very serious crimes), and this is exactly the dilemma in which Huck finds himself in regard to Jim. On the one hand, he knows that his moral barometer, Tom Sawyer, would jump at the chance to have an adventure like this; on the other hand, he knows that a "respectable" boy like Tom would never do something as ornery as steal someone else's slave (although, of course, this belief will be tested before the journey is over).

Slavery is one of the primary states of existence in *Huck Finn* as well as one of the principal forms of commoditization (slaves are, of course, diverted to commodity status by theft, at least originally). Slavery also comes in a variety of forms: characters are enslaved to their belief systems, by their social status, and by wealth or the lack of it.[8] Kopytoff observes that while Western society tends to differentiate between people and things, this is not necessarily true in practice: "People can be and have been commoditized again and again, in innumerable societies throughout history, by way of those widespread institutions known under the blanket term 'slavery'" (64). He argues that the perception of slavery has changed over the years so that it is now "seen not as a fixed and unitary status, but as a process of social transformation that involves a succession of phases and changes in status, some of which merge with other statuses (for example, that of adoptee) that we in the West consider far removed from slavery." While the slave state "begins with capture or sale, when the individual is stripped of his previous social identity and becomes a non-person, indeed an object and an actual or potential commodity," it continues as the slave is made part of the "host group, within which he is resocialized and rehumanized by being given a new social identity. The commodity-slave becomes in effect re-individualized by acquiring new statuses (by no means always lowly ones) and a unique configuration of personal relationships." Thus, the slave changes from commodity to "singular individual occupying a particular social and personal niche. But the slave usually remains a potential commodity: he or she continues to have a potential exchange value that may be realized by resale. In many societies, this was also true of the 'free,' who were subject to sale under certain defined circumstances" (65). The trajectory of the slave described here parallels Jim's course throughout the novel: from commodity to individual back to potential commodity, since in antebellum America there is always the chance that the freed Jim will find himself enslaved again. (The pattern Kopytoff describes also applies to all those others in Twain's text who are "enslaved.")

We first meet Jim at night, sitting in the kitchen doorway of the Widow's house when he hears a noise made by Huck and Tom and comes out to investigate. Unable to detect the source of the noise, he decides to lie beneath a tree until he hears it again and promptly falls asleep, soon to become the object of a schoolboy prank. This encounter is mediated, in fact controlled, by the figure of Tom Sawyer, who sticks Jim's hat in a tree while also leaving a nickel for some candles he takes.

(Tom, of course, will return to torment and "reward" Jim in much the same way at the end of the novel.) Jim also turns this incident to his advantage, creating a story about witches and the devil that gains him fame and admiration throughout the local slave community, even if it does "ruin" him. By trading on his storytelling ability, he is able to turn the nickel Tom leaves behind into much more. Jim's ability to make the best of a situation is also evident in his ability to play a part, albeit in a much more limited way than Huck, and to be deceptive when necessary. His enslaved condition is certainly not by choice, but his position as object has taught him much about ownership and commodity culture. His recognition of his own exchange value means he is able to market himself when the opportunity arises. This is also evident in the hair ball episode, where Jim manipulates Huck as much as the latter does him. Such incidents are important because they ultimately place Jim on an equal footing with Huck, at least in terms of his ability to work a situation to his advantage.[9] Huck understands this equally well, which is why he cannot easily admit it when Jim, in particular, bests him.

Jim's commodity status is never far from view. He is running away not because he has been abused or mistreated, but because he hears he is to be sold for eight hundred dollars and sent to New Orleans. His observation that he now owns himself (a condition most in the novel aspire to without success) provokes some of Huck's strongest feelings of guilt and shame. In addition, Jim intends to perpetuate his subversion of the economic system by returning to buy his wife and buy or steal their children with the help of "an Ab'litionist." Huck observes, "Just see what a difference it made in him the minute he judged he was about free" (74). When he begins to talk about missing his family, Huck is made aware that there may be more to Jim than his status as slave; however, he is ultimately unable to see beyond the other man's commoditized state for more than the briefest stretch of time. Appadurai observes, "The diversion of commodities from their customary paths always carries a risky and morally ambiguous aura" (27), and this is certainly true of Huck's mental state regarding Jim. He can understand and relate to Jim as an object owned by someone and then taken away (with his help), but once he moves into more ambiguous territory—Jim as nonobject (as father, as friend)—he is unsure what to do. His response is to try to find a way to return Jim to the object world as quickly as possible. When Jim begins to talk about being free and one day freeing his family, for example, Huck begins to think seriously about turning him in and even sets out with the intention of doing so. However, Jim's declarations as Huck prepares to paddle off (ostensibly to see if they have indeed reached Cairo) that he is "de bes' fren' Jim's ever had; en . . . de *only* fren' ole Jim's got now" (74) result in spasms of guilt and Huck's ultimate decision not to turn him in, and, from this point on, to do "whichever come handiest at the time" (76). Actual exchange value—what's in it for him—governs most of Huck's decisions, such as when to help someone, when to tell a lie or not, and even what to do about Jim. This is not vindictive on his part; rather, as an aspiring member of the capitalist system, Huck is always considering exchange value. In this particular instance, Huck decides that he would have felt equally as bad had he turned Jim in as he now does having failed to do so. It is only when he stops approaching things from this perspective, when he can begin to think about value in more abstract terms, that he is able ultimately to decide to go to hell for Jim.

Ironically, Jim wants to be part of the very capitalist system that has turned him into a commodity. He describes his earlier financial exploits to Huck: how he started with fourteen dollars, speculated in "stock" (livestock, that is) and then in a bank, and finally ended up poor again. Huck tries to console him by saying, "Well, it's all right anyway, Jim, long as you're going to be rich again some time or other." To which Jim perceptively replies, "Yes; en I's rich now, come to look at it . . . I's wuth eight hund'd dollars" (42). Jim's tale is a parable about investing wisely, but it also shows an entrepreneurial spirit that Twain would have admired. Later, Jim is also able to buy the assistance of the Grangerford slaves, who help him to recuperate and to restock the raft. His innate understanding of the commodity system, which has made him a piece of valuable property, is one reason he plays up those traits and attitudes he knows Huck will find most valuable. For instance, his knowledge of signs and omens, his ability to cook, and his good humor all work to keep Huck from turning him in at various points. Even his subject position as father is calculated to appeal to a boy whose own father is less than loving. Jim also recognizes Huck's value as a traveling companion (he is able to go ashore for supplies and information; he can distract anyone who comes near the raft), which is why when

Jim discovers the dead Pap in the floating house he keeps it to himself. Susan K. Harris points out that the constant threat of bounty hunters and kidnappers means Jim cannot afford to let Huck ever get far away (note, 137), but in order to ensure this he must also make sure Huck does not know his father is dead. (Harris's use of a term from the discourse of commoditization—"afford"—is inadvertent here but apt.) Were Huck to obtain this vital piece of information, there would no reason for him not to return to Hannibal except to avoid the continued attempts of the Widow and Miss Watson to "sivilize" him.

The question of Jim's ownership is, of course, central to a text about a runaway slave set in antebellum America when possession of slaves, escaped slaves in particular, was an important legal and economic issue. However, the object position of "slave" is one Jim moves in and out of throughout the novel, if not literally then at least in terms of his behavior and attitude. When Huck voices his contentment with their lifestyle one day, Jim points out that Huck would not be floating comfortably downstream on a raft, eating fish and hot cornbread, had it not been for him (44). Likewise, when Jim reprimands Huck for tricking him into thinking he has been dreaming when they were separated in the fog, he turns the tables on Huck, associating him with the detritus of a commodity culture, the trash that covers the raft. Jim's reference to Huck as "trash" has very specific class connotations, of course ("white trash"), but it also suggests that someone who tricks his friends in such a way is worthless.[10] This categorization of Huck also places Jim in a superior position, at least for the moment, and leads to Huck's much-analyzed apology. Of course, one of the chief ironies of the text is that Jim is not actually a slave for most of the journey. He is eventually sold by the King and the Duke for forty dollars, but as in so many previous situations, he again manages to get the better end of the bargain; it is Jim who reveals the Nonesuch scam to Mr. Phelps and a neighbor, who then make sure the rest of the townspeople know and can exact their revenge. The next time we see the two scoundrels they have been tarred and feathered; Jim is able to repay the King and Duke for their duplicity without lifting a finger, instead gaining a reputation for cooperation and honesty. By the end of the novel, Jim has again become a commodity, and one whose value has literally increased. The doctor who removes the bullet from Tom describes Jim as being "worth a thousand dollars—and kind treatment too" for staying to help him and not running off as he might have done (223). He is soon literally free and forty dollars richer. Peter Messent argues that "Jim's human value is judged finally in the dehumanizing terms of economic exchange, his worth as property rather than as one with his own voice, his own stake in the social exchange" (237). This may be true, but such a reading ignores Jim's ability to enhance his position and value. When even kindness is a commodity, those who can increase their own worth are far ahead of the game.

While Huck might describe the ideal existence as Tom Sawyer's, an accepted and respected member of society who still has a measure of freedom, it is Jim with whom he has the greater affinity, as Twain makes clear through the discourses of commoditization and authentication in which the two are implicated. Someone like Tom Sawyer is an owner of objects, not an object himself, as evidenced by his tendency to buy his way out of trouble (he leaves a nickel for some candles he takes; he pays Jim forty dollars for his role in the "evasion"). Although not literally a slave, Huck is metaphorically enslaved: to his misplaced regard for Tom, to his desire for acceptance by a community that is biased and provincial, and to the objects he associates with social respectability. Kopytoff posits an analogous relationship "between the way societies construct individuals and the way they construct things." For example, "[i]n small-scale societies, a person's social identities are relatively stable." However, someone who cannot be pigeonholed into one of the socially sanctioned identities "is either singularized into a special identity—which is sacred or dangerous, and often both—or simply cast out" (89–90). The Huck of the hair ball episode is a resident of the small-scale society of Hannibal where he knows his place in the social system, and having finally found his niche by virtue of his new wealth and his association with the Widow (after first being an outcast), he is not inclined to give it up. He knows who he is, who Jim is (Miss Watson's), and he knows his relationships to the objects around him (such as the hair ball). Huck and Jim certainly con one another, but the transaction is relatively unambiguous. Huck gets his prediction and Jim gets his quarter. There is no question about Huck's position relative to Jim's, whose knowledge about turning bad money to good Huck claims also to have, although not at his fingertips; and Huck still has his dollar when all is said and done. Huck and Jim are both able to adapt quickly to situations, sliding into communities and taking up residence. But while Huck moves into the white community where he is subjected to greed, hypocrisy, and violence, Jim moves into the shadow community of the slaves, where he is protected, cosseted, and respected. This "mirror" world is one inhabited by those who know they are all commodities and act accordingly.

Huck straddles the worlds of ownership and commodities, and this conflict is the cause of much of his confusion, especially in his relationship with Jim. Just as Jim's identity is an extension of that of the woman who owns him, so Huck, now the "property" of the Widow Douglas, gets his identity from her, as well as from his "co-owner," Miss Watson. (The gang's acceptance of Miss Watson as a ransom victim validates her position in relation to Huck.) Huck's possible adoption, first by the Widow and then by Aunt Sally at the end of the novel, is a form of commoditization. As a wild thing that has been tamed, Huck is similar to the "exotic and the novel" that the nineteenth-century collector cherished (Schlereth 119). Even Pap treats Huck as a commodity, a value to be cashed in now that he has come of age and is "ready to go to work and do suthin' for *him* and give him a rest." When Pap rails about being kept "out o' my property," it is not clear whether he's referring to Huck or the money (26). Yet Huck has also become invested in his new role as property owner. He does not divest himself of the six thousand dollars (money that has meant his being subjected to the civilizing processes of the Widow) when given the opportunity; instead, he chooses to "sell it" to the Judge. Later, when he must confront the issue of Jim as runaway slave—someone else's property in his keeping—Huck is uncertain what to do with this object that has been *de*commoditized. At some moments he affiliates himself with Jim, the object of pursuit—"There ain't a minute to lose. They're after *us!*" (54; my emphasis)—and at others he claims ownership of Jim, referring to him as "my nigger" (171). Thus, despite his shame at helping to steal a slave, Huck is instrumental in maintaining Jim's status as object. Even his description of Jim as "white inside" resonates with objects, recalling the plaster fruit at the Grangerfords that shows white where it is chipped.[11] Yet Huck's words also signal his entrapment within commodity culture, the world of things, and especially those things that seem to be one thing and turn out to be another. Affiliating Jim with the plaster fruit, made to look even better than the real thing, is not to suggest that Jim is himself a fake. Ironically, that is precisely Huck's dilemma. He expects those with black skin to act a certain way, and by not doing so and instead behaving in a way Huck considers "white," Jim has in fact proved himself to be something other than what he appears on the surface.[12] .

Huck may ultimately be unable to see Jim as anything other than a commodity because he has himself become one as a result of his constant acts of self-creation. While Pap is threatened by his son's newfound literacy, Huck has always been an avid and accurate reader of people, and this ability is far more insidious and even dangerous in terms of his own authenticity and potential objectification. The risk is compounded by Huck's unique ability to empathize with and "become" the other, whether that other is a girl named Sarah Mary Williams, a dead baby named Charles William Allbright, a poor orphan named George Jackson, or an English valet. He is able to copy or mime the salient characteristics of the person he chooses to become, basing his creation on the needs and desires of the consumer. In the case of his first major transformation into Sarah Mary Williams/George Peters, for example, he appeals to the maternal instincts of a solitary woman in a new town, one who does not yet have neighbors with whom to share the latest news about an escaped slave. Immediately seeing past Huck's guise as a female, Mrs. Loftus decides that he must be a runaway apprentice, another form of the commoditized self. More important than this, however, is Mrs. Loftus's advice to Huck about how he should behave when trying to pass himself off as a girl in the future. Her suggestions are designed to produce a more convincing forgery, one guaranteed to fool others as she has not been fooled herself. In his essay "On the Mimetic Faculty," Walter Benjamin claims that humans' ability to mimic "is nothing other than a rudiment of the powerful compulsion in former times to become and behave like some*thing* else" (333; my emphasis). Benjamin's use of the word "thing" is evocative, creating a semantic link between mimicry of persons and forgery in the world of objects.

Huck's mimetic activity is much like the re-creation of an object for sale to someone who cannot afford the real thing. He must adopt a seemingly authentic exterior in order to convince his audience to "buy" his new self; however, this activity has far-reaching effects for the self that is being re-created. There is the possibility that "[o]nce the mimetic has sprung into being, a terrifically ambiguous power is established; there is born the power to represent the world, yet that same power is a power to falsify, mask, and pose. The two powers are inseparable." There is also evidence of "an almost drug-like addiction to mime, to merge, to become other—a process in which . . . *one also becomes matter*" (Taussig 42–43; my emphasis). Huck might easily be described as one addicted to miming, since he adopts new identities even in situations where they are not absolutely necessary, such as when he meets the Grangerfords or is caught by the raftsmen. He is far enough from home that the name "Huckleberry Finn" will be meaningless. However, in *Life on the Mississippi*, Twain gives a possible explanation for Huck's renaming when he discusses the importance of labels on paintings. He writes, "In Rome, people with fine sympathetic natures stand up and weep in front of the celebrated 'Beatrice Cenci the Day before Her Execution.' It shows what a label can do. If they did not know the picture, they would inspect it unmoved, and say, 'Young girl with hay fever; young girl with her head in a bag'" (359). Twain's awareness that labels can change perception, and with it the value of an object, is one he also gives Huck.

As previously noted, one context in which commoditization can occur is through dealings with strangers. This is because "the commodity context, as a social matter, may bring together actors from quite different cultural systems who share only the most minimal understanding (from the conceptual point of view) about the objects in question and agree *only* about the terms of trade" (Appadurai 15). Those strangers who commoditize Huck often do so in order to satisfy a need or desire: the King and Duke, for whom he becomes a source of income; the raftsmen, for whom he becomes a source of amusement; even Aunt Sally, for whom he becomes the missing Tom Sawyer. Huck's position has changed since he was first introduced to the reader in *Tom Sawyer*, primarily because he has become something of value (worth six thousand dollars, to be exact). In effect, Huck has gone from being "singular" and thereby unfit for trade (the singular object is without value because it cannot be exchanged for anything) to being "common" and thus exchangeable for a wide array of other things.[13] Ironically, it is Huck's self-acknowledged "commonness" that makes him suitable as a commodity. This shift in Huck's value position is apparent as he becomes more like Tom and less like himself, a copy rather than an original; it also reflects the paradoxes inherent in the very language of commodity culture: the valuable item is the common one, while the singular item, because it cannot be exchanged, is valueless.

As evidenced in the convoluted hair ball transaction, the discourse of commoditization can hide as much as it reveals, playing with perceptions and established systems. It thus invokes the discourse of authenticity. An example of this tension can be seen in advertisements of the late nineteenth century that describe a product as a genuine fake: an ad for glass that claims "for *true* authenticity there is no substitute for Restoration Glass" (Jones 18) or an ad for a watch that can pass for the genuine article because it "has all the appearances of a movement that you would pay $25.00 or more for" (Orvell 55). Twain acknowledged this tendency to blur the concepts of fake and genuine in *Life on the Mississippi*, where he describes an elaborate hoax involving cottonseed oil (260). He later describes a conversation between two "drummers," one selling oleomargarine, or fake butter, and the other the cottonseed olive oil described; each one prides himself on the ability of his product to deceive the consumer: "Maybe you'll butter everybody's bread pretty soon, but we'll cottonseed his salad for him from the Gulf to Canada, and that's a dead certain thing," says one man to the other (330). The replacement of genuine articles with "real" facsimiles undermines the very possibility of determining authenticity.

Huck's differentiating between "good" and "bad" money in the hair ball episode is another example of the paradoxes that can arise in the discourse of commoditization. While the average consumer would argue that fake money is not really "money" at all, that it is merely a hunk of metal or scrap of paper, Huck and Jim both understand that "money" is simply a value for exchange, whatever form it takes.[14] If it can be traded for something else then it is "good," regardless of the authenticity of its composition or provenance. This doublespeak in the world of commodities was also a concern in the late nineteenth century as consumers began to realize that language could be deceiving and pictures were not always to be trusted.[15] Huck is someone capable of deceiving others, but his deceptions are never initiated for personal gain or advancement (although he does adopt personas in order to acquire information, which can be a commodity in certain contexts). Instead, his counterfeiting is perpetrated in order to become what he believes is expected in a particular circumstance. In turn, he is frequently deceived himself, especially by those he admires. It is the hard lesson of treachery close to home that Huck must learn, the consequences of self-interested and self-aggrandizing impostures like those of Tom and, on a grander scale, the King and Duke (although they may also be a rather pessimistic forecast of what Tom has the potential to become).

The counterfeit quarter that Huck pays to the hair ball is also an apt symbol for his own status throughout the novel; repeatedly attempting to pass as something other, his true nature—his complete lack of hypocrisy—invariably shows through. As a result, he consistently fails to "pass" and is caught in one deception after another. Yet the matter of Huck's "authenticity," like that of the counterfeit quarter, is not so easily resolved. The hair ball scene suggests layers of authenticity at play in the text. After all, Huck is using a fake quarter to fool a magical object that is itself phony, and he does so to preserve a dollar that he has supposedly received in exchange for his six thousand dollars. The authenticity of the quarter is never an issue, since the brass shows through and it is greasy to the touch; rather, the question is whether the coin can be made to appear "real" enough to fool others, and whether these layers of deception will remain intact. These are also the dilemmas that face Huck. In his analysis of the concept, Trilling returns us to the violent origins of the word "authentic": "*Authenteo:* to have full power over; also, to commit a murder. *Authentes:* not only a master and a doer, but also a perpetrator, a murderer, even a self-murderer, a suicide" (131). Huck's series of self-murders and rebirths can ultimately be read as efforts to find or create an authentic self. He is engaged in a constant perfecting of identity, each a variation on a previous one, necessitated by the discovery of his imposture or the destruction of the community he has joined.[16]

Huck exhibits the traits of the authentic self described by the philosopher Charles Taylor; it (A) involves "(i) creation and construction as well as discovery, (ii) originality, and frequently (iii) opposition to the rules of society and even potentially to what we recognize as morality. But it is also true . . . that it (B) requires (i) openness to horizons of significance (for otherwise the creation loses the background that can save it from insignificance) and (ii) a self-definition in dialogue" (66). Huck's various identities are indeed the product of creation and discovery, and they often put him at odds with the existing moral order. He can even lay claim to "openness to horizons of significance," since he alone is able to see through hypocrisy and deceit to the real. But what he lacks is "a self-definition in dialogue"; Huck is forever alone in his quest to find a satisfactory self, even when surrounded by others. Without the availability of such an exchange with another who is also searching for authenticity, Huck's discoveries about the self must always exist in a vacuum, too easily swayed by the whims of others. Considering Huck and the tale(s) he tells as those of someone engaged in a struggle to own himself, in all senses of that expression, creates a new vantage point from which to examine other elements of the text as well, such as the slavery trope. Most important, it implicates Jim in the discourse of authenticity, ascribing a complexity to his character that has not always been recognized.

It is within the context of asserting authenticity that Twain appends the various introductory pieces to *Huck Finn*—the title, the "Notice," and the "Explanatory." However, in the double (and even triple) language of the novel, Twain's elaborate authenticating mechanisms are also designed to give credence to his fictional narrator, who is writing a fiction but who refers to Twain—the author of *The Adventures of Tom Sawyer*—by name in the second sentence. The "Notice" that warns readers not to attempt to find a motive, a moral, or a plot, while very official sounding in tone and diction, is essentially a product disclaimer, a way to forestall readers who might try to examine the contents too closely or try holding these contents to preset standards. It is also a way to account for anything that might seem inauthentic. But this begs the question: why is such a disclaimer necessary? It is not simply his book that Twain is protecting but also his own status as a commodity with a certain reputation as author, humorist, and social commentator. The disclaimer provides protection since the exaggerated threat to shoot anyone attempting to find a plot is calibrated to generate laughter rather than fear. Keeping in mind how Twain struggled to complete *Huck Finn*, however, another reading is possible: a fearful Twain who may himself have believed that the book had no plot, moral, or motive.[17] The humor is intended to make the threat seem less real, but it may have been quite real to Twain. He carefully watched the sales figures and reviews of the book (as always, but those activities seem more pointed in the context I have laid out). If we as readers choose to look too closely, in other words, we may discover the sham behind the mask, to our dismay as well as Twain's. The warning is perhaps a way to protect us from ourselves, from our own tendencies to try to push the mask aside, only to be disappointed by what we find beneath.

The "Explanatory," which addresses the use of dialects in the text, anticipates an audience used to "the culture of the copy" (to borrow a phrase from Hillel Schwartz) and thereby on the alert for fakes. Twain writes, "I make this explanation for the reason that without it many readers would suppose that all these characters were trying to talk alike and not succeeding" (2). This is Twain as the "expert," a trope just beginning to emerge in advertising in the latter part of the century. Thus, the "Notice" and the "Explanatory" represent the twin discourses of commodity and authenticity as well as two sides of the Twain persona. The shadowy figure beneath the surface of these various disclaimers and explanations is simply "The Author," who may or not be Huck Finn, or who may be the voice behind Huck, but it is a voice also "backed" by "G.G., Chief of Ordnance" (2). The process of authenticating that is so essential to the world of goods, and the questions raised by this activity, is an issue from the very first pages of *Huck Finn.*

Chapter 1 expands upon these themes but with even more elaborately convoluted rhetoric. Huck, who introduces himself as the narrative voice, describes Twain as having "told the truth" in *The Adventures of Tom Sawyer,* and then adds the qualifier "mainly" (7), which immediately raises the question of whether, like good versus bad money, truth can be anything but absolute and still be "the truth." This is immediately followed by Huck's attempt to determine who *does* tell the truth all the time. He can come up with a few possibilities—Aunt Polly, the Widow, Mary—but he seems unsure about even these. They are simply the most likely practitioners of a highly unlikely form of behavior. Huck's acquisition of six thousand dollars, which is the next piece of information he imparts, puts him suddenly and squarely in the middle class, the place where the discourses of commodities and authenticity intersect most violently.[18] Like the sham object, Huck is suddenly forced to take on a new identity as an upstanding member of middle-class society in St. Petersburg. He agrees to abandon his former ways, only occasionally sleeping out of doors and skipping school, and gradually finds himself becoming more accustomed to this new self. But it is also clear that the Widow Douglas and Miss Watson, who have adopted the roles of Huck's mentors/guardians, have no idea who he really is. Miss Watson's insistence on calling him "Huckleberry," a name that "contrasts, to comic effect, with the informality of the 'Huck' it artificially formalizes" (Nadel 129), is also an attempt to elevate him in the social order and create an identity commensurate with his new status as a member of the financial elite. For the most part, Huck maintains a facade of obedience, largely out of a combination of guilt, indebtedness, and insecurity; but his place in this society is purely a matter of money, and he knows it. He is with the Widow because he is now wealthy and, like the emerging nouveaux riche at the time the novel was published, he must be made to correspond to a preconceived set of behavioral standards if he is to be allowed to remain.

Huck's new life in town, his acceptance by the community, and his ability to associate freely with other town boys, especially Tom, are possible only because of his newfound fortune. But while money is a preliminary requirement for social acceptance, it is not enough on its own, as Huck eventually learns. When the "gang" is drawing up its oath of membership, he is on the verge of being excluded because he does not have any relative who might be killed were he to give the group's secrets away. (Pap is unsatisfactory since he often cannot be found.) However, Huck suddenly realizes that Miss Watson can serve as a stand-in, and the rest of the boys are satisfied with this.[19] The strict rules and standards created by the gang mirror the rules and standards that govern St. Petersburg society at large, but with ironic effect. Huck is expected to abide by the mores and codes of behavior of a slave-holding society, yet he is also an intruder into the social order, who, by virtue of his status as outsider, is able to cast revelatory light on any group he joins. The stringent rules of the gang underscore this fact, illustrating the reciprocal effect that social membership has on freedom. Social life in St. Petersburg, regardless of whether it is the society of adults or of young boys, is carefully structured. Superstition is part of this system, a complex form of rhetoric that must be understood and internalized if one does not want to be ostracized in certain circles.[20] Huck, for example, often ridicules those who ignore signs or do not know what certain actions mean, such as looking at the new moon over one's shoulder.

Throughout the novel, he searches for his place, even if it is membership in a society of two. Despite the fact that his father accuses him of trying to forget his position and better himself, Huck has no personal interest in climbing the social ladder—his new social status is a result of the interest taken in him by those like the Widow and Judge Thatcher—and he is all too willing to admit his lowly status. His class-consciousness is admirable by the standards of the genteel tradition: he consistently acknowledges the superior intelligence and ability of those above him as well as the relative place of those "below" him. Those above are the "quality," the kind of people among whom one cannot scratch no matter how much one may want to. Similarly, he never forgets his "place" in respect to Jim, that the latter is black and a slave despite the extent to which their friendship develops during the journey down the river. He is reluctant to admit that Jim may know something he doesn't, such as when Jim explains how to "fix" the counterfeit quarter. Huck is able to defer to Tom Sawyer's supposedly greater knowledge on any number of subjects, but as a black man Jim is clearly lower on the social scale, according to the hierarchy of the novel. Apologizing to him is a noteworthy gesture in Huck's world because it requires him to ignore its mores and codes of behavior.

Twain uses one term throughout the novel as a benchmark for all that is false and slavish in middle-class life: respectability. It is in order to become "respectable" that Huck has been placed with the Widow, it is his son's new respectability that Pap most despises, and it is the potential loss of his newfound respectability that haunts Huck as he tries to decide what to do about Jim. Even Tom Sawyer is implicated in this obsession, telling Huck he can join his "band of robbers" if he will "go back to the widow and be respectable" (7). Yet, it is also the "respectable" representatives of society who are most likely to be hypocrites, liars, and scoundrels beneath the surface. As a longtime outsider, Huck has a finely honed sense of the hypocrisies of middle-class life. For example, the Widow will not allow him to smoke, declaring it "a mean practice" and not "clean," but she dips snuff. Huck observes, in a rare sarcastic moment, "that was all right, because she done it herself" (8). The potential for hypocrisy was a growing concern at the end of the nineteenth century, as demonstrated by the way the topic was actively addressed in conduct and success manuals.[21] These matters—respectability and hypocrisy, as well as the discourses of commoditization and authenticity—come together in the Grangerford episode.[22]

The world of the Grangerfords, with its decades-long feud, its obsession with death, its emphasis on the domestic, its object-filled parlor, and its code of behavior that masks hypocrisy is a satirical microcosm of America in the later nineteenth century. From the moment he is stopped by the Grangerford dogs, having nearly been killed by a steamboat and having lost Jim in the process, Huck finds himself in Twain's version of Wonderland. It is a place where men and women can attend church with guns, hear a sermon about brotherly love, and then proceed home to continue killing one another. While the Grangerfords live in the rural South, much of what occurs in this episode also reverberates with life in towns and cities across the country. Twain uses this episode to critique southern attitudes and behaviors, but there is also more general social satire. Huck's first words are symbolic of his rather amorphous state throughout the text: when someone asks, "Who's there?" he replies, "It's me" (79). At that moment he could be absolutely anyone the interrogator wants him to be (including himself), but the suggestion that he is someone the speaker knows also serves to remove Huck from the role of stranger, a gesture he makes whenever he creates a new self. His preferred approach to imposture is to turn himself into someone his audience may be inclined to think they know, or else someone from the vicinity. In one instance he is from "Hookerville, seven mile below" (48), in another "[f]rom a trading scow. She lays up the bend yonder" (240). The result is to establish familiarity and a base level of trust. His description of himself to the Grangerfords as "only a boy" is designed to have the same effect, to downplay his own importance in order to gain confidence. As usual, Huck's ability to come up with a name on the spot is unrivaled. Here he becomes "George Jackson" (reminding us of the island where his journey began), an orphaned boy who has fallen off a steamboat. The disembodied male voice that responds is accompanied by the trappings of authority: a large house, dogs, and guns. Huck's explanation that he "only want[s] to go along by" (79) could be his mantra; it is certainly his dream in a culture that insists he stay put and maintain a single identity. Having determined that he is not a Shepherdson because he does not look like one—a form of knowledge about others that is possible only in a small community where everyone knows everyone else—Huck is given dry clothing, food, and a chance to tell his story. While inventive, the tale he concocts is mainly of interest for the way it foreshadows the events to come: the young girl who runs off to get married, the family wiped out by death, and the young boy who ends up in the river.

Naming has an important place in most discussions of commodity culture. For example, simply knowing the name of a popular item or brand indicates participation in a certain social group, especially where high-end items are concerned.[23] Thus, Buck's ability to repeat Huck's name is a way of giving him value and making him part of an exchange system. However, Huck's constant renaming of himself also subverts this system, since the names he invents have no connection to his real self. They are names created for the moment, designed to sell, and usually intended to be easy to remember. Huck's inability to remember the name he has chosen (and this happens on two occasions) indicates a disconnect between naming and any actual qualities he possesses. Huck must receive the name back, it must be used by the other person in a verbal exchange, in order for it to acquire value. Wearing Buck's clothing, Huck then becomes a mirror image of the other boy, complete with his own slave, and Buck unintentionally adds to the likeness by making sure Huck also has no patience for getting dressed up on Sundays and can take a joke (this one about Huck's old nemesis, Moses). One could say it is Huck's literal-mindedness that prevents him from getting a joke about being in the dark, especially since it reverberates with his own state in a number of ways, but this minor episode also suggests his understanding of language as an economic exchange involving words and meaning. Puns, for instance, undermine exchange value by subverting meaning. Like the dead Moses in whom he cannot "take . . . stock," riddles have no apparent value in Huck's schema. Huck's easy commoditization of the Grangerfords by semantically equating the family with the house in which they live—"It was a mighty nice family, and a mighty nice house, too" (82)—also makes them nearly interchangeable in terms of exchange value.

Names can also have economic value, especially titles (such as *Colonel* Grangerford). A title, for example, is "symbolic capital that is socially and even legally guaranteed" (Bourdieu, *Language and Symbolic Power*

241). The head of the family, and also head of a fighting unit since the entire family is engaged in the feud, Colonel Grangerford is a formidable presence; in his description, Huck evokes both the nobility and authority evinced by his title: he is "very tall and very slim" with "a darkish-paly complexion." He has the thin face, nose (including the nostrils), and hands associated with the aristocracy, as well as deep-set eyes and a high forehead. For Huck, what ultimately elevates the colonel is his wardrobe (his packaging, so to speak): "every day of his life he put on a clean shirt and a full suit from head to foot made of linen so white it hurt your eyes to look at it; and on Sundays he wore a blue tail-coat with brass buttons on it. He carried a mahogany cane with a silver head to it." Whether or not Grangerford really holds military rank is beside the point; his title and presentation indicate wealth and social status (both commodities on the open market), and as such his title is a signifier of his exchange value. Huck's description of the man bears this out, especially his unintentionally amusing observation that Colonel Grangerford "was well born, as the saying is, and that's worth as much in a man as it is in a horse, so the Widow Douglas said" (87).

The homestead that the colonel oversees is a backwoods southern plantation, one where the chivalric tradition is alive and well. The sons toast their parents' health each morning in a ritual in which Huck also takes part, and all the men wear white linen suits. Schwartz observes that "[c]ivility is the habit of masks, like its mirror image, hypocrisy" (78), and behind the mask of civility that they wear, behind their apparent kindness and good breeding, the Grangerfords are renegades and cold-blooded murderers, making them as great a fiction as Huck. It is "Huck's innocent questions about the nature of the feud . . . [that tear] the mask from the Southern aristocratic 'style': that concern with manners and elaborate language and behavior" (Messent 218). In other words, it takes one counterfeit to unmask another, however inadvertently. Even hogs are given greater authenticity in this text: they are the only ones that "don't go to church only when they've got to" (91). The feud, like any war, requires an objectification of the other; the Shepherdsons are not persons as much as they are targets in a deadly game of tag. The feud is also a spectacle, one that brings occasional excitement to otherwise quiet lives. When Huck suggests that the Shepherdsons must be cowards because they attacked an unarmed man, Buck is quick to leap to their defense, and rightly so. They must be figured as brave and equally aristocratic in order to be considered valid enemies and to validate in turn the Grangerfords' perceptions of themselves. The privileging of the visual—even here, where Huck assumes these men to be honorable because they look like gentlemen—is one way Twain undermines the very concept of authenticity. Jim can make a quarter "real" just by making it look so; similarly, Huck is safe because he doesn't look like a Shepherdson. Throughout the novel, what people see or not, what they choose to see or not, is often the foundation of opinions and actions, sometimes to the detriment of others, like Jim. It is because Jim is black on the outside that Huck cannot reconcile his behavior with his expectations. Destabilizing the visual aspect of authentication in the text, Twain mirrors the very dilemma people faced in their everyday lives.

While the description of the Grangerford parlor has been attributed to Twain's satire of the Victorian love of things, it is also emblematic of the family's hypocrisy and lack of authenticity.[24] The room that impresses Huck because it has "so much style" (82) is a mélange of objects, most of them machine-made. It is a testament to commodity culture, with its crockery animals, oil cloth from Philadelphia, pictures, painted curtains, and a clock of which Huck claims, "They wouldn't took any money for her." Central to the setting, however, and sitting on a table in the middle of the room is "a lovely crockery basket that had apples and oranges and peaches and grapes piled up in it which was much redder and yellower and prettier than real ones." Ever ready to appreciate a fellow imitation, Huck points out that the fruit is only recognizable as fake by the chips that expose "the white chalk or whatever it was underneath" (83). Fake fruit that looks even better than the real thing is an apt metaphor for the Grangerfords themselves, who seem so much more glamorous and impressive than anyone Huck has met before, but who will soon reveal the tragic substance beneath their mannered behavior.

In chapter 38 of *Life on the Mississippi*, Twain describes "The House Beautiful, a typical stylish dwelling" of the well-to-do. It contains many of the same features as the Grangerford parlor: "brass door-knob—discolored for lack of polishing . . . several books, piled and disposed, with cast-iron exactness, according to an inherited and unchangeable plan" (317), including plaster fruit "painted to resemble the originals—which they don't" (318). Faced with a feud over which they have no control, the Grangerfords have created a parlor that is a shrine to the man-made.[25] This observation can be extended to Huck as well, who prefers a false identity to the real thing, since it is one over which he, too, has complete control. The Grangerford home is also a perverse version of the domestic ideal celebrated in books such as those by Catherine Beecher (*A Treatise on Domestic Economy*) and *Godey's Lady's Book*. The attitude purveyed in such documents was of "the domestic sphere [as] protected from the corrupting powers of the competitive marketplace and the political arena by the nurturing powers of women" (Trachtenberg, *The Incorporation of America* 146). Rather than a haven from the corruption of the marketplace, however (after all, the feud may have been over land ownership), the Grangerford house, with Emmeline's macabre artwork on the walls and her scrapbook filled with "Graveyard School" poetry, is a nightmare vision. Objects are the means by which the family commemorates the now-dead Emmeline, and one reason they regret her death, at least according to Huck, is because "she had laid out a lot more of these pictures to do" (84). Huck's apparently authentic sorrow for those who die—Buck in particular—is set against the false mourning of Emmeline (although in the small community in which she moved, Emmeline must surely have known many of those about whom she wrote). When he finds the bodies of Buck and his companion in the river, he drags them ashore and says, "I cried a little when I was covering up Buck's face, for he was mighty good to me" (95). However, it is difficult to know whether Huck is grieving for individuals or for a way of life he had found vastly appealing, and his evaluation of Buck is based to an extent on what the young Grangerford was able to do for him rather than his innate goodness or kindness.

As a key episode in Huck's development, his stay with the Grangerfords can be read as crossing over into a different state, one that is more cynical but also more humane. Huck tells the reader that the events on that final day have stayed with him: "lots of times I dream about them" (94). Killed off yet again (Jim thinks he is dead, and Huck is willing to let the remaining Grangerfords think so as well), Huck begins the penultimate leg of his journey, one in which all the negative aspects of a commodity culture treated so far reach their satiric climax. Instead of a colonel, with the authority and privilege invested in that title, we now have a king and duke, men whose entire purpose is to find ways to capitalize on the very naiveté, greed, and desire for social improvement that advertisers at the turn of the century also learned to exploit for economic gain. The raft on which Huck and Jim end up once more becomes, for a short while, an island from all the sordidness and deceptions of the mainland, a place where things are "free and easy and comfortable" (96), and exchange is on their own terms. The arrival of the King and Duke introduces a new level of chaos and more insidious forms of deception because these are carefully planned and executed.

There are varieties of inauthenticity depicted in the novel, and some are more dangerous than others. Messent observes that the "masquerades" of those such as the King and Duke are "much more disruptive to the established order than Huck's" (213). The difference is in the intent, in the planned nature of their deceptions. Except for the case of Sarah Mary Williams, Huck is coerced into his impostures, either by circumstances or by the mistakes of others. The King and Duke have monetary gain as their ultimate goal; they are truly creatures of the marketplace who make conscious use of the commodity culture of which they are a part, creating products for consumption such as the Royal Nonesuch. But the primary difference is that while Huck is an impostor, the King and Duke are impersonators, and the distinction is important because while "imposture [is] the compulsive assumption of invented lives . . . impersonation [is] the concerted assumption of another's public identity" (Schwartz 72).[26] According to this model, "[i]mpostures succeed because, not in spite, of their fictitiousness. They take wing with congenial cultural fantasies. Impostors persevere because any fear they may have of being discovered is overshadowed by their dread of being alone. Their perpetual reincarnations of second bodies arise out of a *horror vacui*, terror of empty spaces within and without" (71). The "congenial cultural fantasies" with which Huck "take[s] wing" include some of the most treasured fantasies associated with America: the myth of the self-made man, the myth of endless frontiers, and the myth of a classless society. In addition, this paradigm allows us to read Huck's adopted identities as a way to conquer the kind of loneliness he feels at the Widow's before Tom shows up to rescue him, as well as giving new meaning to his obsession with death.

Whatever sympathy we may have for Huck, however, does not mitigate the fact that he ultimately allows Jim to become commodified in

ways even Miss Watson would not have tolerated. Jim becomes a spectacle, a sideshow for the amusement of two boys. His humanity is sacrificed to Huck's desire to fit in, to go along, whatever the cost. Huck has
experienced moral growth over the course of the novel, but then he is
unexpectedly pulled back into the comfortable and familiar world of
the Phelps farm, an extension of his life in Hannibal (literally, since
Aunt Sally is sister to Tom's Aunt Polly). This is Huck's opportunity to
see what life will be like should he return to the Widow; the protracted
freeing of Jim, the tarring and feathering of the King and Duke, the ri-
diculous machinations of Tom Sawyer—all of these are necessary if
Huck is to achieve his ultimate realization: that this is not the life he
wants. It may be a life with clean sheets, good food, and safety, but it
is also one in which Jim is a slave, Tom is in charge, and Huck is a non-
entity (they believe he is Tom, but Tom is actually there, which negates
the imposture). Huck must find an alternative to the culture of the commodity if his growth is to continue, and in order to do so, he must leave.
At the end of novel, he stands as a symbol of both hope and despair,
trapped between possibility and reality.

Twain understood that the fake was becoming ever more the norm in
America, yet the very acts of self-creation in which Huck indulges—his
commoditization of himself and his later self-examination and moral
growth, as limited as they are—reenact American ideology, with its emphasis on new beginnings and a potentially ideal future.[27] However, the
only authentic freedom in the novel, the only way to truly own oneself,
is through death, either faking one's own death, as Huck does early in
the novel, or as a result of the death of someone else, as Miss Watson's
death sets Jim free and Pap's death does the same for Huck. But, as Huck
has already informed us, it doesn't make sense to put stock in dead
people. Thus, Twain suggests that there is ultimately no escape from the
commoditization of the self, from the enslavement that comes in so
many forms in modern life. Huck is the product of a society that prefers
lies to truth and valorizes the fake and hypocritical over the real and
genuine. His ability to be something he is not is finally exposed as common, not singular.

This is where we then find Huck in the hotly contested final section
of the novel: a boy who creates a world in which he becomes Tom Sawyer, and a world in which nothing is what it seems. Tom may be the pri-

mary maker of that world, but Huck has the power to unmake it and fails to do so. It is Tom who plans for all three of them, Jim included, to head for the Territory to continue their adventures. It does not occur to either boy, but especially Huck, given what he knows, that Jim will want to remain with his family now that he is free. It is unclear what role the former slave would play, but it can hardly be that of equal adventurer. Once the various subterfuges have been revealed, however, it is Jim who attains the one thing he has most wanted: freedom. It is in the final chapter of the novel that he reveals the truth about Pap, evincing once more his understanding of knowledge as a commodity. Now that the information about Pap is worthless, Jim is willing to let it go. Huck's lack of anger at the deception is a tribute to his understanding of just how such transactions work. As in the hair ball episode, Huck and Jim have manipulated one another, and both have benefited from the exchange. Jim ultimately attributes his success in attaining his freedom to a skill previously associated with Huck, the ability to read; however, in Jim's case it is the ability to read and interpret omens: "I *tole* you I ben rich wunst, en gwineter to be rich *agin;* en it's come true, en heah she *is! Dah,* now! Doan talk to *me*—signs is signs" (228). However, Jim's revelation is followed immediately in the text by Huck's summary paragraph, which contains several crucial revelations.

The first is his realization that Tom has what he has always wanted, namely adventure and glory in the shape of a bullet he wears around his neck, making him once again the victor in the exchange system. It is not enough to say, as Bennett Kravitz does, that Tom, "who seems to control his own fate, earns nothing but a bullet wound for his absurd attempt to free Jim the way 'the book says'" (25). Tom also earns a very potent commodity: the bullet will surely bring him added respect and admiration among his peers back home, which is why he wears it as a badge of honor. If nothing else, Tom knows the practical value of such a talisman, and he is correct in thinking it was worth the cost, at least from the commodity culture perspective. The bullet is in the same category as the nickel Jim received from the devil, an object that will soon have a life of its own and an exchange value far exceeding its actual worth. The second important revelation in the final paragraph concerns Huck's impending restoration to a so-called civilized existence and his reaction. His decision not to return is an unconscious response to the invidious nature of commodity culture in the form of Aunt Sally's plan to adopt and civilize him; he declares, "I been there before" (229). The "Territory" is an ambiguous place, unlike St. Petersburg and the other towns along the Mississippi; it might belong to anyone or no one. It may, in fact, be the one place in Huck's time still relatively untouched by the commodity mentality. However, Twain wrote *Huck Finn* when the frontier was on the verge of closing, so the escape route he provides for Huck is no longer available.

Written at a pivotal moment in American literature by an author who personified many of the nation's concerns and obsessions, what started out as another "boys'" book (like *Tom Sawyer*) became a critique of nineteenth-century life and mores; in other words, a counterfeit boys' book. The discourses of commoditization and authenticity, given expression in the twin figures of Huck and Jim, enabled Twain to explore in new ways the contradictions of American ideology, the trope of slavery, and the effects of commodity culture. Huck is the lens, however flawed, through which we view the contradictions and disjunctions beginning to emerge as the nation approached the new century. The final irony is that Huck the impostor exposes the imposture and impersonations of those around him, their double-dealing and deceptions. Huck's repeated attempts to become free seem always destined to fail, yet it is his ongoing effort that we cling to, apparently, since most analyses of his character tend toward the optimistic and affirmative. His failures, such as they are, expose the counterfeit nature of the American Dream, which is in part a celebration of the ability to re-create the self. Commoditization lies at the heart of this process, treating the self—or the other—as raw material to be molded and packaged for sale to the unwary buyer, with disappointment as the inevitable result when the hoax is revealed. This is one of the consequences of a culture that claims to value authenticity while privileging the commodity. Yet the last lines of *Huck Finn* ultimately give us hope that the real thing—in this case, the freedom of the uncommoditized self—is possible. Poised between the lure of the Territory and a life in Hannibal, Huck decides he will "light out . . . ahead of the rest" (229), leaving even Tom behind. With his own identity restored, with the threat of Pap eliminated, and now free from the moral responsibility of a runaway Jim, Huck finally belongs only to himself.

4

Connoisseurs and Counterfeits

Edith Wharton's *The House of Mirth*

Our stories remain "fluid" as long as we are alive.
—Linda A. Bell, Sartre's Ethics of Authenticity

The crucial opening scene of Edith Wharton's *The House of Mirth* (1905) immediately introduces the central characters in the drama about to unfold—Lily Bart and Lawrence Selden—and does so in a setting synonymous with power, commodities, wealth, and mobility of various types in the nineteenth century: Grand Central Station. Like Huck and Jim in the hair ball episode, Lily and Selden are engaged in a complex system of transactions, with layers and permutations not obvious to the casual observer. They are also from vastly different worlds, although their paths do intersect on occasion. Selden is the observer, the one who initially has the upper hand in the encounter because he sees Lily before she sees him; he even plans to use this advantage for his amusement by seeing how Lily will try to avoid seeing him should she prefer not to be engaged in conversation. She is described here as a woman both distinctive and mysterious. She "[stands] apart from the crowd" (3), and yet she also draws attention from a few of those rushing past on the way to their trains, those who seem to understand that there is a unique item in their midst and take a moment to appreciate the sight. Selden is clearly one of those equipped to enjoy the visual rewards Lily offers, but most of his description is speculative in nature: Why is she in this spot at this particular moment? Is she alone? Is she waiting for someone? To what extent has her beauty been enhanced? He acknowledges the extent of her beauty but also observes that "the qualities distinguishing her from the herd of her sex were chiefly external" (5). The association of Lily, of all women, with animals suggests dehumanization, a necessary step in the objectification process. The same is true of Selden's treatment of Lily as a series of disparate body parts—a "vivid head," a "little ear" (3, 5).[1] Torn between admiration and uncertainty about Lily's value and authenticity, Selden's role as spectator changes to temporary "possessor" when he agrees to find her a place to relax and have tea. From connoisseur to collector, Selden's positions in this scene foreshadow those of every man with whom Lily will come in contact. None of them will be knowledgeable enough to comprehend her full worth, nor will any of them be able to possess her completely. Lily is a commodity who refuses to be owned on the terms set by others; her rejection of the mores of her society threatens to expose the duplicity and lack of authenticity in others, and this ultimately results in her destruction.

In this encounter Lily is depicted as a valuable commodity: she stands out from the crowd, she excites interest and speculation, and she is described in minute detail from head to foot. However, Selden's questions, in particular his reference to her age, raise doubts as to her actual worth. This is indeed a pivotal moment for Lily; not only is she poised between social engagements and destinations, but she is also beginning to realize that she is trapped between society's expectations (that she will marry like everyone else) and her desire for love and self-fulfillment. Unlike the characters in Twain's novel, Lily and Selden live in a world of country homes, dinner parties, and the theater, yet neither is a full-fledged member of that world. While Selden's description emphasizes difference—Lily's from him: "his course lay so far out of her orbit" and Lily's from other women: "Was it possible that she belonged to the same race?" (4, 5)—she and he actually have much in common, beginning with their solitary presence in Grand Central Station on this Monday afternoon. Both are single and of an age when most of those they know are married; both have no immediate family in the form of parents or siblings; both are fastidious in their personal habits and must be surrounded by beauty; and both hover on the fringe of wealthy New York society, although this position is relatively new to Lily, whose star is just beginning to fade. As it turns out, she is currently in need of Selden's assistance; she has missed the train that will take her to Bellomont, the home of Judy and Gus Trenor, and must wait two hours for the next one. As they head out of the station in search of a quiet spot for a cup of tea, Selden's remark that while "[t]he resources of New York are rather meagre," they will "invent something," if necessary (5) paves the way for a narrative steeped in the discourses of material culture and counterfeiting, and one in which the availability of resources and acts of invention are crucial for survival.

Lily has been described by critics as an object for trade, as a commodity in the marriage market, as an ornament, as the object of the male gaze, as an outsider, and as a victim, and these are helpful descriptions as far as they go. In addition, recent essays have focused in various ways on the role of economic exchange in the novel, especially the exchange of women as well as Lily's treatment as "merchandise." However, none of these readings considers Lily as an object per se.[2] But most of these readings suggest that Lily remains somewhat static throughout the text, at least in terms of her object position, whereas a metamorphosis is clearly under way when Selden sees her. From the encounter in the train station until her ultimate death, Lily follows a very specific commodity path. Beginning as a luxury good available only to the most discriminating connoisseur, Lily makes decisions, both good and bad, that compromise her value and her status as a commodity. By the end of the novel, rejected by all those she trusted and loved (except Gerty Farish, the other woman who has rejected the usual path designated for women), she has moved into the final category for commodities: rubbish.[3] Her changing status becomes a barometer for determining the authenticity, sincerity, and even morality of others. In other words, using Lily's downward spiral through the social classes as a vehicle, Wharton is able to explore the greed, treachery, and hypocrisy at the center of American society at the turn of the century.

Lily's commodity status when the text opens is that of a luxury, one that is both "exquisite" and apparently hand crafted, as many such items traditionally are. She possesses all the characteristics attributed to such an item: she is accessible only to the elite, she is difficult to acquire, she "signal[s] fairly complex social messages," one must have "specialized knowledge" in order to acquire her, and acquisition of her is directly linked to "body, person, and personality" (Appadurai 38).[4] From the outset, Lily acknowledges that she is "very expensive" (10) and therefore available to only a few, highly select buyers. She requires a level of maintenance that could be provided only by someone with a great deal of discretionary income and a certain background. (As her cousin Jack Stepney remarks, "we don't *marry* Rosedale in our family" (166), making clear just one of the limitations on possible suitors.) While she is not one of a kind, she is a rare item, primarily because of her beauty. She is also a "highly specialized" product, as Selden observes while they walk through the station (5), and it is this specialized state, in part, that limits her options. She acknowledges that some men (and their mothers) may be afraid of her, and she has also put herself in compromising situations that anyone looking to acquire her must then cope with. Lily also conveys complex—even contradictory—social messages: she "must have a great deal of money" (10) on the one hand, but she would like to have a room of her own, a place where she can arrange the furniture as she pleases and be alone, a sentiment evoked by her visit to Selden's rooms. She has been produced to marry—as Selden observes, "Isn't marriage your vocation? Isn't it what you're all brought up for?" (9)—yet she consistently avoids taking the final plunge, even when she knows (as with Percy Gryce) that she is running out of options. She loves beauty and comfort, but she also refuses to take the easy route to acquiring them. While she is in many ways the product of her cultural moment, a voracious consumer who looks to things to fill the emptiness within, she is an anachronism. Like the item of an older period that Wharton privileges in *The Decoration of Houses,* Lily harkens back to "a mellower civilization—of days when rich men were patrons of the 'arts of elegance,' and when collecting beautiful objects was one of the obligations of a noble leisure" (184).[5] While this is an apt description of Lily, it hardly applies to the men who would like to own her—Gus Trenor, Simon Rosedale, and Selden; they desire Lily not for her truly valuable qualities—her gentleness, her innate honesty, her style—but simply for her value as an investment, one that should bring a greater return over time. Their interactions with Lily point to some of the consequences of consumer culture woven throughout the novel: wealth has become the arbiter of taste rather than a means to acquire it; the connoisseur has simply become the one with the largest bank account; and buyers privilege expense over actual worth in the objects they purchase.

It is ironic that the two men with the specialized knowledge needed to fully appreciate and understand Lily, Selden and Rosedale, are so dra-

matically different in almost every way. Selden's surprise when he first
sees Lily at the train station (and it is his "seeing" her, his intense close
observation that is the essential activity in the scene) stems from his
inability to place her in this particular setting, and Selden is a man
who does not like to be surprised. In fact, he prides himself on "knowing" things, which is one reason he immediately attempts to restore his
psychic equilibrium by testing Lily, aware that "if she did not wish to
be seen she would contrive to elude him." Like a detective gathering
clues, he works to piece together what he sees and what he thinks he
knows or surmises in order to account for her. His interest is almost ethnographic in its close description of her features, her habits, and her
mannerisms. He observes that "her simplest acts [seem] the result of
far-reaching intentions" (3), and he admires "the modelling of her little
ear, the crisp upward wave of her hair . . . and the thick planting of her
straight black lashes" (5). The chance to observe her even more closely
and without interference is too good to pass up, and he agrees to keep
her entertained until her train arrives. However, while Selden uses the
comparative method of the ethnographer, his intention is not to draw
conclusions about the culture that produced Lily. Instead, this scene is
primarily about Selden's pleasure at Lily's expense: the pleasure of his
first sight of her in this unlikely place ("his eyes had been refreshed by
the sight of Miss Lily Bart"), the pleasure he will receive by trying her
social skills, his pleasure in her physical appearance, his enjoyment of
her indiscretions, and even his pleased surprise when she agrees to come
up to his room for tea (an indiscretion for which she will pay dearly
while he will pay nothing). This rare opportunity to be close to Miss
Bart is a "luxurious pleasure," akin to that of holding a rare piece of
porcelain—he even describes her in such terms, as having a "fine glaze
of beauty" (5)—or a leather-bound first edition of one of his favorite
books. The effect on the senses is almost narcotic, and he seems a bit
dazed by her proximity.

Although he would prefer to be an actual collector, Selden is more
appropriately a "cicerone," a specific type of connoisseur. While the actual definition of cicerone is "one who shows and explains antiquities
and curiosities to foreign visitors" (*OED*), the word has come to mean
"a learned escort in museums and private collections. As such, it suggests someone who has access to hidden domains of art and treasures.

In the capacity of disseminating arcane knowledge and gaining access where none is thought possible, the cicerone regulates the act of spectating. By doing so, such a guide enhances his or her own value at the same time as the value of the art objects increases through explanation. . . . the cicerone must market himself or herself as an arbiter of taste, not just a possessor of facts" (Hepburn 36).[6] The cicerone can also, like the connoisseur, be one who appreciates without necessarily owning. Selden serves as guide for the reader in critical moments, presenting a view of Lily that only he is able to provide because he has access to her in ways no one else does. He is also an aspiring collector, but one without the means or courage to acquire Lily, which makes him envious of other potential collectors.[7]

Watching Lily at the station, Selden's is the reaction of the connoisseur coming upon a rare find, someone who has spent years honing his taste for the beautiful and the singular (even though he cannot afford to own the things he loves). His appraising gaze recognizes and appreciates a valuable item, and she is the ongoing object of his attention (she is still, at this point, something in which the right man might invest with hope of a good return). As a product designed to elicit male desire, inhabiting a world in which men control the wealth, it is only fitting that Lily is introduced to the reader through the male gaze. Much has been written about "specularity" and the function of the gaze.[8] As objects (in both meanings of the word) of the gaze, women occupy a position that is both subjective and commodifying. It seems fitting that a novel about a woman who is expected to become the property of a man opens with a man taking visual ownership of her, ownership that he maintains until the last page—when he also gets the last word.[9] The dispassionate way in which Selden evaluates Lily—trying to determine whether her inner and outer selves are compatible, whether "the material was fine, but . . . circumstance had fashioned it into a futile shape" (5)—deftly places her the category of lovely but inaccessible object d'art. Yet this is also a moment in which Selden's pleasure is tempered by the possibility of deception, the suspicion that haunts their entire relationship. For example, seeing Lily in the station, he realizes that her "air of irresolution . . . might . . . be the mask of a very definite purpose," while he also notices that beneath her hat and veil, "she regain[s] the girlish smoothness, the purity of tint, that she was beginning to lose after eleven years" (3); he even wonders if her hair has been "brightened by art" (5). As a connoisseur, Selden is interested only in authentic objects, not fakes, regardless of how well made they are; the very reputation of the connoisseur rests on his ability to differentiate the real from the false. Thus, a misappraisal in regards to Lily would also be a black mark against his knowledge and expertise. However, there is also something of the voyeur in Selden, the one who wants to look without necessarily touching. He has clearly been watching Lily for some time; he knows her habits and mannerisms, and he knows enough about her "discretions" and "imprudences" (4) to draw some conclusions about her character. He then spends the rest of the novel watching her, even when he doesn't expect to be, as when she exits the Trenor house.

Immobile in a moving crowd when Selden first spots her, standing in a venue that suggests motion and change, Lily seems like an object in a dream (which will later become a nightmare).[10] This connection between Lily and the world of objects/dreams is reinforced in several later encounters with Selden. During their solitary afternoon at Bellomont, it is as if time is temporarily suspended and "they [seem] lifted into a finer air," while after her role in the tableaux vivants, she and Selden stand in the garden "accepting the unreality of the scene as part of their own dream-like sensations" (76, 144). In the latter episode, Lily invokes the dream state after one of her most highly charged moments as a commodity.[11] Her connection to dreams also suggests an unreality that is expressed in persistent speculation about her, such as the questions Selden asks himself at the station. The connoisseur must, of course, verify the authenticity of the object he is evaluating. He then proceeds to describe her in language that validates his own finely honed perceptions. In a period when "newness" was valorized and even preferred, it is in the field of art that newness is still risky, that the antique and the masterpiece are privileged categories. Therefore, a Lily who is not "new" (as Selden observes) (3) is more valuable, more emphatically a luxury, than a new Lily would be. Even the "argument from design" (4) to which Selden refers in his description of Lily, while it generally refers to a theory for the existence of God, suggests the creative energy behind artistic creation, including Lily's creation of her "self."[12]

As they stroll down Madison Avenue—a "dream street" in the American cultural imagination, and one that has immediate associations with consumer culture—Selden's doubts and "confusion" continue. The narrator observes that Selden "had a confused sense that she must have cost a great deal to make, that a great many dull and ugly people must, in some mysterious way, have been sacrificed to produce her" (5). She is indeed a production, one on whom many resources have been expended, including some of her own, but also one whose purpose is purely decorative. She is both a work of art and artifice, and Selden, whose perspective we share in the important opening sequence, seems torn between admiration and repulsion. Ultimately, however, it is his frustration that is most apparent: he is able to appreciate Lily's beauty and grace, but his lack of wealth means he will never be able to truly possess this rare item, except in odd moments such as this when she takes herself temporarily out of her usual path.[13]

While she seems at first glance to be a viable commodity for the marriage market—beautiful, malleable, and charming—there are crucial ways in which Lily never fits that classification. She understands and seems to accept that she is an object for exchange, yet her subconscious acts of subversion send Percy Gryce and other suitors running at the very moment they should be proposing. As Carry tells Selden, "That's Lily all over, you know; she works like a slave preparing the ground and sowing her seed; but the day she ought to be reaping the harvest she over-sleeps herself or goes off on a picnic. . . . Sometimes . . . I think it's just flightiness—and sometimes I think it's because, at heart, she despises the things she's trying for. And it's the difficulty of deciding that makes her such an interesting study" (197). These contradictions and paradoxes contribute to the picture of a woman who is indeed "singular," although not in ways her society is likely to appreciate. She is beyond the means of all but one or two potential buyers; conversely, she is also subjected to ongoing questions about her authenticity and her singularity, as are all collectibles. Carry's language casts Lily as a case to be studied rather than a flesh and blood woman with needs and desires; or, if she has them, they apparently do not count for much. Eventually, she will be held up as an example for other young women of what not to do or become, and society will continue on its destructive, commodifying way.

Wharton herself did not collect art, but she did write frequently about collectors and collecting between 1902 and 1913 in such stories as

"The Moving Finger," "The Dilletante," and "The Pot-Boiler." In these, "she exposes the complex relation between those who produce art, those who are the subjects of art, those who appreciate art, and those who collect art" (Hepburn 26).[14] (And in *The House of Mirth* she considers the subject *as* art in the form of Lily Bart.) Collecting as an activity is introduced early in the novel in connection with the Gryce Americana collection, which has the reputation of being the best in the world. Questioning Selden about Americana and collecting during their afternoon tea in his apartment, Lily later makes use of the information when she meets Percy Gryce, the current overseer of the Americana collection, on the train to Bellomont. She entertains visions of becoming "what his Americana had hitherto been: the one possession in which he took sufficient pride to spend money on it" (51), until she sabotages her own plans by spending the afternoon with Selden and angering Bertha. Part of the reason for this is that Lily is only beginning to understand what it will mean to be "collected," to become one more rare item owned by a connoisseur, and to lose her singular identity in the process.

Collecting is a complex and socially constructed activity, and as such the collector represents many of the tendencies of the larger social order. Selden's attitude toward Lily says much about consumer society at the turn of the twentieth century as well as about desire, gender roles, and the construction of authenticity. He recognizes her potential as a collectible the day he rescues her at Grand Central Station, and his appreciation is fueled by desire, the primary motivation for all collecting.[15] Because he does not possess the means to collect on a grand scale, Selden has learned to enjoy instead the "heightened emotions" that accompany desire (Belk, *Collecting in a Consumer Society* 4). This is what he experiences when he meets Lily at the station and what he feels with increasing intensity later at Bellomont, where he goes specifically to see her. Selden admits he is not a collector, telling Lily that he "simply like[s] to have good editions of the books [he is] fond of" (11).

Yet he is, in fact, a collector; he simply accumulates experiences and sensations rather than objects. One reason for his interest in Lily is that she always provides a "spectacle," a unique experience to entertain him, and one he gets free of charge (although she frequently pays a price for these moments), which most certainly would not be the case were he to marry her. Without the means to collect actual objects, Selden must live vicariously through the collections of others, enjoying the fruits of their labors without spending anything himself.[16] He attends functions like the Welly Brys's entertainment because, as the narrator observes, "he enjoy[s] spectacular effects, and [is] not insensible to the part money plays in their production: all he ask[s is] that the very rich should live up to their calling as stage-managers, and not spend their money in a dull way" (139). Lily, who can be uncommonly insightful about such things as a result of her own precarious social position, confronts Selden on several occasions with the discrepancy between his attitude toward the elite and his actions. During their afternoon at Bellomont, for instance, she turns the table on him and remarks, "It seems to me . . . that you spend a good deal of your time in the element you disapprove of." He counters with the rationale that he has managed to "remain amphibi-ous; it's all right as long as one's lungs can work in another air. The real alchemy consists in being able to turn gold back again into something else" (72). This is clearly what Selden believes he will be able to do with Lily, because he is convinced that he alone can help her live up to the gift of her physical beauty. However, his desire is not without its limitations, just as the desire of any collector for the cherished object is tempered by conditions such as availability, authenticity, and cost.

Being added to a collection transforms objects, as Lily seems to know intuitively. Belk compares collecting to a form of ritual in which "the empowering (priestly) collector brings special objects into the collec-tion, and in so doing decommoditizes, singularizes, and sacralizes them" (*Collecting in a Consumer Society* 62). There is a sacramental quality about collecting, first because it often involves sacrifice of some kind (time, money), and second because the collectible, once obtained, is ex-pected to transfer some of its uniqueness to its possessor. The fact that a collected item is one that has been sacralized (no real collector of Americana would compromise the condition of a book by actually read-ing it) suggests another reason for Lily to aspire to this status. As a rare kind of collectible, Lily can achieve several ends. She can make her-self even more valuable, her availability is limited to a few of the very wealthiest collectors, and she can be assured that her potential owner will perceive her as something too valuable to use. In other words, Lily

as collectible will not have to worry about having sexual relations with
the man who ultimately owns her. (This may be the "price" Rosedale
will be expected to pay if she agrees to marry him [266].)

Lily's status as a collection-worthy item has various stages. Initially
she is one of the rarest of objects, out of reach of all but a few. However,
two things ultimately affect her value: her refusal to compromise her
own happiness and mores for the sake of marriage (which is the equivalent of collecting herself) and her change in status after her appearance
in the tableau vivant, which begins her shift from exclusive object to the
more common collectible, the bibelot. Failing to attract as a luxury item,
and with rumors about her relationship with Gus Trenor beginning to
surface, Lily must find a way to restore interest and make herself desir-
able once again. The social-climbing Wellington Brys's decision to host
a "general entertainment," one that will include tableaux vivants, provides her with a golden opportunity, one for "displaying her own beauty
under a new aspect: of showing that her loveliness was no mere fixed
quality, but an element shaping all emotions to fresh forms of grace"
(138). Rather than being something no one wants—and whose value is at
the mercy of women like Bertha Dorset—Lily attempts to affirm her
status as something worth possessing because, as she readily acknowledges, "people [are] tired of her. They would welcome her in a new character, but as Miss Bart they knew her by heart" (105). Unfortunately,
the tableau has the reverse effect. When the curtain parts on Lily's re-
creation of Reynolds's Mrs. Lloyd," "the unanimous 'Oh!'" that follows
indicates the extent to which she has succeeded in making herself be
seen in a new way (141). While the others have merely enacted scenes,
Lily has literally turned herself into a work of art, a living portrait available to only the most discriminating connoisseurs. As it turns out, however, the single true connoisseur on hand that evening—because he recognizes Lily's value as a collectible—is Rosedale, who later tells Carry
Fisher, "My God, . . . if I could get Paul Morpeth to paint her like that,
the pictur'd appreciate a hundred percent in ten years" (167).

As in the opening scene of the novel, Lily is presented here through
the eyes of Lawrence Selden, who is convinced that he is now seeing "the
real Lily Bart." (The irony that Lily seems most herself in this static
pose, when she is imitating another woman (Mrs. Lloyd), who is also
imitating someone else, is apparently lost on Selden.) But while Selden

would like to think he appreciates Lily for who she is at this moment
(or who she might become)—"[t]he noble buoyancy of her attitude,
its suggestion of soaring grace, reveal[ing] the touch of poetry in her
beauty"—his assessment of her relies almost exclusively on her physical
beauty and his appreciation of it, not on any sense of her inner value.
His flawed connoisseurship is underlined by the words of the supposedly "experienced connoisseur" (a description of Ned Van Alstyne that
drips with sarcasm) that follow: "there isn't a break in the lines any-
where, and I suppose she wanted us to know it." Van Alstyne's focus is
also exclusively on Lily's physical appearance, something he and Selden
have in common despite the latter's feeling of "indignant contempt" for
the speaker (142). The tableau vivant presents Lily for the first time as a
sexualized object of desire, a change that is reflected in the responses of
the various men watching her, during but especially following the event.
It is in response to the tableau, after all, that Selden expresses his love to
her for the first time, Gus Trenor tries to seduce her, and Rosedale pro-
poses marriage.

Although his seems the more chaste response, Selden's desire for Lily
as collectible has always been deeply intertwined with his physical desire
for her as a woman.[17] With her appearance as "Mrs. Lloyd," Lily crosses
the very fine line between an ideal and a more common object of desire;
she now enters the world of the bibelot. Defined as a "small curio or
article of *virtù*" (*OED*), the bibelot has far richer cultural implications.
Rémy G. Saisselin describes such objects as occupying the "ambiguous
space where love of possession, love of art, and social ambition meet"
(xv). It is a locus inhabited by women as well, to such an extent that
woman and the bibelot have become almost synonymous. In the nineteenth century, "the work of art . . . becomes a luxury item. It also becomes a 'collectible,' an apt if inelegant term sometimes used by antique
dealers. Finally, the work of art functions as an object within an intimate interior space inseparable from woman herself." Woman becomes
both "the most expensive bibelot and . . . at the same time, a voracious
consumer of luxury and accumulator of bibelots" (53).[18] Lily exists at
the center of this confluence: she is a work of art/expensive bibelot,
something to be added to an existing collection, and she is a "voracious
consumer," so much so that she is usually deeply in debt for her own
bibelots. She also recognizes that consumption is the key to success in

her milieu, and that she must give the impression of wealth even if she does not actually have the means to support it. (Her mother prided herself on this very sleight of hand: the ability to make a little seem like a lot.) It is her ability to create impressions, her ability to counterfeit, that causes the greatest trouble in the long run.

For example, even though she is not actually anyone's mistress, once Lily takes money from Gus Trenor she unwittingly cast herself into this role, one that affects all future transactions with men and women alike. Trenor clearly believes his money has purchased a stake in Lily, and after the tableau, when she seems to be moving beyond his reach, he reacts with the anger of someone who believes he has been cheated. "I didn't begin this business—kept out of the way, and left the track clear for the other chaps, till you rummaged me out and set to work to make an ass of me—and an easy job you had of it, too. That's the trouble—it was too easy for you—you got reckless—thought you could turn me inside out, and chuck me in the gutter like an empty purse. But, by gad, that ain't playing fair: that's dodging the rules of the game" (153–54).

His analogy about being tossed in the gutter "like an empty purse" suggests a robbery, and even more specifically, someone whose pocket has been picked. He accuses Lily of blatantly ignoring "the rules of the game" in which they are engaged; it never occurs to him that she may not understand either the rules or the game. In Trenor's world, this is a fairly common economic exchange, and he thinks he knows what he should be able to expect in return. Lily, however, still under the impression that the money she has received is hers by right, however naïve, is shocked by Trenor's advances, even more so because he clearly thinks she has done this sort of thing before. Her lack of knowledge is not solely her own fault, however; it is fostered first by her mother and her social circle, then sustained by the inexperience and naiveté of Aunt Peniston. If *The Decoration of Houses* is Wharton's rejection of the bibelot way of decorating (Saisselin 71), then *The House of Mirth* is her equally strenuous rejection of woman as bibelot, as well as her critique of a society that turns women into useless objects easily discarded.

Unlike most collectibles, which have no control over their fate, Lily makes very specific choices that lead her away from the life for which she has been groomed and toward her eventual destruction. She is a "self-consuming artifact" (Agnew 155), destroying herself even as she is destroyed by others.[19] Yet while she must bear responsibility for most of her decisions, she is abetted by Selden, who has neither the means nor the courage to own Lily himself but who does not want anyone else to own her, either. His repeated subversions of her efforts to find someone to take possession of her through marriage—his conscious manipulation of her so-called better self, the way he insinuates himself back in her life at decisive moments—makes him complicit in her destruction. His ambivalence about Lily, so evident in the opening scene, reveals a level of dissatisfaction that will increase over time, manifesting itself in repeated attempts to tear her down so he will no longer desire her. Even in the opening scene, while he can sense that Lily might be as fine underneath as she appears on the surface, he can't bring himself to a definitive evaluation. Selden is correct when he says he is not an actual collector (although he is referring to books at the time), but his avoidance of this activity is not purely financial; he also suspects the commitment that "collecting" Lily will entail and ultimately decides she is not worth the risk.[20]

Lily's appearance in the tableau vivant validates her as an object whose value is purely decorative, but as if to deny this, she continues to assure herself of her usefulness, to believe that her taste and artistic sense (her ability to trim hats, a claim that will be proved false in the most devastating way) set her apart from the other objects on the marriage market. However, the terms of transaction have changed. Before, Lily was a lovely object for exchange on the marriage market, but it was still an arrangement in which she might hope to find, if not love, at least sympathy and congeniality, and one in which she had a say. At least in the early stages, marriage in *The House of Mirth* seems to include congeniality and the union of like-minded persons, although that may change later. The marriage of Percy Gryce and Evie Van Osburgh may not be a love match, but neither is it strictly a business arrangement. Such a transaction is also perceived as an exchange: the wife brings social position and a conduit for the conspicuous display of wealth and in return she gets stability, comfort, and a measure of power. Now, Lily has become completely objectified, a lovely item for sale to the highest bidder. While diversion can sometimes lead to the "decommoditization" of an object, it can also result in "the (potential) intensification of commoditization by the enhancement of value attendant upon its diversion" (Appadurai 28). Lily's conversion to bibelot has the latter effect, increasing her value but also increasing her status as commodity.[21] It is because the terms have changed that each man advances his particular cause, certain he will be successful. Selden, as we have seen, believes he has finally discovered the true Lily and that he alone can save her. Trenor no longer sees Lily as a woman who must be treated with deference. In fact, having already paid for this particular item, her appearance at auction prompts him to attempt to take possession of something he believes he already owns. Finally, Rosedale is emboldened to ask Lily to marry him because he believes she understands the kind of business arrangement he is proposing.

Rosedale, who is the other important connoisseur of Lily, has the money and wants a mannequin on whom he can display his wealth.[22] That Lily is briefly seduced by "the clink of Mr. Rosedale's millions" testifies to the accuracy of his reading (186). It is Lily's cousin, Jack Stepney, who makes the connection between the tableau and that other commodity arena, the art auction, when he remarks to a small group the next evening at Mrs. Fisher's, "Really, you know, I'm no prude, but when it comes to a girl standing there as if she was up at auction . . . " (158). According to Baudrillard, "the essential function of the auction is the institution of a community of the privileged who define themselves as such by agonistic speculation upon a restricted corpus of signs" (*For a Critique* 117).[23] The competitive speculation to which Baudrillard alludes is a subtext throughout *The House of Mirth*. While Lily realizes she is unsuited to participate as a player in the competition (just as she does not have the means to continue to play bridge), she recognizes that the system can be made to work for her if she establishes herself as the object of agonistic speculation rather than as a speculator, as she has been to date. Having tried to establish herself as a type of masterpiece in the tableau, Lily confirms her rarity by keeping herself aloof afterward, appearing again only as the guests enter the drawing room on the way to dinner. As Wharton acknowledged, "a beautiful object is certainly enhanced when it is known to be alone of its kind" (*Decoration* 187), and Rosedale has an eye for the unique object. But he also knows it is ownership alone that ultimately confers the status of singularity upon an object. He gradually acquires the skills and knowledge needed to succeed in the highest social circles and considers trying to secure Lily for himself, moving him into the ranks of those with the specialized knowledge needed to acquire her. Association with Lily will most certainly enhance her "buyer" in ways both physical and social, as Rosedale is well aware. (Later association with her, of course, will have the opposite effect, as Rosedale also knows when he rejects her belated acceptance of his marriage proposal.)

From their initial meeting outside the Benedick, when he appears with his "small sidelong eyes which gave him the air of appraising people as if they were bric-a-brac" (14), Rosedale is associated with commoditization, connoisseurship, and collecting. He is especially interested in those things that, like Lily, are hard to come by; as the narrator observes, "It was perhaps her very manner of holding herself aloof that appealed to his collector's passion for the rare and unattainable" (121). On another occasion he looks at Lily "with a steady gaze of his small stock-taking eyes, which made her feel herself no more than some superfine human merchandise" (268). As he becomes more knowledgeable and his taste more refined, Rosedale becomes even more aware of Lily's value. It is to his credit that, even when her value as an object has declined in everyone else's eyes, he is able to recognize Lily's "*external* rarity, an air of being impossible to match. As he advanced in social experience this uniqueness had acquired a greater value for him, as though he were a collector who had learned to distinguish minor differences of design and quality in some long-coveted object" (315). It is for this reason that Rosedale emerges as the true connoisseur of Lily.[24] Unlike Selden, he knows intimate details about Lily's dealings with Gus Trenor and about the letters she has from Bertha to Selden; he also knows that she refuses to use the letters to save herself. As much as her beauty, it is Lily's "unexplained scruples and resistances" (280) that attract him to her as time goes on, qualities he admires but does not possess.[25] Pearce argues that "[o]ur collections, with all their potential for selection and dismissal, offer us the romantic chance to complete ourselves, to create significance and meaning out of nothing by the power of need and imagination, and so to sustain a sense of dignity and purpose. They are both autobiography and monument" (*On Collecting* 254). For Rosedale, Lily would indeed be a way to complete what he has begun; she would be a monument to his wealth and his status as both connoisseur and collector. While her rejection of him is initially rooted in the anti-Semitism of her circle—he is described by Judy Trenor as "the same little Jew who had been served up and rejected at the social board a dozen times within her memory" (17)—Lily eventually refuses Rosedale out of an instinct for self-preservation in its truest sense; to use the language with which she describes Mrs. Hatch's milieu to him, a life with Rosedale would also be too soft a berth where "one might [sink] in too deep" (306). On the other hand, Rosedale's appreciation of Lily does not mitigate what she describes as his other "standard of values" (316), which entail blackmail, trading on the lives of others, and the willingness to commodify or destroy anything or anyone for the purpose of social advancement. Not that any of these traits are exclusive to Rosedale; they can also be found in the Trenors, Dorsets, and other supposedly upstanding citizens who inhabit Lily's world. Her refusal to engage in such practices is perceived as tacit condemnation, which is exacerbated by her naiveté and her indecisiveness. The result is that the group she is so desperate to join turns on her instead.

As long as she continues to resist the market for which she has been designed, Lily's social value will continue to decline, although her situation is exacerbated by the rumors about an affair with Gus Trenor, her failure to inherit Aunt Peniston's fortune, and her inability/unwillingness to secure a husband. Perhaps worst of all, the beauty that has been her one asset is beginning to fade; she can now see fine lines in the mirror and shadows under her eyes. Lily has been in circulation for thirteen years, since her debut at sixteen, and like the items in a museum (the natural home for artifacts), which arrive there through "extremely complex blends of plunder, sale, and inheritance" (Appadurai 21), Lily passes through a number of hands over the years.[26] Starting with her parents, who have since passed away, she moves into the hands of Aunt Peniston, who is not quite sure what to do with her new acquisition. Her aunt's strategy is to allow Lily to fend for herself, assuming that she will eventually end up in the right hands. Lily has also slipped from the hands of one potential suitor to another, making her way through the circuit of eligible men without allowing herself to be possessed by any of them. As the novel progresses, she continues to change hands, going from Gus Trenor to Carry Fisher to Gerty Farish, and each time she is passed on to someone new her worth is diminished even further. Her resistance to the values of her social circle puts Lily in the position of "other" to most of the women she knows, just as it makes her anathema to the men. It throws a spotlight on their own complicity in the marriage market, just as her natural loveliness (although even this is questioned by Selden in the opening scene) makes others appear less attractive and even false by comparison.

The difference between the authentic and the mass produced is a concept Wharton addressed in her very first book. *The Decoration of Houses,* written with Ogden Codman, Jr. and published in 1897, offered an alternative to the Victorian "gilded age of decoration" (191), the multi-layered effects and accumulations of pointless objects of all kinds. The final chapter is devoted to "bric-a-brac," the myriad things that filled Victorian homes, with a detailed discussion of such objects and their relative worth. Wharton's stance is encapsulated in the final paragraph: "To sum up, then, a room should depend for its adornment on general harmony of parts, and on the artistic quality of such necessities as lamps, screens, bindings, and furniture. Whoever goes beyond these essentials should limit himself in the choice of ornaments to the 'labors of the master-artist's hand'" (190). Her emphasis is on authenticity, usefulness, and artistry.

In the same way, Lily's uniqueness and fine quality, even at her worst moments, set her in contradistinction to the kind of knickknacks Wharton detested and which are analogous to many of the other women in the novel: "costly horrors" that are neither useful nor artistic. Wharton's standard for assessing the "real object of art" (as opposed to other types of objects) can also be used to evaluate Lily: Does she "adequately [express] an artistic conception" (besides Wharton's own, that is)? (*Decoration* 184). This criterion raises two related questions: Is Lily-as-art-object "real" or just an expensive knockoff? Is she a collectible to be cherished or a knickknack to be enjoyed for a time and easily discarded? On the surface, at least, she appears to be a fraud: she no longer has a "legitimate" claim to the social circle inhabited by the Trenors and Dorsets, nor to any of the others she attempts to join in her descent through the New York social order; her lack of personal fortune and/or an old family name makes her a trespasser among the elite, and she does not share the sensibility of either the Gormers or Mrs. Hatch. However, if the truly elite are distinguished by fineness of perception, appreciation of the beautiful, and independence of spirit, then Lily has more right to a place in that sphere than any of those who refuse to allow her to remain. Certainly a woman like Bertha Dorset or even one like Judy Trenor, who claimed to be Lily's friend yet abandoned her at the first suggestion of trouble, are hardly "elite" in either their attitude or their behavior. Wharton is measuring them against a standard that had all but vanished by the time she wrote *The House of Mirth*, the Old New York of her girlhood; it was a world in which Lily might well have prevailed, as opposed to the highly competitive, commodity-driven world in which she now finds herself.[27]

Lily's very digressions from the norms—her refusal to accept her fate as well as her recognition of the falseness and hypocrisy of others—attest to her authenticity. However, her struggle to own herself eventually undermines her value as a collectible object. When she fails, she is easily discarded as one more bit of the "conspicuous waste" that Thorstein Veblen described as the by-product of conspicuous consumption (118).[28] She is ill-equipped (for a variety of reasons) to cope with a world in which every gesture is a form of economic exchange and everything is for sale, including one's morals. Selden compares her to "a captured dryad subdued to the conventions of the drawing room" and adds that "it was the same streak of sylvan freedom in her nature that lent such savour to her artificiality" (34). The tension between the outer self that seems to conform, that is highly stylized and fashioned, and the inner self that struggles to make sense of a world in which everything is for sale for the right price, is central to any consideration of Lily, even to consideration of her as an artifact. The question of what is real haunts *The House of Mirth*, from the opening scene where Selden questions Lily's intentions and wonders if she is wearing a mask until the final moments when her "sleeping face . . . seemed to lie like a delicate impalpable mask over the living lineaments he had known" (334).[29] It is true that Lily is not what she seems in many cases: she is described as hard on the outside but "malleable as wax" inside, she has "the art of blushing at the right time," and she has a "real self" that only Selden seems capable "of drawing out of the depths" (55, 6, 99). But she also understands all too well the artificial nature of the world to which she aspires, a world where "one [can] never do a natural thing without having to screen it behind a structure of artifice," where the "ambiguous . . . atmosphere" of Bellomont is the norm, and where everything is a "show" (16, 53, 56), including her liaisons with Selden. Welly Brys's house epitomizes the inherent deception of this existence. It is a place where "one ha[s] to touch the marble columns to learn they [are] not of cardboard, to seat one's self in one of the damask-and-gold arm chairs to make sure it [is] not painted against the wall" (139). The novel is filled with references to clouds, illusions, masks, veils, shadows, and spells, language that suggests disguise, the unseen, and the mysterious.[30] Although she is attributed with a "vivid plastic sense" and a "dramatic instinct" (138), it is actually Lily's refusal to fake, to deny her genuine integrity, that dooms her to the penultimate commodity position she will occupy, that of waste.

Once the authenticity of an object has been questioned, its status is also compromised, and this is true of people as well. This is even more the case in a commodity culture, where "[t]inged by commercial interests, art assumes the status of suspect endeavor because it attracts both the phony artist and the effete dilettante." In this environment, "[t]he collector . . . emerges as a cultural inevitability: an expert who distinguishes the authentic from the fake and buys accordingly" (Hepburn 27). As we have seen, Lily's authenticity is an issue for Selden from the first pages of the novel. A work of art is, by extension, a work of artifice, a human creation, one that the collector has a vested interest in authenticating and appraising. For Selden, it is Lily's questionable authenticity that prevents him from taking a chance on her. Given the opportunity to think good or ill of her—when she pulls back from their moment of intimacy at Bellomont, when he sees her emerging from the Trenor house, when she is ejected from the Dorset yacht in Monte Carlo—Selden always chooses to think the worst. His antithesis is Gerty Farish, who insists on thinking the best of Lily despite the rumors. In between these two extremes is Simon Rosedale, who sees Lily for what she is because he is the only one who has taken the time to discover the truth.

While Lily's trajectory from luxury item to bibelot to waste or rubbish can be traced to specific moments in the text, her changing status is also foreshadowed in the opening scene of the novel, where she is described by the narrator as being "in the act of transition" (3), a phrase that refers to more than just a simple pause between trains and country houses. Because Lily does not have a "legitimate" right to move in the Trenor-Dorset circle, she is tolerated as long as she serves a useful purpose (amusing and distracting husbands, playing bridge, filling in as secretary).[31] Once that ends, however, and Lily makes it clear that she is not willing to give the final seal of approval to this form of existence by committing her life to its perpetuation, she becomes a liability; her existence is an affront and she must be removed. In other words, when she fails to take advantage of the "opportunities" she has been given, the understanding is that she should, like Gerty, find a nice flat somewhere and withdraw from society. She is the first to acknowledge that "there is nothing society resents so much as having given its protection to those who have not known how to profit by it: it is for having betrayed its connivance that the body social punishes the offender who is found out" (109). Yet it is not about herself that Lily reaches this conclusion but about Bertha Dorset, whose letters she has just purchased; ironically, this dictum will eventually be applied to Lily, and at the instigation of Bertha. That Lily's authenticity of motive and action hinges on whether or not to use the letters of a known adulterer—and that she does not do so because the letters are to a man she loves and admires, and who is himself an adulterer—suggests the layers of reality and illusion that permeate the text. Lily is authentic by virtue of what she won't do (marry someone she does not love, seek revenge against Bertha), but these are also the reasons she is cast out.

One of the focal points of Lily's fall from grace is her increasing invisibility, both to herself and others. Gary Lindberg writes of Lily that Wharton "remov[es] her from even the illusory identity she maintained within her social class. When Lily has fallen far enough from her original circle to be excluded from the activities she had learned to regard as real, she seems to herself to have no being at all" (54). To have no being is the equivalent of being trash, something that can be easily discarded because it has no value to anyone. (Trash is also the one thing the women in Lily's set never come in contact with.) In *Rubbish Theory*, Michael Thompson outlines the various paths commodities can take—from transient item to rubbish and possibly to durable good—and provides a way to understand the various stages Lily passes through as an object for trade, particularly in her final stages. According to Thompson, most goods fall into two categories, they are either "transient" or "durable." Those in the first category lose their value over time "and have finite life spans," while the opposite holds for so-called durable goods (7). However, there is a third, "covert category" of goods: *rubbish,* that "is not subject to the control mechanism (which is concerned primarily with the overt part of the system, the valuable and socially significant objects) and so is able to provide the path for the seemingly impossible transfer of an object from transience to durability." Thus, "a transient object gradually declining in value and in expected lifespan may slide across into rubbish" (9), but it may then be recuperated by its very longevity as a durable object. Rubbish itself is "socially defined" and not an inherent quality of objects (11), which means that an item once perceived as rubbish can, in the right circumstances, actually become durable or worthy of collection again (much the way Huck loses his status as "white trash"—or human rubbish—over the course of Twain's novel). Nor is this shift possible only with inanimate objects; people, because they are "physical objects" and "subject to the same process [of human social life]," can become rubbish—or durable—as well (77). Finally, we also consign to this category "those things or areas we conspire not to see. When these latter intrude, and we cannot help but see them, we banish them from view (or, alternatively, neutralize their visibility) by assigning them to a unique cross-cutting cultural category which may be labeled 'rubbish'" (88). Thus, the value of an object is often related to its visibility, the extent to which it is seen and acknowledged as valuable.

With nothing to enhance her value—no personal wealth, no wealthy husband—there is nothing to prevent Lily from slipping out of her privileged place in the social order. To use Thompson's expression, Lily's "slide" inexorably follows the usual course of transient items into the category of rubbish. Having been abandoned by her friends, Lily makes her way through a series of interim phases, linking herself to the Gormers and then Mrs. Hatch, becoming ever more invisible at each stage, until the final humiliation of her disinheritance. It is at this moment that she "feel[s] herself for the first time utterly alone. No one looked at her, no one seemed aware of her presence; she was probing the very depths of insignificance" (233). Aunt Peniston's decision to cut her off with only ten thousand dollars ends all hopes Lily may have had of recovering her place in society on her own terms. While a luxury item is intended to be "useless," a simple commodity is expected to serve a purpose of some sort. She acknowledges her new status in her final encounter with Selden, when she describes herself as "a very useless person" and asks, "What can one do when one finds that one only fits into one hole?" She then provides her own answer: "One must get back to it or be thrown out into the rubbish heap—and you don't know what it's like in the rubbish heap!" (324-25). Lily realizes she has been cast off by the very society that has been the single focus of her existence, and she is now left to watch as society "simply drift[s] by, preoccupied and inattentive" (275). The invisibility of rubbish—or rather our refusal to see it—is its essence, and it is her gradual invisibility, and the accompanying loneliness, that Lily finds hardest to endure.

The perception of women as easily disposable is not a new one.[32] The phrase "damaged goods" as a way "to describe a girl who had lost her virginity as well as one tainted with venereal disease" became part of the vernacular at the turn of the century (Robinson 346-47). The rumors suggest that Lily is just such a commodity, having ostensibly prostituted herself to Gus Trenor, an act even more egregious than simply losing her virginity. Aunt Peniston's equation of Lily's behavior to having a "contagious illness" in the house (133) is indicative of this attitude. As rubbish, Lily is now associated with contagion and disease, and she must be banished before she infects others. However, like other forms of trash, she is a reminder of other things as well, such as greed, selfishness, and wastefulness; society must either eliminate Lily or acknowledge its own sins. Her status is a determination made by her peers based on her behavior, real and implied, not one based on her actual merits or her value. She is allowed to become waste because discarding her permits a supposedly outraged society to make known what it will and will not tolerate without having to change the way its members go about their own business. The scapegoat is what we discard in order to assure our own continuity and righteousness. In Wharton's own words, which have been quoted countless times but bear repeating in this context, "a frivolous society can acquire dramatic significance only through what its frivolity destroys" (*A Backward Glance* 207).

It is only in death—the human state most associated with waste—that Lily is able to make the transition from rubbish to durable object. That change actually begins in Selden's apartment when she finally burns Bertha's letters. In that moment, Lily transcends the limitations of her upbringing and her social order (both of which would put public advancement before morality) and enacts her authentic self. Able to see herself, Selden, and her position with complete clarity for the first time, Lily escapes from the rubbish heap to which society has consigned her. She takes responsibility for her existence, aware that, as much as she would like to, she cannot leave the "old Lily" with Selden and remains true to her desire for happiness on her own terms. Even Selden cannot avoid the "reality" of that instant: he describes it as "one of those rare moments which lift the veil from their faces as they pass" (326), although he is unable to take advantage of it in time. Influenced by the rumors about Lily, unable to trust his instincts, he loses his final opportunity to rescue her—and himself.

Lily is rescued, although by the least likely of all those she meets in her final hours: Nettie Struther and her child. The encounter with Nettie, whom she meets after leaving Selden's apartment, gives Lily a vision of what is possible even for "damaged goods." Nettie was also, at one time, "one of the superfluous fragments of life destined to be swept prematurely into that social refuse heap of which Lily had so lately expressed her dread" (330), and she credits Lily with her survival and success. Nettie's husband, able to look beyond her mistakes and love her despite her status as a fallen woman, "made her renewal possible"; as Lily later observes, "it is so easy for a woman to become what the man she loves believes her to be!" Holding Nettie's child against her chest in the Struther kitchen, Lily starts to understand what has been missing from her life all along: stability, a place to call her own, but primarily the faith of another that confers value where society says there is none. As opposed to the "wild centrifugal dance" of the men and women she has known and struggled to emulate, she now has a sense of "the continuity of life" (337) and, to use Thompson's term, a sense of what it might mean to be durable. Her meetings with Selden and Nettie make Lily "visible" once again and reinstate her sense of her own value. But the realization cannot make up for the fact that in the morning she will be penniless. Paid her inheritance earlier than expected, she forces herself—before the "momentary exultation of her spirit" passes (338)—to write a check to Trenor and repay the money he gave her as well as settling her other debts.

The House of Mirth ends as it began, with Selden and Lily alone, the former watching and speculating about the latter. Their final encounter is laced with ironies: that he is able to rise above his own limitations but too late to save Lily; that a check to Gus Trenor once again threatens to undermine his faith in her; and, of course, that it is only when possessing her is no longer fraught with questions and difficulties that Selden is able to imagine that Lily finally belongs to him. Now that she is gone, he can manipulate her as an object in new ways, creating understandings and connections that can never be disproved. He can "read into [her] farewell all that his heart craved to find there," he can imagine that their final moment has been "saved whole out of the ruin of their lives," and he can even imagine that "the word which made all clear" passes between them (347). In her final state as pure object, Lily can be made to stand for anything; but she has also become "durable" as opposed to transient. A tragic figure, she leaves behind a series of people who will remember her courage and generosity at important moments: Nettie, Simon Rosedale, Gertie, even Selden. (And we have Wharton's novel, where woman-as-commodity, and the culture that created her, is immortalized.) Having been raised and cultivated for one purpose, Lily is destined for destruction once she rejects that path. The description of her as "some rare flower grown for exhibition, a flower from which every bud had been nipped except the crowning blossom of her beauty" (334) emphasizes her uselessness, her terminality, and her uniqueness.[33] However, a flower without additional buds is unnatural, destined for the rubbish heap as soon as its single bloom fades and dies. In the world of the commodity, where the artificial and the ostentatious have become objects of worth, Lily has no place. Instead, by remaining true to her own sense of worth, by refusing to sell herself and her potential happiness to the highest bidder, she is finally able to escape the demands and limitations of a society that consumes individuals as well as goods. A lovely memory, Lily has become the ultimate collectible.

5

Dressing to Kill

Desire, Race, and Authenticity in Nella Larsen's *Passing*

> To pass is to sin against authenticity, and "authenticity" is among the
> founding lies of the modern age. . . . And the Romantic fallacy of
> authenticity is only compounded when it is collectivized: when the
> potential real me gives way to the real us.
> —Henry Louis Gates, "White Like Me"

The letter Irene Redfield holds in her hands in the opening passage from
Nella Larsen's novel *Passing* (1929) has been sent to her by Clare Kendry,
a childhood friend who has emerged for the second time in two years
from the shadows of the white world into which she "passed" twelve
years earlier. The letter is mysterious, difficult to read, uncertain of origin, and impossible to ignore, much like the woman who wrote it. By the
end of the story, Irene will also hold Clare's very life in her hands as well
as her own future, the existence she has created since her marriage to
Brian Redfield, a prominent local physician. Two worlds collide in this
novel—that of the "passing" woman who has rejected her race for the
material comforts of the white world, and that of the light-skinned
black woman who remains in the African American community but
within the narrow precincts of Negro society in the 1920s—with profound results. Thinking of the letter as a form of "correspondence"—
with all that word signifies—opens up and complicates readings of this
scene. It suggests the connections and even similarities between Irene
and Clare, business dealings, sympathetic response, analogous relationships, congruity, and even sexual intercourse, for those interested in
readings of the novel that focus on the latent homosexuality in the text
(*OED*). The string of events that Clare's letter initiates—renewed friendship, a possible affair, and murder—is the provocation for a complex examination of race, identity, and authenticity in Larsen's novel.

The letter in question contains Clare's plea for Irene's help and understanding as she ostensibly attempts to reconnect to the life she abandoned when she married John Bellew, a white businessman who has no
idea that his lovely and sophisticated wife is actually a black woman. Declaring that she is "lonely, so lonely" for those of her own race, Clare
rambles on for several incoherent pages, comparing her estrangement to
"an ache, a pain that never ceases." However, in a rhetorical move that
will be repeated in various forms, Clare also "blames" Irene for her current unrest, tracing it back to the day in Chicago two years ago when
the two accidentally met at the Drayton Hotel, where both women were
passing. What Clare feels is a "wild desire" that cannot be ignored, regardless of the cost to herself or others (174). What Irene feels, on the
other hand, is the combined fear of and desire for the other that is often
directed *at* African Americans, an irony that attests to Larsen's complex
treatment of race in this text. Rather than examining constructions of
race through the binary of black and white, Larsen focuses on the more
subtle and complicated racial issues in the African American community: racial guilt and pride, the connection between skin color and class,
the objectification of the self that began in slavery and continues under
the mantle of commodity culture, and the way these various issues are
implicated in racial passing. In order to do so, she co-opts the discourse
of consumer culture; terms such as cost, value, exchange, speculation,
desire, and envy are laced throughout the text. Irene, the casual "passer"
who has created a life built on manipulation of others, denial, and self-
deception, is forced to face her greatest fears in the person of Clare, the
permanent passer who admits she will do anything to get what she
wants. The latter's "having way," as it is referred to throughout the novel
(a trait that Irene shares, as we shall see), and the repeated references to
the "cost" of getting what one wants, especially since that cost includes
the denial of one's race, link desire and race to the marketplace and consumer culture.

Larsen's novel has finally begun to receive its share of critical attention after an extended period of neglect. However, like many works in a
specific mode (in this case the "passing narrative"), critical analyses
have tended to privilege certain elements at the expense of others. Judith
Butler has accurately captured the critical dilemma of *Passing*, that readings of the novel are traditionally of two kinds: those that focus on "the

historical and social specificity of the novel, as brought to light by Barbara Christian, Gloria Hull, Hazel Carby, Amritjit Singh, and Mary Helen Washington," and those that focus on "the psychological complexity of cross-identification and jealousy in the text as discussed by Claudia Tate, Cheryl Wall, Mary Mabel Youmans, and Deborah McDowell" (173). In particular, recent readings (such as Butler's own) have emphasized the lesbian subtext in Irene's attraction to Clare, which raises interesting questions about the intersection of race and gender but has come to subsume other interpretations.[1] While these studies have enriched our understanding of the novel, Larsen's examination of race and racial authenticity, especially the construction of blackness and whiteness in this critical period, should also be considered within the context of commodity culture, which infiltrated all areas of American life in the early twentieth century.

From the outset, Clare represents a problem that the recipient of her letter would rather ignore, but one she must inevitably confront. Irene opens the letter last, once she has dealt with her other correspondence, but she must eventually act, reading it or discarding it, and either action will have consequences. The Italian paper contributes to the letter's exotic presentation, but the conflation of English words and "foreign" paper creates a combination that is at once familiar and strange, which may be one reason for Irene's reaction. The letter strikes her as "furtive," "sly," and "alien" (171)—terms later used to describe Clare herself—but it is also "flaunting" and "extraordinary." Irene seems torn between distrust and admiration, between fear and envy, which is typical of her response to Clare as the novel progresses. Without a return address, the letter's provenance can only be guessed at; but in fact Irene already knows the identity of the sender based on a similar, previous letter as well as her knowledge of her friend (awareness of Clare's visits abroad, recognition of Clare's handwriting). What one knows or does not know, how one knows, and when one knows it are crucial in *Passing* (and in "passing"), especially in the novel's depiction of the construction of race.[2] The ability to "read" others is critical, and those who are unable to do so are in danger of being badly, even dangerously, deceived. But race is also about the relationship between the actual or real self and the surface presentation—or, at another level, whether there is an essential self at all, and if so, whether that self is raced.

Larsen situates her characters squarely within the black bourgeoisie, where consumerism, desire, and race meet. Sitting in her bedroom holding Clare's letter, Irene is surrounded by the trappings of black middle-class culture: a large and beautiful house with a black maid (Zulena) and cook (Sadie), a physician husband (Brian), and enough money to consider sending one of their two sons (Junior) to school in Europe in an attempt to distract Brian from his restlessness and unhappiness. Irene is part of the black bourgeoisie of the early twentieth century, a group that emerged to challenge the dominance of the old "aristocrats of color," to borrow the title of Willard B. Gatewood's 1990 study. This group "came in time to constitute a parallel elite" of professionals and businessmen, similar to the white nouveau riche who emerged at the turn of the twentieth century to challenge the social dominance of "the 'old Knickerbocker set' of New York and the 'old Philadelphians.'" Although not as wealthy as their white counterparts, the black bourgeoisie had much in common with the equivalent class in white society, in particular "a penchant for conspicuous consumption and publicized social affairs" (334). The black bourgeoisie was marked by feelings of both self-hatred and insecurity, according to E. Franklin Frazier, perhaps as a result of internalizing white attitudes. Those who succeeded generally worried that their achievement would result in "hatred and revenge" on the part of other African Americans (228); conversely, because they were still black and could not "escape identification with Negroes," members of the black bourgeoisie "experience[d] certain feelings of insecurity because of their feeling of inferiority [to whites]" (216). In order to protect themselves from the truth about their unstable place in the American social system, they "created a world of make-believe . . . out of the myth of Negro business, the reports of the Negro press on the achievements and wealth of Negroes, the recognition accorded them by whites, and the fabulous life of Negro 'society'" (229). (Of course, creating a world of make-believe is also the goal of a consumer culture.)

It is just such a make-believe world that Irene Redfield has created and that Clare's appearance threatens to destroy. It is a world of tea parties, dances, bridge games, and shopping, the life of the bourgeois woman of the twenties, irrespective of color. It is also an existence that suits Irene's desire for "security of place and substance" (221), for constancy and safety. Harlem in 1927 is a place where famous white people and those who follow them attend Negro Welfare League (NWL) dances, where "the race problem" is something Irene can conveniently ignore and even hide from her sons. Behind the doors of the Redfield house, race is a nonissue, certainly not something to be discussed at the dinner table if Irene can help it. When Brian brings up a recent lynching, she is horrified and refuses to let him answer their son's questions about the episode. Irene, however, is light enough to pass—assumed to be "an Italian, a Spaniard, a Mexican, or a Gypsy" (178) by white people with whom she comes in contact—which means she can take on and discard the mantle of race at will. But her husband and at least one of her sons are dark, so that for them race is an ever-present fact of life, not something they can escape, along with the heat, on the rooftop of the Drayton Hotel. Beneath the "make-believe" and colorless (in several respects) world that Irene has erected lies a troubled marriage based on manipulation and fear, a child-rearing strategy that relies on the denial of racial problems in America, and the specter of blackness both in the form of race and her unacknowledged fears. Having refused to move with Brian to Brazil in the early years of their marriage, Irene must now contend with lingering doubts about her husband, his occasional expressions of profound dislike for his profession and his country, and her decision to place her own happiness above his. Irene has convinced herself that she acted with the best interests of Brian and her sons at heart, not her own, "never acknowledging," as the narrator observes, "that, though she did want [Brian] to be happy, it was only in her own way and by some plan of hers for him" (221). Yet she has not completely calculated the cost of her actions and will not do so until faced with the possible destruction of her marriage by Clare, the woman for whom no cost is too high for something she truly desires.

Envy and the desire to possess the belongings and status of others are the impetus for the collective practices that Veblen referred to as pecuniary emulation; they are also the primary motivators for most of the women in *Passing*. Much of Veblen's analysis centered on the role of women (regardless of race) in a social order based on envy and conspicuous consumption, although his focus was primarily on (white) females as emblems of male wealth and power.[3] In "Frocks, Finery, and Feelings: Rural and Urban Women's Envy, 1890–1930" Susan J. Matt con-

siders the ways middle-class women at the turn of the century—and I
include women of the black bourgeoisie in this category—reacted to the
sudden proliferation of goods as evidenced in magazines, catalogues,
and other sources. Female envy in this period centered on dress and the
ability (or inability) to keep up with the latest fashions, and the "occasions for envy" increased with the increasingly open display of luxury
goods (such as in department store windows); as a result, "Such a situation frequently produced envy and desire in those who saw with new
clarity and detail what they could not possess" (377). One response was
to feign social status, and women soon realized that the right apparel
could send messages about the self within the social order that were not
necessarily accurate or even true. This situation—the feelings of envy
and desire, the realization that outward appearance can be manipulated
to create a specific impression—is compounded by the construction of
racial identity in Larsen's text, where the envious women are black and
either passing as white (such as Clare) or in denial about the role of race
in their lives (such as Irene).

A seemingly simple act of communication, Clare's letter is the correspondence of a wealthy and fashionable woman, but one who is also
consumed with desire for the things she does not possess. I would like
to concentrate for a moment on the purple ink in which the letter is
written. A color formerly reserved for royalty, according to Elizabethan
sumptuary laws,[4] it now alludes to the status and affluence of the sender.
Taking this connotation a step further, the entire letter signifies an interest in presentation that is consistent with the world of fashion, in particular the world of fashionable clothing. The ink color, the foreign paper, even the lack of return address indicate a production designed to
send a very specific visual impression about the writer. This is a letter
with flair and drama, with a sense of style (and an aura of secrecy long
associated with clothes of all kinds) that is an accurate representation
of the woman who sent it. Self-presentation, especially in terms of attire,
is an ongoing theme in Larsen's novel and inextricably connected to
the very act of passing. (For, while it is a central activity in the novel,
passing is merely a trope for the various kinds of disguises and subterfuges that many of the characters enact in one form or another.) That
Irene's random thoughts about Clare as she holds the letter lead her very
quickly to a memory that involves clothes, the image of a young girl

sewing what we will later learn is a new dress for a Sunday school picnic, marks the extent to which Clare—and race—are associated with fashion in Irene's mind. Equating race and fashion may seem disingenuous and even frivolous, but, as William J. F. Keenan argues in his introduction to *Dressed to Impress*, fashion is a much more serious field of inquiry than many scholars have been willing to acknowledge (7). Clothing has long been understood as a means for constructing identity, for asserting boundaries, and for identifying the other among us. Larsen's text is particularly interesting for the ways its author is able to exploit the near obsession with fashion in the early twentieth century while also engaging issues of race and class construction and deconstruction. The epitome of this is the woman who uses clothing to completely re-create the self as white, either occasionally (as Irene does, so she can shop in stores that would not otherwise admit her) or permanently (as does Clare).[5]

Clothing envy begins at an early age in Larsen's novel when, as a young girl, Clare withholds money from her father in order to buy fabric to make herself that new red dress. Irene recalls that "in spite of certain unpleasantness and possible danger, she had taken the money to buy the material for that pathetic little red frock," and that she continued to sew as her inebriated parent "bellow[ed] curses and made spasmodic lunges at her" (172). After her father is killed in a saloon fight, Clare is taken in by her two maiden aunts (who are white, as was their brother, Clare's grandfather); they provide her with "a roof over [her] head, and food, and clothes—such as they were." On those occasions when she returned to the old neighborhood, she now tells Irene, "I used almost to hate all of you. You had all the things I wanted and never had had" (188). When the teenaged Clare is later seen in the company of "another woman and two men, all of them white," it is the fact that she is "*dressed!*" that strikes a cord with her former girlfriends. The stories all point "in the same glamorous direction" (181), to a life of beautiful clothes, fancy cars, and chauffeurs, and the envy they evoke is revealed in the way Irene describes what she remembers: "how, when they used to repeat and discuss these tantalizing stories about Clare, the girls would always look knowingly at one another and then, with little excited giggles, drag away their eager shining eyes and say with lurking undertones of regret or disbelief some such thing as: 'Oh, well, maybe she's got a job or something,' or

'After all, it mayn't have been Clare,' or 'You can't believe all you hear'"
(181–82).

The girls ultimately attribute whatever Clare has done to her "having
way," meaning her ability to get the things she wants by whatever means
necessary, a trait Irene assumes has led to Clare's current position as a
wealthy "white" woman married to a man "with untold gold" (182, 189).
It seems fitting then that Clare may have returned specifically to flaunt
her social position and wealth after a girlhood of deprivation (Cutter
91). The tea party to which she invites Irene and Gertrude, the only two
friends from her youth not likely to raise the suspicions of her husband because they are light-skinned, is a perfect venue for "flaunting" (a
word Irene also uses in connection with both the letter and with Clare
herself in describing her attire for the Negro Welfare League dance)
what she has gained: beautiful surroundings, beautiful things, a "white"
daughter, and a doting and wealthy husband. The dress she wears for
the occasion, which is the same shade of "startling blue" as the draperies
hanging in the sitting room where the women gather (194), associates
her with the space, a room at the Morgan where she would not be per-
mitted to stay were it known she is black.

Irene's descriptions of Clare consistently spotlight what she is wearing, but race is almost always a subtext. There is the "fluttering dress
of green chiffon" in which she first appears at the Drayton Hotel (176),
a place where a black woman would never normally be admitted; the
"priceless velvet" of a dress that Clare's tears splatter when she cries
about being lonely (227); "the stately gown of shining black taffeta" that
Clare wears to the NWL dance (233), which makes Irene feel "dowdy and
commonplace" in comparison (234); and Clare's "superlatively simple
cinnamon-brown frock" and "string of amber beads that would easily
have made six or eight like one Irene owned" (253), which she wears to
afternoon tea at Irene's house the same day the latter first suspects she is
having an affair with Brian. One of Irene's very first observations about
Clare, when she sees her at the Drayton and is unaware of her identity,
is that she is wearing "[n]ice clothes"; however, once she learns who the
woman is, her admiration becomes qualified. Clare becomes "almost too
good looking," and her previous behavior is called into question—"It's
hardly any wonder that she . . . " (177, 185)—a speculation that remains
unfinished. In addition to her expensive designer dresses, Irene pays me-

ticulous attention to Clare's hats, shoes, and furs, so that every encounter between the two women is as much about what Clare is wearing (and
how that makes Irene feel) as it is about Clare's wanting to return to the
race or her possible affair with Brian.

Larsen's fascination with clothing as a means to construct race and
class is evident in other instances as well. When Irene's friend Felise
Freeland shows up at a tea party in a dress Irene admires, she remarks,
"Felise . . . Really, your clothes are the despair of half the women in Harlem . . . How do you do it? . . . Lovely, is it Worth or Lanvin? . . . Oh, a
mere Babani" (252). The casual tossing around of designer names marks
both the wearer and the viewer who can identify them as among those
who "know." Conversely, Irene's negative opinion of Gertrude Martin,
who is married to a white man (although one who knows her race) is in
direct proportion to the tastelessness of Gertrude's apparel: she wears
"an overtrimmed georgette crepe dress" that is "too short and show[s]
an appalling amount of leg, stout legs in sleazy stockings of a vivid rose-
beige shade." All of this follows Irene's initial observation that Gertrude
"looked as if her husband might be a butcher" (196). Dress is a visual
statement, and it conveys very specific messages about the self, whether
intentionally or not.

A number of important studies of dress, such as Alison Lurie's *The
Language of Clothes* and Ann Hollander's *Seeing through Clothes,* have
helped us to understand the personal and cultural functions of clothing.
Lurie reminds us that the first purpose of clothing was "magical," "to
attract good animistic powers and ward off evil" (29), while Hollander
addresses the visual importance of dress. What we admire is simply a
reflection of what we expect to see in a given cultural moment, according to Hollander; it is about both "perception" and "artistic convention"
(311). However, women's ability to use clothing to reinvent the self was
also a concern for social critics at the turn of the century. As Susan J.
Matt observes, "In a society filled with strangers ignorant of each others' true economic circumstances, a woman might wear particular styles
in order to signal a higher social status than she actually possessed. . . .
It was because of their perceived usefulness in creating social identities
that articles of dress gained new importance for women" (381). Social
commentators and spiritual leaders reacted to this intense female interest in emulation with stern warnings about the sinfulness of envy and

the need to be satisfied with one's position (385), partly because emulation erased social boundaries, or at least called them into question.[6] Articles in magazines such as the *Ladies Home Journal*, the *Saturday Evening Post*, and the *Christian Advocate* and sermons delivered from the pulpit advised women "to be 'sincere' in their self-presentation, that is, to restrain their emulative instincts. To the moralists, a 'sincere' woman was one whose clothing accurately reflected her social status" (Matt 385).[7] Among the various female deceptions that others were warned to be on guard against were "prostitutes disguised as shoppers and saleswomen appearing to be 'ladies,'" women whose beauty was illusory, and, of course, "light-skinned octaroons passing into white society" (Peiss 320).

The concern that a woman might present herself as something she was not was symptomatic of a larger problem: the increasing difficulty of distinguishing the authentic from the fake based on visual evidence alone. This reaction to female imitation also masks fears about the possible eradication of class and racial boundaries at the turn of the century. The inability to distinguish the real from the false meant that "[p]ossessions, particularly clothing, became crucial markers of class in urban America because judgments about people's background, position, and prospects gradually came to depend less on close acquaintance and more on appearances" (Matt 380). Just as the right apparel could allow a white woman to "pass" as a member of a higher social class, so, too, could it provide a way for a black woman to pass as white. Because African Americans could rarely shop in the most exclusive stores, a woman wearing the kinds of clothes that Clare sports was not likely to be identified as a Negro. In fact, her ability to outdress every other woman in a room is a clear indicator of Clare's social standing and economic clout, but it is also the way she constructs herself as white.

Irene also acts on the assumption that what one is wearing can be a racial marker. When she notices Clare staring at her, she immediately thinks it must have to do with her appearance and reaches up to see if her hat is on straight. However, after a few moments she starts to wonder if the other woman suspects she is black, only to dismiss this possibility and scoff at the criteria white people presumably use to distinguish race, such as "fingernails, palms of hands, shapes of ears, teeth, and other, equally silly rot" (178). She believes that her general appearance is enough to allow her to pass for white, and the other criteria by which she might be identified are unreliable at best. The disjuncture between race and physical appearance is introduced in this initial encounter between the two women, just as clothing—the package in which one presents oneself—is also introduced as part of the game of artifice. This is why, on her way to the Drayton, the first thing Irene does is check her appearance in a mirror. What Irene describes when she talks about Clare's appearance is in effect a sartorial elegance designed to fool white observers who may have reason to suspect that she is black, especially since Clare seems to be getting darker as she gets older (at least according to Jack Bellew). The appropriate clothing is essential, whether one is passing as someone of a higher social class or someone of another race.

That one might pretend to be something "other" also threatened to undermine essentialist notions of identity. Woman, in particular, was supposed to have a "self" that was "an unchanging, unchangeable set of qualities with which she was born," not one that was created for a specific purpose. While it was fine for men to re-create the self—although, as we will see in the case of Gatsby, even this has its limits—"such a model seemed unsuitable for women, idealized as moral and submissive beings" (Matt 387). Race has also typically been perceived as an unchangeable quality or essence, especially when inherent difference was essential to the privileging of whiteness. (This is one reason Huck has so much trouble categorizing Jim; the best he can ultimately come up with is that Jim is "white inside.") Passing, of course, undermines these preconceptions about racial identity. As Elaine K. Ginsberg observes, "presumably one cannot pass for something one *is not* unless there is some other, prepassing identity that one *is*." Acknowledging "that 'maleness' or 'whiteness' or ethnicity can be performed or enacted, donned or discarded, exposes the anxieties about status and hierarchy created by the potential of boundary trespassing. For both the process and the discourse of passing challenge the essentialism that is often the foundation of identity politics . . . disclos[ing] the truth that identities are not singularly true or false but multiple and contingent" (4). *Plessy v. Ferguson*, which resulted in the so-called one-drop rule (a person was considered legally black if any ancestor, regardless of how long ago, was black), was essentially a response to this problem, an attempt to force racial identification regardless of skin color. It was also a tacit admission of the fact that race, like class status, was possible to fake.[8] The criteria Irene lists for the ways white people try to identify their darker brothers suggests the extent to which some would go to separate the races and the unreliable nature of the evidence on which such a judgment could be based. Even proximity to other Negroes was dangerous, which may be why Clare refuses to hire a black maid (something Bellew points out); she is concerned that this will somehow reveal her racial ancestry.[9]

Passing challenged notions about racial identity and authenticity in the same ways social critics warned that wearing clothing not suited to one's social position could destabilize class structures; but passing also served to undermine the new emphasis on the visual in the early twentieth century.[10] Whether it was photographs, advertisements, museums, or the plate glass display windows that became defining features of major department stores, the visual was suddenly given primacy as a source of knowledge. The importance of the visual was announced, with unintended irony, by one advertising marketer: "You may forget what you read—if you read at all. But what you see, you know instantly" (Leach 43). It is precisely this relationship between seeing and knowing, and the all-too-frequent discrepancies between the two, that is both embodied in and undermined by the passing figure. Larsen's novel is replete with references to knowing and/or being known, to what one does and does not know, wants to know, can and cannot know. And in almost every instance "knowing" is connected to "seeing": Irene holding a letter in her hands and knowing at once who the sender is; Clare pleading with Irene, "You can't know how in this pale life of mine I am all the time seeing the bright pictures of that other that I once thought I was glad to be free of" (174); Irene suddenly wondering whether the woman staring at her knows she is a Negro; until, finally, we are left with a distraught Irene wondering if anyone in the apartment has seen and therefore knows what she has done to Clare, a scene that fades to black (where seeing is impossible) as Irene faints. While the knowing/seeing trope is used primarily in association with Clare, it appears whenever Larsen wants to raise questions about what someone is trying to hide, either from others or from themselves. For example, Bellew believes he "knows" about Negroes, but all his information is secondhand ("I know people who've known them"); he cannot "see" three black women sitting in his own living room, one of whom is his wife (202).

However, the inadequacy of the gaze when trying to determine/

construct race is not confined to Bellew. Irene is also unable to recognize Clare as a black woman at first sight, and when she does finally come to understand who Clare is, what she "knows" about her also changes. Irene is perfectly willing to attribute certain positive qualities to her Negro blood, such as her "polite insolence" and her "[m]ysterious and concealing" eyes (190–91). Conversely, while she is ready to excuse what she sees as too-flirtatious behavior when she thinks Clare is a white woman, once she knows the truth she decides that Clare's "odd upward smile" is "too provocative for a waiter" (180). Irene's attribution of certain qualities to Clare's Negro ancestry is as essentialist as Bellew's preconceived notions about blacks. Her attitude also enables her to erect boundaries between herself and black women of whom she disapproves, such as those who have chosen to marry white men, without guilt. When Irene arrives at Clare's apartment for tea, for example, her reaction upon seeing both Clare and Gertrude is " 'Great goodness! Two of *them*.' For Gertrude too had married a white man" (194; my emphasis). While she classifies Clare and Gertrude as women who have rejected their race, Irene has done essentially the same thing in more understated ways.[11]

Larsen is clearly aware of the dangers inherent in social advancement. Brian Redfield's ostensible reason for wanting to take his family to Brazil is the pervasive racism in America, but he is no friend of struggling blacks. In reply to Irene's comments about the amount of work she must do for the NWL dance, he responds, "Uplifting the brother's no easy job."[12] He also grumbles about having to care for those who live in "smelly, dirty rooms" and "climbing filthy steps in dark hallways" (217). Brian will admit he does not know "what race is" (216) in a conversation about why those who pass inevitably try to return, but it is hard to imagine a black man from the folk having trouble with such distinctions. His privileged position has made race something about which he can speculate—and something he can even afford to run away from—even if he is too dark to pass in America.[13]

As we have seen, Irene is also firmly embedded in the black middle class, and although her envy may be expressed in the language of the bourgeois woman who covets the possessions of her wealthier, elite counterpart, it is envy complicated by racial ambivalence. The latter is signaled by her refusal to engage in discussions of racial problems, by her unwillingness to acknowledge her occasional passing for what it is, and by her fears about the possible destruction of the tenuous world she has created, one in which race seems to be incidental. Even Clare realizes that for Irene maintaining the status quo is more important than race, although she may complain about the "restrictions and distinctions" of Negro society (186). Clare's arrival brings these problems to the surface. Irene is suddenly torn between race loyalty and a host of other emotions: pity, envy, fear, and revulsion. The situation becomes nearly unbearable once she suspects an affair between Clare and Brian. She finds herself "caught between two allegiances, different, yet the same. Herself. Her race. Race! The thing that bound and suffocated her. . . . For the first time she suffered and rebelled because she was unable to disregard the burden of race. It was, she cried silently, enough to suffer as a woman, an individual, on one's own account, without having to suffer for the race as well" (258). She also refers to her feelings as "[t]hat instinctive loyalty to a race," something she is unable to be free of (260).

But there are more subtle allusions to the burdens of race as well. An anecdote about a broken teacup (which Irene drops when she sees Brian with Clare at her tea party) can also be read allegorically:

> Did you notice that cup? Well, you're lucky. It was the ugliest thing that your ancestors, the charming Confederates, ever owned. I've forgotten how many thousands of years ago it was that Brian's great-great-granduncle owned it. But it has, or had, a good old hoary history. It was brought North by way of the subway. Oh, all right! Be English if you want to and call it the underground. What I'm coming to is the fact that I've never figured out a way of getting rid of it until about five minutes ago. I had an inspiration. I had only to break it, and I was rid of it forever. So simple! And I'd never thought of it before. . . . Still, . . . I'm perfectly willing for you to take the blame and admit that you pushed me at the wrong moment. What are friends for, if not to help bear our sins? (255)

Like the despised teacup (and Clare, who is also easily broken), race is something Irene would prefer to be "rid of . . . forever;" it haunts her marriage, her relationship with her sons, and even her social life. However, Clare is the one made to help bear Irene's "sins" by the sacrifice of her death, just as Irene must help bear Clare's sins when she hears her race denigrated by Jack Bellew and learns of the affair. To drive home the analogy even more firmly, the episode concludes with Irene asking Clare if she'd like more tea.

While blackness itself is traditionally figured as mysterious and alien, in *Passing* it is the person of mixed race—more specifically, the person who attempts to ignore race because she can—who represents the strange and unknown. This is manifested in Irene's conflict between attraction to and revulsion toward Clare, who is frequently likened to a wild creature: in addition to being catlike, she appears as snakelike in her green chiffon dress, and her "dark secret" is "forever crouching in the background" (233). Even as a teenager, Irene recalls, "no matter how often she came among them, she still remained someone apart, a little mysterious and strange, someone to wonder about and to admire and to pity" (239). Clare describes herself as "not safe" and as having no "morals or sense of duty" (240). (Ironically, these things actually turn out to be true of Irene as well.) The furs she wears when she visits Irene also signal her affiliation to animals. Lurie explains: "Fur is more likely than leather to turn its wearer into an animal symbolically"; the message it sends is "'I am a very expensive animal'" (233). But Clare is also a dangerous animal, as Irene suspects from the start, primarily because she represents a challenge to everything in which Irene believes. She is the unknown quantity that Irene has consistently avoided in her quest for security.

The feeling of something "lacking" is a recurring theme in *Passing*, and it is the emotion Clare most inspires in Irene, who realizes that the former has an "ability for a quality of feeling that [is] to her strange and even repugnant" (226), a level of emotion Irene will never know because it is the antithesis of the safety and security she desires above all else. She has worried about propriety for so long that she has cut herself off from legitimate emotion. Clare, on the other hand, rejects the safe and secure. She epitomizes the "quest for the new" that was so prevalent in this period (Leach 91). Envy is triggered by exposure to what one does not have, and this happens for Clare just as it does for Irene. In a reversal of the usual pattern, Clare finds herself desiring the middle-class life Irene has created, chiefly because it has the additional allure of being a life she was denied as a child and a life among other blacks. The thing long denied elicits a special kind of desire, and Clare is determined to achieve it this time, regardless of the cost to herself or others. There is also an implied critique of upper-class white existence, where fashion and appearances are paramount. After their initial encounter in Chicago, Clare writes to Irene: "*It may be, 'Rene dear, it may just be, after all, your way may be the wiser and infinitely happier one. I'm not sure just now. At least not so sure as I have been*" (208). Another "lack" is Clare's inability to associate with her own kind. Two years later, when she shows up in New York, she has convinced herself that she must see other Negroes again, and that she will not be denied the fulfillment of this desire regardless of the consequences.

The notion of "lack" also evokes consumer culture at its most basic level, one where need and desire are interchangeable. Clare and Irene represent various types of female consumer: Clare is the elite woman who must have the new, fashionable thing each year, regardless of the cost. She is the incarnation of "the economy of desire" with "its support of the cult of the new and its indifference to past loyalties" (Leach 302). Irene, on the other hand, is the envious middle-class woman who sees what those above her have and wants it for herself. Both women represent the tug of "fashion," which "demanded constant change, incessant newness"; it "pressed people to buy, dispose of, and buy again. It dealt not with the utility or the enduring artistry of goods but with their fleeting appeal" (92). Clare has wealth and security, but she has had to abandon her racial heritage to attain them; Irene has managed to have social prestige, financial stability, and renowned acquaintances while retaining her place in the black community, but she has also paid a price for this balancing act. Unfortunately, Irene is unable to see just how much she has paid, or will pay, until it is too late.

Envy is "selective blindness. *Invidia*, Latin for envy, translates as 'non-sight,' and Dante has the envious plodding along under cloaks of lead, their eyes sewn shut with leaden wire. What they are blind to is what they have . . . in themselves" (Aldrich xv). It is the result of being unable to see the self clearly, and this is an apt description of Irene. Her entire life is based on the avoidance of self-analysis. She "passes" when comfort or necessity dictate it, although it is an activity she does not acknowledge. There is no acknowledgement of Irene's "passing" when it occurs in the cab, by either Irene or the narrator and, in effect, passing has become "so natural for [her] . . . that she is not even conscious that she is doing so" (Brody 1057). Similarly, Irene passes with the reader, who does not find out she is black until several pages into the second chapter of the novel. Irene acknowledges her "outward sinking of self" (224), but not the falseness that this suggests. She also begins to realize that she may not even have loved Brian or been loved by him. In fact, it becomes clear that, like Clare, Irene will "do anything, risk anything" (268), but in her case it is to preserve her bourgeois existence (which is at some level the same thing: a fixed relationship to money, status, and goods).

One effect of Irene's blindness is her belief that she can direct not only her own life but also the lives of others, especially Brian's. Her husband is a possession to be controlled, to be guided "in the right direction" (218), meaning in the direction she has determined. Her willingness to manipulate situations is evident early in the text. In an apparently minor episode, Irene intentionally distracts Brian from noticing that she is again late by handing him the letter from Clare to read while she finishes dressing, a gesture she acknowledges with "a little mental frown" (213). A short while later she tries to use the same technique to distract him from his own happiness, but with much less success; she is brought up short when he refuses to agree that Junior's "queer ideas" about sex are troubling. Instead, Brian takes the opportunity to point out, "The sooner and the more he learns about sex, the better for him. And most certainly if he learns that it's a grand joke, the greatest in the world. It'll keep him from lots of disappointments later on" (220). His bitterness is a product of Irene's machinations, but she is dismayed rather than regretful, unable to understand why he can't be happy in the way she wants him to be. She cannot tolerate the fact that something may be out of her control or beyond her understanding, and she is ruled by "fear" and "panic" (212), especially in regard to Clare.

Her refusal to allow her husband to discuss a lynching reported in the local papers is one of the more obvious examples of her willful blindness, but she is also blind to the intense anger she harbors. This manifests itself in abrupt explosions of emotion, such as when she vows that Brian's restlessness "*would* die. Of that she was certain" (218). Ironically, Clare's arrival has the effect of lifting the veil that Irene has allowed to fall between herself and reality. She must now face issues about her marriage, her race, and herself that she has been able to ignore for years. As she tells Clare, "I'm beginning to believe . . . that no one is ever completely happy, or free, or safe" (227), an observation that seems more typical of Clare.

There is yet another facet to Irene's blindness: her inability to see that she and Clare have more in common than she would care to admit. For example, when Brian describes a remark made by Irene about Clare as "slightly feline in its implication," the comment recalls Irene's own description of Clare as "cat-like" (249, 173). Clare's determination to go to the dance is like "an image of the futile searching and the firm resolution in Irene's own soul" (231). Even the letter Irene holds in the opening passage might represent her as much as it does Clare, since Irene is also sly and furtive, out of place and alien.[14]

That the two women are foils for one another is clear, but Larsen explores their connectedness in a more pointed—and ironic—way, through the use of the gaze, especially her use of mirrors and windows in which the two women are reflected or which serve as "frames" for their duality. The repeated occurrence of surfaces that either reflect images or allow for public display is part of the trope of commodity culture, specifically the world of fashion. Shop windows, mannequins, and mirrors were central to the new turn-of-the-century world of commodity display, and the "shop window" was one of the new "visual media" created to attract consumers (Leach 40). Clare is so sure of her ability to deceive that she willingly invites the gaze of others, and Irene comments on her "deliberate courting of attention" (234). But while Clare may seem to be dressing to attract the male gaze, in the world of fashion both the object of and the owner of the gaze are undeniably female. It was originally for women that shop displays were created, and it is women who notice the details and expense of garments, which in turn arouses envy and continues the cycle of desire. And just as color was used to attract consumers (Leach 65), the vivid colors of Clare's clothes—the reds, cinnamons, and golds—are a way to attract the gaze of women. Clare's decision to wear black to the NWL dance is especially significant. It is a color associated with the "sinister," with "fear of the blind darkness of night and the eternal darkness of death; and in small, carefully flavored doses, such deliberate conjuring is always attractive" (Hollander 365–66). Clare is sporting a color that both announces her race (although only to those with enough other information to understand the allusion) and warns Irene, whose reaction—she feels inferior and insignificant—suggests the strategy is working. A black dress such as Clare's has serious connotations for the viewer: it suggests not only a "self-conscious theatricalism" but also "fatal sexuality. A lady in black is not only dramatic and dignified but also dangerous" (376). Clare declares as much, telling Irene she is "not safe," that she will "do anything, hurt anybody, throw anything away" in order to get something she really wants (240). She is meeting Brian for the first time on this occasion, and the insinuation is that she does indeed pose a threat.

Irene's envy of Clare is also articulated in visual terms. She frequently claims that Clare is too beautiful, as if her attractiveness were a liability. She expresses an appreciation for Clare's "decorative qualities" but also derogates her intelligence and social skills. Clare provides "aesthetic pleasure" yet is unable to contribute much to dinner party conversation; she is "easy on the eyes" but "intelligent in a purely feminine way," a description Brian interprets to mean "[i]ntelligent enough to wear a tight bodice and keep bowing swains whispering compliments and retrieving dropped fans" (239, 248, 249). Like advertisements of the late nineteenth century in which "'eye appeal' had begun to rival copy for prominence" (Leach 43), Clare has appearance without substance.

Yet there is a more negative connotation to this depiction: Clare's association with sexual danger and even death affiliates her with another type of femme fatale, the prostitute. The possibility is actually alluded to by Irene, when she explains to Clare that she cannot attend the dance without a date because she might be mistaken for one of the "ladies of easy virtue looking for trade." It is a possibility Clare responds to by laughing, saying, "Thanks. I never have been. It might be amusing" (230). Also, when she is seen in the company of white men after going to live with her aunts, it is assumed she has decided to trade in on her beauty in the most basic of ways. The figure of the prostitute is "commodity and labor collapsed into one" (Solomon-Godeau 117), making it the ultimate icon of a marketplace which already depends so heavily on female sexuality. While Clare is certainly not a prostitute in the classic sense, she is not above doing whatever it takes to get what she wants, including selling herself to the highest bidder. Larsen may also be alluding here to the traditional connection between mixed race women and prostitution. Finally, because she had to attract the gaze of men, the prostitute is generally associated with eye-catching garments and often depicted as the best-dressed woman in town. The well-dressed black prostitute (actual or implied) is the epitome of the dangerous, man-consuming, boundary-obliterating woman.

The connections among female desire, consumer culture, and the gaze have other negative—and racialized—connotations in Larsen's text. Before she bumps into Clare at the Drayton, Irene is shopping for gifts on a hot August afternoon, on a street where "the shopwindows [throw] out a blinding radiance." When a man faints nearby, the incident has no more effect on Irene than to make her feel "disagreeably damp and sticky and soiled from contact with so many sweating bodies" (175). The setting for this early episode—with its references to "rays . . . like molten rain," "sharp particles of dust," and breezes like "the breath of a flame" (174)—is hellish in all its aspects. Nearly fainting herself, Irene is whisked into a passing cab by its solicitous driver and brought to "another world": the rooftop restaurant at the Drayton Hotel (176). But in order to enter that world she must become something she is not, a transformation that, as noted earlier, she undergoes without qualm or hesitation. A short while later she is staring through the windows of the cafe to the street below when Clare appears, taking her seat at an adjacent window, so that the two women are framed in their respective apertures. Women in the novel are often "framed" as in store displays: the tableau created by Gertrude and Clare in the latter's hotel room when Irene arrives; Irene and Clare before the mirror in Irene's bedroom; the dancers at the NWL dance as seen from a box overlooking the floor, where Clare and Ralph Hazleton are a "study in contrasts" (235). This technique serves to set such moments apart, to be recollected and deciphered later by the viewer (much like the tableaux vivants in *House of Mirth*). Even Irene's memories of events involving Clare suggest the experience of the viewer before department store windows, where the consumer is both reflected and able to gaze on the objects of desire, where both the objects within and the viewer without are framed, depending on one's perspective. The techniques intrinsic to the manipulation of consumer desire—"[f]ashion, interior display and decoration, and facades of color, glass, and light" (Leach 111)—resonate with the scenes in the novel involving Irene and Clare. Similarly, the mannequin at the heart of the window display is the focus of the gaze and the focus of desire, and as a copy of the real thing, it is a fake, a counterfeit, as is Clare (and Irene as well).

One of the most significant of these scenes is when Clare appears at Irene's for the first time, intent on learning why her letters have gone unanswered. Clad in furs and her "priceless" velvet dress, Clare takes Irene by surprise, "drop[ping] a kiss on her dark curls" (224). Because she is seated at her dressing table mirror when Clare appears behind her, the narrator's reference to Irene's "[l]ooking at the woman before her" is intriguing in its ambiguity. The uncertainty of the reference serves to conflate the two women in ways that are repeated throughout the novel, as does the fact that Clare sits in Irene's favorite chair; the connection is reinforced by the omnipresence of mirrors and reflecting windows in which the two appear as well as the twin reflections of one another's eyes. Mirrors are significant in constructions of the self. Yet the ambiguous reference to the woman in the mirror is immediately followed by Irene's exclamation, uttered "with something like awe in her voice: 'Dear God! But aren't you lovely, Clare!'" (225); the words are a testament to Clare's desirability and visual appeal. Irene's is the appreciation of the connoisseur, but it also objectifies Clare; she is a lovely object, something distinct—at least for a moment—from the actual emotions Irene experiences upon her arrival.

While some may read Irene's desire for Clare in sexual terms, it is also a matter of economics. First, Irene envies and desires the capital Clare represents: in beauty, in nerve, and in actual dollars. These assets enable Clare to ignore the boundaries of race, even if only for a time, and move from the black world to the white; the same disregard for boundaries marks her attempt to move back again to the black world. Yet Clare is also exchange value for Irene. She is at first perceived as a distraction, a way to keep Brian entertained and keep his mind off other matters; she is someone to send to events Irene does not want to attend, and she is a way for Irene to justify the choices she has made. In comparison to Clare's abnegation of race, her cavalier attitude toward her daughter, and her betrayal of their friendship, Irene's manipulations seem barely worth mentioning. Unlike Clare, however, Irene is not prepared to pay for what she has received, having neither the assets nor the desire to do so. Instead, she makes Clare pay, the one who has already declared that passing and all it entails have been "worth the price" (190). It is a comment in which several discourses intersect: that of the commodity, that of authenticity (since passing is itself about the authentic), and that of racial construction (since it is Clare's mixed-race status that enables her to pass).

These elements of passing—identity creation and confusion, commodity culture, objectification of the self, specularity—are all in evidence at the NWL dance, particularly during Irene's conversation with Hugh Wentworth, the well-known white author. When Irene joins Hugh in an empty box, she "let[s] her gaze wander over the bright crowd below" (234). The spectacle before them is carnivalesque, a blur of men and women of all shapes, sizes, ages, and colors. Their ensuing analysis of the attraction of one race for the other, a conversation that suggests the very cultural anxiety Ginsberg describes, is initiated by the sight of Clare dancing with Ralph Hazelton, the one "fair and golden, like a sunlit day" and the other "dark, with gleaming eyes, like a moonlit night" (235). It is an attraction Irene attributes to "a kind of emotional excitement. You know, the sort of thing you feel in the presence of something strange, and even, perhaps, a bit repugnant to you, something so different that it's really at the opposite end of the pole from all your accustomed notions of beauty" (236). Like the display in the shop window, this scene is about desire and lack, about the manipulation of reality, and about the role of the gaze in the construction of meaning. Clare embodies the great American drive for social advancement and economic security and especially the American dream of class mobility. However, her passing suggests a kind of mobility that is threatening rather than salutary or mythic. As a white woman, she can have much of what she desires, especially since she has married a wealthy man; as a black woman masquerading as white, however, she must be punished for her transgressions of race and class. Clare, like Irene, attempts to ignore race. Her fate is sealed with her attempt to transgress the boundaries of race again, this time by moving in the opposite direction and back to the black world. But as the object with exchange value, Clare has transgressed boundaries besides those of race. She has no purchasing power of her own beyond what she has acquired through Bellew, but she behaves as though she can exchange herself on the open market, as if she can be both the desired object and the seller of that object. Clare is trapped by the limitations of the market where women are concerned as much as she is by her race.

Irene is also trapped by the workings of the market; she is the consumer being manipulated by means of her envy and desire. As Rachel Bowlby observes, "the model in the window is something both real and other. It offers something more in the form of another, altered self, and one potentially obtainable via the payment of a stipulated price" (34). This is the essence of Irene's relationship to Clare. Like the object of desire in a department store window, Clare represents what Irene wants *and* what she lacks as well as the cost that must be paid. Like windows and mirrors, eyes can also serve as reflectors, and on a number of occasions Irene sees her desires, and her fears, reflected in Clare's eyes. For example, when Bellew declares that he would never marry a "nigger," Clare looks at Irene "with an expression so deep and dark and unfathomable that she had for a short moment the sensation of gazing into the eyes of some creature utterly strange and apart. A faint sense of danger brushed her, like the breath of a cold fog" (201). Irene eventually knows herself to be strange and apart—and potentially dangerous—as well. This is most evident in another "mirror" scene when she discovers the relationship between Clare and Brian. Having just learned that Brian has, of his own volition, invited Clare to a tea in honor of Hugh Wentworth, Irene suddenly realizes from his reaction that something is going on between the two. Once he leaves the room, she sits "in strained stiffness. The face in the mirror vanished from her sight, blotted out by this thing which had so suddenly flashed across her groping mind. Impossible for her to put it immediately into words or give it outline, for, prompted by some impulse of self-protection, she recoiled from exact expression" (250). She must admit that she has been "something—oh, very much—of a damned fool" (251).

This scene before the glass is repeated on the evening of the party at the Freelands'. Clare shows up as Irene is dressing and, facing the woman she is now convinced is about to ruin her life, and having just met Jack Bellew downtown the previous day in the company of the distinctly black Felise, Irene must confront her own ruthlessness. She fails to tell Clare of the possible danger that lies ahead—unwilling to deal with a Clare who is free to be with Brian—and "pass[es] a hand over her eyes to shut out the accusing face in the glass before her. With one corner of her mind she wondered how long she had looked like that, drawn and haggard and—yes, frightened. Or was it only imagination?" (265). Just as she is momentarily conflated with Irene in the mirror, Clare serves as a mirror for the side of Irene that would like to ignore race, the side that wants social place and material comfort, the side that would kill another who threatened those things. Irene's antipathy toward Clare could well be the result of her subconscious awareness of Clare as the mirror image of herself and what that might mean for Irene's security and artificial existence.

Mirrors have long held fascinating implications, such as "the fear of being either trapped or attacked by something that lives inside the mirror itself and is only released by the viewer's gaze. . . . Behind the reflecting surface is something waiting to be born." Ultimately, what we fear about the mirror is that "the infinite and wayward power of the human eye [will] turn on itself and make an uncontrollable, destructive creature out of the self-image" (Hollander 392). In other words, we fear that we will become the very monster we believe is hidden in the mirror. Clare is on the one hand the danger waiting to be released by Irene's gaze; she is both trap and destructive creature, and her presence brings out these characteristics in the other woman. She begins as spectacle or object of the gaze only to become a specular object, reflecting back to Irene what she does not want to see or know. However, Clare's arrival also brings out the very worst in Irene, turning her into the very deceptive, marriage-killing monster she believes Clare to be.

In several key episodes Irene is positioned before an actual mirror confronting the truth about the self she has created: it is one who has used emotional blackmail to force her husband to stay in a country he despises, one who passes when convenient but will not allow race to be an issue in the raising of her black children, one who would do anything to make sure her privileged existence is not threatened in any substantive way. For most of the novel, Irene believes the "menace" comes in the form of change, not in the guise of race (258), but she has mistaken stability for safety. Clare's arrival precipitates Irene's acknowledgement of the extent to which race matters; it also compels her to confront her ambivalence about being black and the extent to which she has fashioned an identity that is neither white nor black. With her casual passing and attempts to ignore the racism around her, Irene lives as if blackness were a garment to be donned—or removed—at will, not an essential part of her identity. Yet she is equally willing to accuse Clare of a lack of racial consciousness. Passing is in part about individuation, about creating an identity for oneself apart from race (although, ironically, one uses race to pass), but it also means separating from the larger community, both black and white. Mark Jones argues: "Each society, each generation, fakes the thing it covets most . . . fakers are above all creatures of the market" (13).[15] Passing, like other varieties of counterfeiting, is about desire; it is about obtaining what one covets, whether material goods, social position, or simply the ability to ignore race that comes with being white.

Larsen's novel ultimately poses several questions: Where does race end and the self begin? To what extent is race something we can fashion for ourselves (if at all)? What are the consequences for both the self and the larger community when we attempt to ignore or escape the influence of race in America? After all, it is only when she begins to find race a burden—when she starts to acknowledge some of the feelings she has long since buried or ignored—that Irene also begins to wonder who she is and what it is she truly wants.

These elements come tragically together in the novel's conclusion, which takes place at a party at Felise and Dave Freelands' sixth-floor apartment. Irene, convinced that Clare and her husband are having an affair, is determined to keep Brian and the life she has created with him. Following Clare's example, she has learned that the price of success is sacrifice, even if that means the sacrifice of another. "Brought to the edge of distasteful reality," Irene no longer has any illusions about herself or her life, but she is also not willing to give up what she has acquired through a lifetime of self-denial (268). The evening begins with Irene's final confrontation with her true self—her reasons for not telling Brian and Clare about seeing Bellew; her own desire to "do anything, risk anything to prevent [Bellew] from learning the truth; the fact that "security was the most important and desired thing in life" (268, 267)—and ends in blackness and denial. Even in the depths of her despair, however, she observes that Clare is wearing "a shining red gown," and that she is "a vital glowing thing, like a flame of red and gold" (265, 271). When Bellew appears in the apartment and confronts his wife about her race, Irene rushes to Clare's side and, in what must have seemed to the casual observer as a possessive and protective gesture, places her hand on Clare's arm. Clare is standing before an open casement window, framed against the blackness of the evening, mannequinlike in her calm. The gaze of those in attendance is split between her and the enraged newcomer, and it is this that provides Irene with the moment she needs to act.

When Clare vanishes from sight, no one suggests that Irene may be to blame. Left alone in the apartment as the others race downstairs to Clare, Irene is at first struck by the physical loss of the other woman: "Gone! The soft white face, the bright hair, the disturbing scarlet mouth, the dreaming eyes, the caressing smile, the whole torturing loveliness that had been Clare Kendry. That beauty that had torn at Irene's placid life. Gone! The mocking daring, the gallantry of her pose, the ringing bells of her laughter" (272). Irene's final description of Clare is reminiscent of the types of phrases found in advertising copy for beauty products, the kind that hold out the promise of future happiness if only one wears the right lipstick or the right clothes. As the woman Irene would like to be, Clare is also the manifestation of a consumer culture that values presentation over substance, fashion over sincerity.

Glass is the barrier that separates the consumer from the object of desire, but it is also a key element in the provocation of desire, according to Leach. Pushing Clare through an open window (one Irene has opened just moments before) essentially allows Irene to remove her from the market, to destroy the one thing that testifies to her own lack. Clare is no longer something to be admired and not touched, something inviolate and privileged. The missing glass also turns Irene from what Leach describes as the "compulsive viewer" into one who acts, however negatively. The open window reverberates with the class issues raised in the novel as well. As Leach points out, "glass democratized desire even as it dedemocratized access to goods" (63); without glass, everyone has access to the objects on display, even those who can not actually afford to buy them. The cost Irene finally pays is the destruction of the ideal world and self she has constructed. Despite Clare's red dress, the final images of the novel are variations on a theme in black and white: the group of black men and women confronting Bellew, the solitary white man; Clare's "black" body lying prostrate in the snow; everything going black as Irene finally faints.

At one point in the novel Irene observes, "It's funny about 'passing.' We disapprove of it and at the same time condone it. It excites our contempt and yet we rather admire it. We shy away from it with an odd kind of revulsion, but we protect it" (216). This may be in part because the passing figure embodies a very recognizable desire—the uniquely American dream of success and social mobility—while also subverting any possibility of using race as a signifier. Although not merely a turn-of-the-century phenomenon, passing is a powerful metaphor for much that transpired in that period. It is about marketing, about selling a newly created self, and about packaging. It also raises questions of authenticity for black and white alike. Irene's feelings about Clare are produced by the recognition of her own deceptions. Her desire to destroy Clare, who has already been established as her double, is in effect an attempt to destroy the evidence. The supposed affair provides Irene with much-needed justification for her actions, but Clare has been made the scapegoat for all the varieties of deception that fill the novel. In a tale that is in many ways about the inability to authenticate or prove things, especially in regard to race, Irene utters what may be the definitive statement: "Appearances . . . had a way sometimes of not fitting facts" (185).

The passing figure complicates the question of racial authenticity for both white and black alike. Is Clare black, even though she has renounced her race? Is she white, having been accepted by the white community, even though she has black blood? Those who pass are a threat to both communities; for the black community they represent the possibility of race annihilation, while for the white community they suggest that racial identity is one more area of uncertainty in an uncertain time. But the very existence of the mixed-race person, whether or not she chooses to pass, subverts the notion of racial authenticity. When one is both white and black, which identity is "real"? In effect, the person of mixed race is always a fake, regardless of the choice she makes. Larsen's decision to include several mixed-race women in her text (Irene, Clare, and Gertrude) illustrates not only the variety of choices available but also the inherent falseness of any choice. The mixed-race woman, whether she passes completely, occasionally, or not at all, reveals the ways in which race is socially constructed (a new concept in the early twentieth century) as well as the insufficiency of such terms as "white" and "black" for establishing identity. By taking full advantage of the expanded access to products in a consumer culture, she also spotlights the ways consumerism threatened to undermine the traditional ways of identifying the other. Finally, the authenticity of whiteness is itself subverted, and with it the notion of white superiority.

Passing thus engages many of the issues that were paramount when Larsen wrote: the nature of the self, the effects of consumer culture on female desire, and the meaning of race. What each has in common is the potential to subvert authenticity and call into question the traditionally accepted means for understanding what constitutes identity. Larsen suggests that authenticity—racial or otherwise—is a misnomer, a label for a category that does not exist. The events that Clare's letter initiates are explored in part through the discourse of consumer culture, and in particular through the lens of fashion, where women are encouraged to create new selves and covetousness is praised and even rewarded. Fashion may seem frivolous to the uninitiated, but the consuming woman understands how essential it is to the construction of a new identity and one's ability to pass, whether one is passing as a member of the elite or as white. The fashionable woman, like Irene, has been well trained in the art of dressing to kill.

6

A World of Wonders

Collecting and the Authentic Self in *The Great Gatsby*

Collecting—at least in the West, where time is generally thought to be
linear and irreversible—implies a rescue of phenomena from inevitable
historical decay or loss. The collection contains what "deserves" to be
kept, remembered and treasured. Artifacts and customs are saved out
of time.

—James Clifford, *The Predicament of Culture*

On the afternoon he meets Daisy Buchanan again for the first time in
five years, Jay Gatsby takes her to see his magnificent house. He has
planned this meeting so she can see the building at close proximity,
hoping to impress her immediately with its size and grandeur, and a
tour is the natural culmination of his quest to win Daisy and convince
her that he is worthy of her love. In order to create the strongest possible
effect, they go down the road and through the front gate, a route that
suggests the long years Gatsby has waited for this moment (although he
has taken a shortcut on his route to wealth). Daisy might be a princess
being escorted into a palace by her long-lost prince (with Nick along as
a kind of gentleman-in-waiting); emitting "enchanting murmurs," she
admires "this aspect or that of the feudal silhouette" of the house (built
by a brewer with dreams of "Found[ing] a Family," and mounts marble
stairs past the "pale gold odor of kiss-me-at-the-gate," a fitting scent to
mark the arrival of the "golden girl" (89, 92, 120). The hushed and vacant
interior is a far cry from the scene during one of Gatsby's parties, as
Nick observes; the silence is so eerie he imagines guests hiding "behind
every couch and table" until they have passed (92). The group wanders
through "Marie Antoinette music-rooms and Restoration salons," "the
Merton College Library" (described earlier as "a high Gothic library,
paneled with carved English oak, and probably transported complete
from some ruin overseas"), "period bedrooms," "dressing-rooms and

poolrooms, and bathrooms with sunken baths," and even one "living exhibit": Mr. Klipspringer, who currently resides with Gatsby and is discovered in one of the rooms doing "liver exercises" (92).[1] All these rooms are anachronisms, no longer connected to their original and actual context; like a series of tableaux in a variety of styles, they seem to have nothing in common besides the four walls in which they coexist.

What they do have in common, however, is the desire of the collector who has brought them together. In the hushed reverence of what seems much like a museum visit, Gatsby, Daisy, and Nick Carraway, the narrator of F. Scott Fitzgerald's *The Great Gatsby* (1925), make their way through the world Gatsby has created, a series of spaces and objects suspended in time, wonderful in their variety, and a testament to the wealth and suitability of their owner. Gatsby's suite of rooms is the centerpiece of the tour, an austere set of spaces except for the Adam study, which in all likelihood would have been quite ornate.[2] Like the music rooms and salons, a study in the style of Robert Adam alludes to earlier periods in history. The only ornament, the solid gold toilet set on Gatsby's dresser, continues a theme that began with the epigraph to the novel; it includes Gatsby's attire in this scene—he is wearing a "gold-colored tie" (85)— and is given life when Daisy uses the gold brush to tidy her hair while Gatsby looks on in wonder. This is, after all, "the king's daughter, the golden girl" (120), who has entered his world; she is able to transform a gold brush from a mere ornament to an item of value simply because she has used it. As if overwhelmed by the sight, Gatsby "[sits] down, [shades] his eyes, and [begins] to laugh" in amazed pleasure, unable even to articulate what it means to have the one possession he has desired for years suddenly in his house, using one of his other possessions.[3] Yet the actuality of Daisy, her sudden "realness," has several profound results. The first is the way her presence causes Gatsby to appear as if he is "running down like an overwound clock" (93), an image that suggests the temporal nature of dreams, of desire, and especially of the objects that fuel desire.[4] There is also a paradigm shift that leads Gatsby to "[revalue] everything in his house" depending on the reaction he sees in Daisy's "well-loved eyes" (92). He has worked hard to create a setting for Daisy and to assemble the proofs of his worthiness. Instead, her arrival has the inadvertent effect of exposing first the unreality of his creation and then its crassness. Even the meaning of the notorious green light, a

kind of avatar, is altered by her presence. When Gatsby mentions it a
short while later, telling Daisy, "You always have a green light that burns
all night at the end of your dock," Nick notices that he "seem[s] absorbed in what he ha[s] just said. Possibly it had occurred to him that
the colossal significance of that light had now vanished forever . . . it
was again a green light on a dock. His count of enchanted objects had
diminished by one" (94).

But there are still some enchanted objects available that Gatsby can
turn to in order to reassert the world he has created. He suddenly throws
open the doors of "two hulking patent cabinets" to reveal his infamous
shirts. Before considering the contents, however, it should be noted that
the receptacles holding Gatsby's clothes have ramifications of their own.
The word "hulking" is also one Daisy has previously used to describe her
husband, Tom, much to his displeasure. By employing a word associated
with him, Fitzgerald brings Tom back into the picture, even if only for
the reader, just before what is probably the most memorable scene in the
novel: Daisy sobbing over Gatsby's shirts. We are not allowed to forget
that she is a married woman and as such "belongs" to someone else. The
reference to "patent cabinets" evokes a far different association but one
also associated with commodities and ownership; like the patent cases
in Specimen Days, which hold the patent models, the cabinet storing
the shirts gives them the aura of an exhibit, although Gatsby has not
assembled this particular collection himself, which begs the question:
What is the value of a personal collection that has not actually been collected by its owner? Gatsby has "a man in England who buys [him]
clothes" (93), and it seems very likely that everything else in the house
is someone else's doing. The fact that someone else has done the buying also establishes some objective distance between Gatsby and the
things he owns. Like Whitman, he is not a materialist in the traditional
sense, and unlike the usual consumer, who buys things in order to satisfy a deep-seated and never sated desire, Gatsby has only one motive
for everything he does: the attainment of Daisy and the dream she represents.

The cabinets contain the only possessions of his that elicit a strong
emotional response from her, perhaps because, unlike the other objects
that fill his house, they are a vivid and tangible symbol of the depth of
his desire, recognizable even to someone as lacking in imagination as she

is. The shirts, like Daisy, are "actual" and "astounding" (92), but her re-action is as questionable as Gatsby's provenance and his possessions. For one thing, it is hard to believe, given Tom's wealth and his apparent affinity for fine clothes, that Daisy has never seen such beautiful shirts before. Knowing what we do about her ability to adopt specific personae in order to get an emotional response, it is very likely that Daisy's reac-tion is a show for the benefit of Gatsby and Nick. Her response would be more convincing if there were any evidence in the text that Daisy had the capacity for wonder, and this is exactly the reaction Gatsby's house is designed to elicit.

The house is a carefully assembled collection of beautiful and exotic things, and as such it is a success. It is also intended to convince others of the discrimination and wealth of its owner. As an advertisement for good taste, of course, the house is a dismal failure.[5] It is unconvincing in the same ways Gatsby himself is: while the individual pieces seem fine, it is trying too hard and a bit overdone. Finally, the house is also the ultimate container for the final precious object Gatsby has been waiting for, but it is equally a failure in this capacity. Daisy does not really un-derstand what she has wandered into, although she tries to rise to the occasion. She admires and smiles, but her response even to something as glorious as "a pink and golden billow of foamy clouds above the sea" is to tell Gatsby, "I would like to just get one of those pink clouds and put you in it and push you around" (95). Rather than a response equal to his efforts and the depth of his desire, Gatsby is instead treated to what passes for romance with Daisy: sentimental and meaningless chatter.

The Great Gatsby is a novel about wonder,[6] and just as Whitman needed to find a specific form for his experiences in order to provide meaning and a context, Fitzgerald had to find a form to hold the fantas-tic (as in "incredible") people, objects, and places he pulled together to furnish his tale of life in America in the early decades of the twentieth century. What the novel most resembles is a *Wunderkammer,* or Cabinet of Wonders, that Renaissance invention that was a precursor to the mod-ern museum and one of the earliest examples of commodity fetishism. While a Cabinet of Wonders was a personal collection, what made it of interest to others were the strange and exotic bits and pieces assembled, preserved, and often catalogued by its owner (in this case Nick Carra-way, standing in for Fitzgerald).[7] Nick is the primary "collector" in the text, and his own prized possession is Gatsby; the novel then becomes a catalogue, so to speak, of the items he has collected during his summer in the East.

While Fitzgerald's version evokes the sense of a Cabinet of Wonders in prose, a Wunderkammer was originally an actual cabinet—"a cupboard with shelves and drawers that held small physical objects"—filled with bits of bone, plant samples, old coins, bits of stone and metalwork, feathers, and so on. (A room-sized display might have animal specimens, curious instruments and devices, costumes, and unusual weapons.) By the seventeenth century the term was being applied to almost any space that housed a collection of "curiosities (whether cupboards, a closet adjoining a bedroom, a summerhouse, or other rooms) and to designate the collection in its entirety" (Swann 2). Thus, a patent cabinet, a room, a house, or a novel may be a Cabinet of Wonders, as long as what is collected within that space is designed to elicit wonder (it may not generate the type of wonder intended, of course, but that is a different matter). This is a novel overflowing with "things," with objects of all shapes and sizes: furniture, magazines, pools, gas pumps, cuff links made from molars, photographs, books, and the list goes on.[8] It is through association with objects that characters are not only given substance but are also able to "prove" their provenance and signify their social status. In this text, you are what you own, or *who* you own. Objects also ground the text in its place and time, a period in which rampant consumerism was becoming a defining aspect of American culture. The Cabinet of Wonders, and collecting in general, represents many of the recurring themes considered throughout this study: commodity fetishism, the construction of identity, the dubious nature of authenticity as a concept, and the tenuous connection between authenticity and value.

Others have already made a case for the influence of earlier texts on *The Great Gatsby*, and we can see Fitzgerald's interest in the past even in his references to Adam studies and Restoration salons. George Monteiro, for example, sees the influence of both Columbus's *Journals* and Washington Irving's *A History of New York, from the Beginning of the World to the End of the Dutch Dynasty*, texts that reinforce the theme of Old World versus New World that pervades the text. In addition, Mitchell Breitwieser's "Jazz Fractures: F. Scott Fitzgerald and Epochal Representation," while it does not focus on textual influence, contains some intriguing language for the purposes of my study. Reflecting on the differences between his current reading of the novel and his understanding of it as a younger man, Breitwieser writes, "Fitzgerald's writing seems to me now less an expression and celebration of pure longing than an *archaeology of American desire*—not the unbroken lineage from Dutch explorers to Jazz Age dreamer that Fitzgerald posited at the end of his most famous work, but a sedimentation of desires, like the layers of Troy or the layers of meanings Freud peeled away in the analysis of the symptom—'America' as a condensation, aggregate, *or depository of subject-residues,* rather than a mystical being" (359; my emphasis). The phrases I've highlighted, especially the terms "archaeology" and "depository," suggest a way of thinking about the novel that can be explored more fully. It is Fitzgerald's interest in the past and history, his effort to link 1920s America to the discovery of the New World, that suggest he might have been aware of Cabinets of Wonder; this awareness seems especially probable in light of the popularity of collecting in the early twentieth century (which had its institutionalized form in the museum). If Nick can turn the clock back on a late summer evening on Long Island to invoke the arrival of the first Dutch settlers, then it is surely just a few more steps from collections of baseball cards and matchboxes back to one of the earliest forms of the organized personal collection, the Wunderkammer.

Cabinets of Wonder were a direct product of the Age of Discovery. In *Marvelous Possessions: The Wonder of the New World,* Stephen Greenblatt asserts that "Columbus's voyage initiated a century of intense wonder" (14). As he explains:

> Wonder—thrilling, potentially dangerous, momentarily immobilizing, charged at once with desire, ignorance, and fear—is the quintessential human response to what Descartes calls a "first encounter." Such terms . . . made wonder an almost inevitable component of the discourse of discovery, for by definition wonder is an instinctive recognition of difference, the sign of a heightened attention, "a sudden surprise of the soul" . . . in the face of the new. The expression of wonder stands for all that cannot be understood, that can scarcely be believed. It calls attention to the problem of credibility and at the same time insists upon the undeniability, the exigency of the experience. (20)

The many unusual objects brought home by explorers and their crew members then led to a passion for collecting, particularly among private citizens (Swann 23).[9] Two types of collections became especially popular in this period: the *Kunstkammern* of the wealthy, which contained art objects, and the Wunderkammern or "cabinet[s] of wonders" or curiosities, assembled by those "[l]ower down the social scale" (2). The Cabinet of Wonders, in its truest form, was intended as a microcosm of the world, which was indeed perceived to be a wondrous place.

Greenblatt's characterization of wonder is helpful when thinking about the way this concept functions in *The Great Gatsby*, especially in terms of collecting and even authenticity. Wonder characterizes Gatsby's early encounters with Daisy: he is "amazed" by the beauty of her house, by the "ripe mystery about it" (148), and by Daisy herself. Although he knows she is a diversion from his plans, he is unable to stay away and eventually finds his desire has turned to love. But even before Daisy appears, Gatsby is a creature motivated by wonder. As a young man, "grotesque and fantastic conceits haunted him in his bed at night. A universe of ineffable gaudiness spun itself out in his brain." Unwilling to face the reality into which he was born, one of "shiftless" and "unsuccessful" parents, he indulges in "reveries" that afford "a satisfactory hint of the unreality of reality, a promise that the rock of the world was founded securely on a fairy's wing" (99, 100). Then, like an explorer arriving on the shore of the New World, Dan Cody, Gatsby's mentor and savior, sails into Lake Superior, "represent[ing] all the beauty and glamour in the world" to the young James Gatz (100–1). Gatsby is like a curiosity or wonder himself at this point, taken away by Cody and then set adrift again when Cody dies and Gatsby is unable to claim the twenty-five thousand dollars bequeathed to him. Gatsby then discovers his own New World when he meets and falls in love with Daisy Fay of Louisville. The collection he assembles in West Egg is an attempt to re-create that world, one with "a ripe mystery about it, a hint of bedrooms up-stairs more beautiful and cool than other bedrooms, of gay and radiant activities taking place through its corridors, and of romances that were not musty and laid away already in lavender but fresh and breathing and redolent of this year's shining motor-cars and of dances whose flowers were scarcely withered" (148).

As we have seen in previous chapters, collecting is about creating order, about fashioning a self for public consumption, and about the possible reification of that self. What distinguishes Fitzgerald's text from the others I have examined to this point is partly the form collecting takes. In *Specimen Days,* Whitman uses the natural history museum as the model for his collected experiences in order to provide a context and significance. *The House of Mirth* is a novel where the decision to collect or not, and to be collected or not, has profound results. The activity of collecting in Fitzgerald's novel contains these elements, but it is also a way to link the past and the present and, even more specifically, to restore the past to the present. Because collections of all types record what has transpired as opposed to what is to come, the activity of collecting is uniquely suited to serve as a vehicle for examining the interrelatedness of the past and the present. Of course, not all collecting is the same. In *Museums, Objects, and Collections,* Pearce identifies three types of collections: "collections as 'souvenirs,' as 'fetish objects,' and as 'systematics'" (68–69), and each type is in evidence in here. Nick is a souvenir collector, and the novel becomes much like the catalogue for a Cabinet of Wonders, this one containing all the various and sundry mementoes of his summer in the East; Gatsby is a fetish collector, gathering objects purely for the work they can do to establish a milieu fit for Daisy, who will be the defining object in his collection; finally, Tom Buchanan is a systematic collector whose primary interest is the acquisition of things, especially women, because they bolster his sense of manhood. Whatever the mode, however, the urge to collect is the logical consequence of a culture that gives objects a central place in the construction of meaning, value, and authenticity. The collection is also the way identity is established, and many characters in the novel are associated with specific items.

Collecting is a defining activity in *The Great Gatsby,* yet it is significant that all the collectors are men. One obvious reason is that men control the means to collect, but they also have desire, an emotion that is patently missing in the women (except, perhaps, for Myrtle Wilson). Nick, for example, refers to Daisy and Jordan and "their impersonal eyes in the absence of all desire" (12). Also, because women are themselves collectable, they are not in a position to be collectors (as we saw with Lily). Daisy speaks to the female condition of the objectified woman when she tells Nick her response to giving birth to a daughter: "Well, she was less than an hour old and Tom was God knows where. I woke up out of the ether with an utterly abandoned feeling, and asked the nurse right away if it was a boy or a girl. She told me it was a girl, and so I turned my head away and wept. 'All right,' I said, 'I'm glad it's a girl. And I hope she'll be a fool—that's the best thing a girl can be in this world, a beautiful little fool' " (17). Although this little speech ends with Daisy's exaggerated posturing as a cynic and with a smirk, as primarily objects for trade, women are indeed better off if they cannot understand this. Gatsby's description of meeting Daisy for the first time illustrates both her position as a collectible object and specifically her role as a fetish.

Daisy Fay is simply one of the many expensive things her family's money has made possible, like the large house, the wide lawn, her road-ster, and her "many clothes" (150). She is a "nice girl," a phrase that reso-nates with the language found in the success manuals and etiquette books so popular in this period, and one synonymous with "marriage-able." But "niceness" is a product of wealth and class status rather than anything to do with actual behavior. (After all, would a truly "nice girl" in 1920s America be having sex with a young soldier she has just met?) Gatsby has never before had access to such a girl, and it takes a world at war to give him admission to Daisy's world, temporarily eliminat-ing the "barbed wire" that has kept his kind at bay until now (148). The uniform of an army officer admits him to the Fay house because it erases all sartorial evidence of class status. But the experience, true to Veblen's theories about the workings of pecuniary emulation, serves chiefly to sharpen Gatsby's desire for the thing he has seen from afar. He wants exactly what he was never intended to have. Daisy, the "ob-ject" of his desire—in both senses of the word, for she is both "goal" and "thing"—is reminiscent of a mannequin in a department store dis-play such as might have been created by L. Frank Baum.[10] Surrounded by "the bought luxury of star-shine" and sitting in "a wicker settee" that "squeaked fashionably" (149), she represents desire, beauty, wealth, status, and power, the driving elements of a consumer culture (but no-tice that the star-shine is "bought" and the fashionable squeak of the settee may be artifice as well).[11]

She is "safe" when Gatsby meets her (that is, worth investing in), a luxurious object on the marriage market, whose value is determined by the simple rules of supply and demand: many men have desired Daisy, and so she is clearly worth having. Daisy has not always lacked desire of her own. For example, Nick tells us that Gatsby "kissed her curious and lovely mouth" (149); either of two meanings of "curious" is possible here. Daisy is certainly curious about Gatsby, who is so different from the other boys she has known, but Daisy's mouth is also curious to him because she represents a type he has never experienced before.

The word "curious" has interesting connotations for collecting, and especially in terms of Cabinets of Wonder. From the French *curieux,* it is "associated . . . with the theme of totality," with someone who "decides, dissatisfied with a knowledge of the common and the normal, to seek greater knowledge of the singular" (Pomian 56, 57). Gatsby's experience with Daisy initiates him into the world of the remarkable, and he can never again be satisfied with less than this. In other words, he is filled with curiosity, with "a desire and a passion: a desire to see, learn or possess rare, new secret or remarkable things, in other words those things that have a special relationship with totality and consequently provide a means of attaining it" (Pomian 58–59).

Daisy is also "curious" about Gatsby, but she lacks any way of achieving this "totality." While her relationship with him may begin as a summer fling with a handsome soldier, by the time Gatsby leaves Daisy has apparently committed herself to him. However, having been raised to be acquired by a man (much like Lily Bart), and as someone who has always had her every need gratified, Daisy does not have the emotional reserves needed to wait for Gatsby. A one-of-a-kind item, she is intensely sought after (Jordan Baker describes her as the most popular girl in Louisville), and both Gatsby and Tom single-mindedly pursue her in their turn. This situates her as more than just a common consumer item; she is a prized collectible, and whoever wants her can expect to pay dearly, which is exactly what Tom Buchanan does (his wedding gift to her is a 350-thousand-dollar pearl necklace). However, this logic also locates Daisy as an object without inherent worth; her only value is that bestowed on her by others and is in large part a result of her inaccessibility and the extent to which she is sought after by others (Gatsby is "excited" by the knowledge "that many men had already loved Daisy—it increased her value in his eyes" [148]).[12]

If Gatsby wants to own Daisy "legitimately" (a loaded word in this text, in which most things are false or illegitimate), he must first acquire the means to "purchase" her. In the interim, she will continue to incarnate for him "the youth and mystery that wealth imprisons and preserves" (150), a state much like that of a rare insect preserved in amber. However, like most highly valued and inaccessible items, Daisy is not destined to be the first thing one acquires. The objects a collector is able to accrue are typically determined by class status—unless he steals them. And in some way Gatsby does indeed "steal" Daisy, as Nick observes: "he took what he could get, ravenously and unscrupulously—eventually he took Daisy one still October night, took her because he had no real right to touch her hand" (149). Richard Godden describes Gatsby as engaging in "economic subversion," referring to his acquisition of Daisy as a theft and connecting it to Veblen's language in *The Theory of the Leisure Class;* thus, Gatsby is "a thief who steals the 'badge,' 'prize,' or 'trophy' of a group" (83). However, in the context of collecting, this is not theft as much as it is getting a good deal and acquiring something for less than its actual value.

While she was once a treasure just waiting for the right collector, Daisy is now a married woman with a child, wealth, and social status, but little else. There are moments when her awareness that something is missing is apparent and even touching. Leaving Gatsby's party, she glances past Nick and toward

the lighted top of the steps, where "Three O'Clock in the Morning," a neat, sad little waltz of that year, [is] drifting out the open door. After all, in the very casualness of Gatsby's party there were romantic possibilities totally absent from her world. What was it up there in the song that seemed to be calling her back inside? What would happen now in the dim, incalculable hours? Perhaps some unbelievable guest would arrive, a person infinitely rare and to be marvelled at, *some authentically radiant young girl* who with one fresh glance at Gatsby, one moment of magical encounter, would blot out those five years of unwavering devotion. (110; my emphasis)

What she is describing is the girl she used to be, the version of Daisy that Gatsby still believes in. Collecting is a way to deny the passage of time and the changes it brings. This is because, as Bourdieu explains, owning things from the past—especially those that can only be inherited or passed down—is one way to possess time (*Distinction* 71).[13]

While Gatsby's primary motivation for collecting objects that signify his wealth and apparent class status seems to be the reacquisition of Daisy, he is actually also attempting to eliminate the last five years because in that time he has lost something else as well. He believes that given the right combination of things (the right house, the right lawn, the right clothing), he can "repeat the past" (111) and find not only Daisy but himself. Nick rejects the possibility of reliving the past, but Gatsby is not the only one who believes in second chances. Jordan claims: "Life starts all over again when it gets crisp in the fall" (118). The idea of the fresh start is commonly evoked in advertising, where products are typically touted as having the ability to make the buyer better, cleaner, smarter, or more attractive; but even more than that, advertising is the machine behind the culture of consumption, which is "founded upon a lack" (Baudrillard, *System of Objects* 204–5).[14] Looking for a way to identify what distinguishes Gatsby, Daisy has no recourse but to turn to the language of consumption. Telling him, "You resemble the advertisement of the man . . . " effectively removes him from the temporal realm. Instead of an actual man, he becomes instead an "advertisement" of a man. Daisy becomes "new" as well in this moment; or, rather, she returns at least briefly to what she once was. Suddenly aware that his wife is in love with Gatsby, Tom "look[s] at [him], and then back at Daisy as if he ha[s] just recognized her as some one he knew a long time ago" (119).

Daisy has a different relationship to the temporal; instead of consciously trying to relive the past, her desire is to find ways to forget it by filling the present with meaningless activities. She wonders aloud, "What'll we do with ourselves this afternoon? . . . and the day after that, and the next thirty years?" (118). This evasion of time—whether it takes the form of trying to recapture or trying to avoid the past—has one thing in common with collecting: both are about the avoidance of death.[15] The novel is dense with images of death: the Valley of Ashes one must pass through on every trip to Manhattan, the funeral cortege Nick and Gatsby pass on their way to the city, Daisy's voice as a "deathless song" (97), the death of Dan Cody, not to mention Gatsby's own death. Col-

lecting has a paradoxical relation to death in that the act of collecting
saves objects from becoming waste and being discarded, but in order for
that to happen the object must be taken out of circulation. The collected
item has an existence in limbo.

Another way to ensure the continuity of life is to find ways to control
time, and collecting is effective here as well. Because objects either predate the collector or represent specific moments in the collector's life, a
collection is inevitably about the past. Objects in a collection can serve
"as mystical bridges between imagination and the past regarded as eter-
nally present and presentable through its physical traces" (Pearce, *Collecting in Contemporary Practice* 160–61). Gatsby has created his own
"mystical bridges" in order to return to a very specific moment in his
past, that moment when he decided to link his future to Daisy's. It is
immediately after he makes his remark about repeating the past that we
are told of his decision to commit himself to Daisy. Abandoning the
typical model of the American success story—the lone man on a quest
for fame and fortune—Gatsby decides to link his fate to Daisy's, to "forever wed his unutterable visions to her perishable breath" (112), and he
remains true to that decision for five years. What he never realizes, however, is that the wonder he experiences as "Daisy" is only a cipher for the
dreams of others; even Jordan, recalling that she admired Daisy most
"of all the older girls" (76), can provide as reasons for her admiration
only the size of the Fay house and lawn and the whiteness of Daisy's
clothes and car.

Gatsby's method for repeating the past is to collect it in various forms
(period furniture, mementos, photos), and this is the unifying theme in
his fetish collection.[16] His house, his car, his parties, and even his shirts
are part of an attempt to recapture the elegance and gaiety he associates
with Daisy's old home in Louisville and with the young idealist he was
then; his house on West Egg is simply a grander, gaudier version of that
other life, "vast, vulgar, and meretricious," to use Nick's words (99). It is
the creation of the same seventeen-year-old boy who conceived of and
wrought Gatsby himself. The fetish collection is unique in that it is "removed from the sphere of actual social relationships with all the tensions, efforts of understanding and acts of persuasions which these im-
ply. This detachment is, indeed, a very substantial part of the attraction
for their collectors, who use them to create a private universe, but its

sterility gives to the material [a] peculiarly lifeless quality" (Pearce, *Museums, Objects, and Collections* 83).

Except for Meyer Wolfsheim, who is really a business acquaintance, Gatsby seems to have no social connections to another human being. His behavior at his parties is also reminiscent of the fetish collector. While these are crowded, garrulous affairs, Gatsby rarely appears and remains aloof when he does so, watching from a distance rather than participating, as one might with a display or exhibit. Nick observes that "no one swooned backward on Gatsby, and no French bob touched Gatsby's shoulder, and no singing quartets were formed with Gatsby's head for one link" (50). While the parties are very public affairs, they are filled with strangers. There are also elements of Gatsby's world that remain hidden to most observers, like the uncut pages of the books in his library. (As I have observed earlier in this study, items in a collection are devalued by use. Thus, the uncut pages both illustrate this point and epitomize a specific form of conspicuous consumption.)[17] It also turns out he has been collecting clippings about Daisy for years, following her progress since her marriage to Tom; and Nick is the solitary witness to the moment of silent homage Gatsby pays to that other iconic object in his collection: the green light at the end of Daisy's dock on the other side of the sound. But, of course, it is the stacks of shirts of all colors and patterns—"shirts with stripes and scrolls and plaids in coral and apple-green and lavender and faint orange, with monograms of Indian Blue" (93)—that represent the most memorable exhibit in Gatsby's fetish collection.

Whereas Baudrillard might argue that such a collection represents Gatsby's "frustrated social aspirations" (*For a Critique* 50), the reaction they elicit in Daisy suggests a somewhat different function, one that Gatsby instinctively understands since he pulls them out at a climactic moment. The word "fetish" derives from "the Portuguese *feiticos,* meaning 'a charm,'" but it also "means 'made by man' and carries the idea of something 'artful' or 'magically active'" (Pearce, *Museums, Objects, and Collections* 82).[18] They do indeed work a kind of magic on Daisy; she is again the young woman weeping the night before her wedding, in love with one man but on her way to marrying another. The green light is also a kind of charm, an ordinary object turned into an object of veneration (in fact, Nick sees Gatsby with his arms outstretched toward it in the darkness). Similarly, Daisy can become a "grail," a rallying point for all Gatsby's dreams and desires (149).

His hope that permanent possession of Daisy will "fix everything just the way it was before" is not uncommon in the world of collecting, especially in the collection of art and other rare objects. He knows that something has changed in the years since he knew Daisy, that things have become "confused and disordered since then" (111), and part of the problem is the way he has earned his money. Involved in any number of unsavory deals, and now in all likelihood a bootlegger, Gatsby needs Daisy to redeem his wealth. In order to do that, he must own her, but trying to win a woman like Daisy with tainted wealth will not be easy, and Tom exploits this knowledge. For despite his belief that he can rescue the past, Gatsby must now contend with the fact that Daisy belongs to someone else. Having been part of Tom's "collection" (and prior to that her family's), she has already been removed from the secular world and thereby been sacralized. If he is going to add Daisy to his own collection, Gatsby must first return her to the secular world of the commodity.[19] Of course, in the meantime, hovering as she is between two potential owners, she can no longer be considered magical. Gatsby is engaging in what Appadurai refers to as a "tournament of value," one example of which is the art auction.[20] Daisy is iconic, and so to possess her is to also possess wealth, power, and the ultimate object of desire, but to win her Gatsby must pit his own resources—wealth, power, prestige—against Tom's.

The latter's obsession with the downfall of Western civilization gains added significance when one considers his part in this particular tournament. He sees himself as the watchdog of civilization as he knows it, and Gatsby (and his kind) are a threat to that way of life.[21] Thus, losing Daisy would be about far more than losing a woman or wife; such a loss would compromise the boundaries of class and social distinction for which Tom lives. While his fears about these boundaries are expressed primarily in racial terms—he worries about interracial marriage and "The Rise of the Colored Empires" (the title of the book he has been reading)—he is just as concerned about class infiltration and makes a point of learning about Gatsby, especially the source of his wealth.

At their confrontation in the Plaza Hotel, when Gatsby finally reveals his love for Daisy, Tom's strategy is to draw attention to Gatsby's questionable past and business dealings, thus undermining his social capital in Daisy's eyes. In a deliberate process of devaluation, Tom describes him as "Mr. Nobody from Nowhere," someone who would never have been allowed near Daisy "unless [he] brought the groceries to the back door," "a common swindler who'd have to steal the ring he put on her finger" (130, 132, 134), a common bootlegger, and perhaps even worse. And, the more he talks, the further Daisy withdraws from something she seems never to have intended in the first place (Nick describes her looking at one point "as though she realized at last what she was doing— and as though she had never, all along, intended doing anything at all. But it was done now. It was too late" [132–33]). Daisy has no choice but to remain with Tom because she realizes, with the decimation of Gatsby as her example, it is the only way she can continue to exist as she has, "safe and proud above the hot struggles of the poor" (150). Tom first consigns Gatsby to nothingness, and then he does the same thing to Daisy by making her leave the hotel room with him. Once they leave, Nick observes, they are "snapped out, made accidental, isolated, like ghosts, even from our pity" (136).

Objects have two possible functions: to be used or to be owned (Baudrillard, *System of Objects* 86). One way objects can be used, and are in *The Great Gatsby*, is in the construction of an identity, whether the kind of fraudulent identity that Gatsby creates or the "genuine" identity of someone like Tom Buchanan, who has supposedly come by his position and his wealth "honestly" (although the Nordic connection Tom refers to—if he is casting himself as the descendent of an original settler— aligns his ancestors with those who robbed and pillaged the New World in their quest for wealth). If we are what we own, as advertisers and other purveyors of the dream would have us believe, then the objects in our possession, inanimate or otherwise, represent our beliefs, our desires, and our very sense of self. By extension, then, the items in a collection must represent the purest version of these ideas. But objects also serve a social function, as the characters in the novel well know.[22] What we own says volumes about class status, wealth, and power. It is Tom's ability to buy things—"his freedom with money" (6)—that is one source of resentment among his peers. His string of polo ponies, rather than his house, is the primary example of his ability to buy anything he desires *and* take it with him wherever he goes. The tensions between the

personal desire for social advancement and society's tendency to maintain the status quo have long been recognized as a fundamental concern
in this novel. James Gatz becomes Jay Gatsby in order to win Daisy Fay,
who is not of his social class. He realizes his position relative to hers and
that he is able to associate with her only "by a colossal accident" (149);
his army uniform is a form of disguise that hides his true background
for the time being. However, he also realizes that he must acquire money
and manners in order to finally secure Daisy for himself. To that end he
becomes involved in a series of shady but lucrative ventures, one involving the selling of grain alcohol at "drug stores," as Tom discovers (134).

The source of Gatsby's wealth has already been established as problematic, but there are greater obstacles in his path. His "manner" is
never quite right; even Nick is able to detect the "real" Gatsby through
the pose at their first meeting, the "elegant young roughneck, a year or
two over thirty, whose elaborate formality of speech just missed being
absurd" (48). His paraphernalia—a huge house in the "wrong" part of
Long Island, a yellow car, clothing that includes a pink suit—are similarly inappropriate, ostentatious in the wrong way.[23] Gatsby's over-precise
diction is typical of what Bourdieu describes as the "correctness or hyper-
correctness [that] betrays an imitation" (*Distinction* 95). It is one of the
reasons Nick questions his host's provenance, noting that even before he
learned Gatsby's identity he was aware of the other man "picking his
words with care" (48). In contrast to Gatsby's strained-for poise Fitzgerald situates Tom Buchanan, who exudes privilege and confidence, even
arrogance. His are the "legitimate manners" which are evidence of "a
social power over time" (Bourdieu, *Distinction* 71). Yet the correct manners in a given situation are more than merely a gloss on behavior; they
also give those who possess them "an absolute, arbitrary power to recognize or exclude" (95).

This dynamic is apparent in an episode midway through the novel,
when Tom unexpectedly shows up on Gatsby's doorstep, arriving on
horseback with a man by the name of Sloane and an unnamed woman,
also members of the social elite. The cool condescension of his guests is
highlighted by Gatsby's intense desire to please, an eagerness that manifests itself from his first words—"I'm delighted that you dropped in"—
to which Nick mentally observes, "As if they cared!" (102). When Gatsby
decides to accept an invitation from the woman, now slightly inebriated,

the class divisions become palpable. Tom evinces shock at Gatsby's intention to join them despite the subtle signals being sent to the contrary; the three ride off just as Gatsby emerges from the house, hat and topcoat in hand. If manners are "the stake in a permanent struggle" (Bourdieu 69), then Gatsby has just lost a major battle.

Gatsby's ostentatious and perennial house parties are in the same category as bad manners. Lavish affairs that draw people of all types (this failure to recognize class distinctions is crucial), they resonate with music and dancing and a general level of hilarity that gradually moves into the realm of the fantastic and even bizarre: performances by young women dressed in baby costumes, people crying for no apparent reason, and women carried out bodily by irate husbands.[24] The parties exist on the periphery of real time, one event rolling into the next and each one seeming to go on indefinitely. Couples argue about how long they have remained, and Nick worries whether he has outstayed his welcome by being among the last to leave. These weekly events are where Gatsby begins to emerge, the hazy product of rumor and anecdote. The stories that circulate figure him as everything from a murderer to a member of royalty, although almost none of those in attendance have actually met him. He is the one nonparticipant in the carnival atmosphere, simply setting the stage and then awaiting the arrival of Daisy, for whom this world has been specifically created.

The house in which the parties take place is, like Gatsby, a copy masquerading as the real thing, "a factual imitation of some Hôtel de Ville in Normandy, with a tower on one side, spanking new under a thin beard of raw ivy, and a marble swimming pool, and more than forty acres of lawn and garden" (5). When Nick arrives home one evening to find the place "blazing with light," he tells Gatsby, "Your place looks like the World's Fair" (82). The comparison is significant. World's fairs, so popular at the turn of the century, were sites where the display of representative objects, collections, and consumer culture intersected most vividly. The world's fair is the modern version of carnival, but carnival with consumerism at its heart (and even carnival was affiliated with the marketplace).[25] Gatsby's private version of the fair contains many of the features of the traditional, popular events, including the re-created foreign locale (his imitation French hotel), theatrical presentations (a full orchestra provides music each night), redundant quantities (books, stacks of shirts), and parties that feature a collection of "human oddities," from the elegant to the crude, the famous to the infamous, the wealthy to the working class.[26] In a Whitmanesque catalogue, Nick lists the partygoers who are part of this living exhibit, those who "accepted Gatsby's hospitality and paid him the subtle tribute of knowing nothing whatever about him" (61). Most of the names underscore the sense of the fantastic and playful associated with fairs: Endive, Snell, Dancie, Flink, Hammerhead, Ferret, Smirke, and Beluga, as well as a doctor named Civet, and "the Willie Voltaires" (61–63). Like the Crystal Palace, which was "'a monument to consumption' to which people made a 'commodity pilgrimage'" (Belk, *Collecting in a Consumer Society* 13), Gatsby's exhibition on Long Island is a destination, a place people end up whether or not they have been invited. Nick recalls the scenario: "They got into automobiles which bore them out to Long Island, and somehow they ended up at Gatsby's door. Once there they were introduced by somebody who knew Gatsby, and after that they conducted themselves according to the rules of behavior associated with amusement parks. Sometimes they came and went without having met Gatsby at all, came for the party with a simplicity of heart that was its own ticket of admission" (41).

Once there, they have free run of the house, the gardens, the beach, while Gatsby looks on "with approving eyes" (50). Like a stage manager or director, he enjoys the spectacle he has put together and waits for Daisy to wander in one day from her house across the sound. However, he is as much a product in this world he has created as is the house, its contents, and the visitors that constitute this particular part of the collection.

Gatsby and his collection occupy a liminal space somewhere between the past and the present, which is why he and it seem unreal and even impossible. The first response to either the man or the items he has amassed is not wonder but disbelief, until some piece of information or some bit of evidence suddenly makes Gatsby seem vitally real. This is the moment of wonder: when the owl-eyed man examines the books in Gatsby's library and discovers with pleasure that they are genuine, if uncut; when Nick hears that everything Gatsby has done has been to win back Daisy and exclaims, "He came alive to me, delivered suddenly from the womb of his purposeless splendor" (79); when Daisy sees the shirts.

It is the kind of collection that, to use Pearce's words, "seems to have grown up around him as an extension of his physical person" (*Museums, Objects, and Collections* 81), but it is a collection doomed to be forever incomplete.

While the reality of this is not apparent for some time, Daisy's inability to bear the burden Gatsby has prepared for her—to be the iconic symbol of his youthful dreams and desires—is obvious almost immediately. Preparing to leave him alone with Daisy, Nick notices an "expression of bewilderment" on Gatsby's face: "Almost five years! There must have been moments even that afternoon when Daisy tumbled short of his dreams—not through her own fault, but because of the colossal vitality of his illusion. It had gone beyond her, beyond everything. He had thrown himself into it *with a creative passion, adding to it all the time,* decking it out with every bright feather that drifted his way. No amount of fire or freshness can challenge what a man will store up in his ghostly heart" (97; my emphasis). Nick's description of Gatsby's pursuit of Daisy reverberates with the discourse of collecting, but Gatsby's apparent disappointment also engages one of the fundamental paradoxes of collecting and of consumer culture in general. Both consumption and collecting are based on a desire that can never be completely fulfilled. For every object obtained, another and better one appears. In fact, the satisfaction of desire is the antithesis of consumer culture. Consequently, no single item can ever be the thing that satisfies desire and, conversely, no object can ever quite measure up to the significance with which we have invested it.[27]

The need to collect the same thing over and over again sounds much like the behavior of another collector in the novel, Tom Buchanan, who collects women the way other men collect works of art. The women we are told about—Daisy, the chambermaid in Santa Barbara, and Myrtle, as well as an unnamed woman in Chicago—represent different types of the same object. A man who owns things and people—polo ponies, the house, Daisy (or so he thinks)—Tom's current object of desire is Myrtle Wilson, the wife of a local gas station owner. Myrtle's class status signifies her as something exotic, certainly different from the women with whom Tom would typically associate. (However, her husband has apparently come into possession of Myrtle under false pretenses. According to her, George convinces her he is a "gentleman" and then marries her in a borrowed suit.) Having acquired Daisy, the type of woman he is supposed to marry as the heir to a great American fortune, Tom proceeds to add to his collection as he might to his string of polo ponies. It is his interest in various "types" that identifies Tom as a systematic collector in Pearce's taxonomy.[28] Rather than having affairs with versions of Daisy, Tom is working his way through the socioeconomic system, collecting women as he goes. When he refers to Myrtle as "my girl" (24), it is an expression one cannot quite imagine him using for Daisy, who floats above coaches like a spirit and whose voice sounds like money. Myrtle may be made from a substance that is base, but she also exudes a "panting vitality" (68) that is its own brand of authenticity. In Myrtle, Tom has found a woman he can possess through her own desire for things. The dog she buys in the city becomes part of the world she creates, a world "that has been previously invented by magazines. Some of them are scattered all over her apartment, and her apartment embodies what they have to say about the good life of acquisition" (R. Berman 62).[29] Myrtle is the stereotypical consuming woman whose desire is fueled by advertisements and department store windows.

Daisy, on the other hand, embodies a very specific form of value for Tom as both status object and charm, which is why he cannot afford to lose her. While he is generally disliked, Daisy's allure and beauty provide a buffer between him and other people; it is she who is missed in Chicago, according to Nick, while Tom admits, "I'm not very popular" (130). Yet while he is able to allude to several romantic moments he and Daisy have shared as he attempts to win her back, Tom's eventual success in the tournament with Gatsby has more to do with his ability to discredit his opponent and arouse Daisy's fear than with actual love or valor. Tom never even tells Daisy he loves her when she says she loves Gatsby; instead, he promises "to take better care of [her] from now on" (134), as if she were a fine piece of porcelain. Unlike the fetish collector, who enjoys a passionate relationship to objects, the systematic collector is interested in classification and organization. Ironically, Tom's sudden interest in the quasi-scientific theories of racial supremacy is suggestive of the ethnographic work of the natural history museum, where systematic collecting is the standard. Tom is essentially aligned with the three activities of museums: "exhibition, eugenics, and conservation" (Harraway 55), and, like a museum, he is inherently conservative and elitist.[30] He values Daisy because others do and for her pedigree, not for any sense of her as an individual with desires of her own.

Daisy suddenly reawakens Tom's interest because his claim to exclusive and perennial ownership is challenged, and by someone whose victory would upset the natural order he has taken to espousing. Like the explorers to the New World who were both fascinated and repelled by the strange peoples and customs they encountered, Tom imagines himself "standing alone on the last barrier of civilization" (130). His implications about Daisy's provenance—in particular her racial status—should be considered within this context. When Tom first mentions the idea of Nordic superiority to Nick, he includes Nick and himself in that designation, only adding Daisy "[a]fter an infinitesimal hesitation" (14). And later, when confronted by Daisy's affair with Gatsby, he rails against those who "begin by sneering at family life and family institutions, and next they'll throw everything overboard and have intermarriage between black and white," to which Jordan responds, "We're all white here" (130). Daisy's reference to her "white girlhood" is followed by another reference to "the Nordic race" when she jokingly tells Tom that this subject was part of her conversation with Nick on the veranda (20). The suggestion that Daisy is somehow tainted—the "taint" can be read as her loss of virginity prior to marriage—could serve to undermine her potential value, and thus her desirability as a collectible. However, racial ambiguity actually casts her as the exotic "other" and something to be prized by collectors. The questions about her status and worth are part of the discourse of authenticity in the text, especially since objects are the way authenticity is validated or not.[31]

The perennial irony about collections is that the object that could complete the set increases in value as a result of its absence, raising the question of whether collections are ever meant to be completed.[32] The missing final object in a collection comes to represent the entire series (Baudrillard, *System of Objects* 92). Thus, when Daisy fails to appreciate his collection, Gatsby's instinctive response is to alter its intrinsic nature, which he effectively does by shutting the doors and replacing all the servants. The collection has now become something new, something sedate and, hopefully, something acceptable (because familiar) to Daisy. While collectors would generally appear to be working toward completion, there is also "a paradoxical fear of completing a collection. For if one is a collector and there is nothing left to collect, who is one then?" (Belk, "Collectors and Collecting" 324). Thus, when Gatsby tells Nick, "I didn't want you to think I was just some nobody" (67) and produces his artifacts (a medal from Montenegro, the photograph of him at Oxford), he is testifying to the inextricable connection between material objects and the self that collecting exemplifies. While Gatsby believes possession of Daisy will complete him, acquiring her will also alter the identity he has created as the man who seeks Daisy. Possession of the desired object, in this case, will both complete and destroy. And, eventually, the very attempt to possess Daisy leads directly to Gatsby's destruction.

As a harbinger of death, both for Gatsby and Myrtle Wilson, Daisy is a memento mori, a traditional reminder of the inevitability of death.[33] In this role, it is not unlikely that she is both the thing that "preyed on Gatsby," the "foul dust that floated in the wake of his dreams" (2), and the grail that inspired those dreams. All we need to do is compare Gatsby's "heightened sensitivity to the promises of life" to Daisy's preference for gestures over emotions, Gatsby's "unutterable visions" (2, 112) to Daisy's empty small talk. Like any memento, she is a "reminder of a past event or condition, of an absent person, or of something that once existed" and, invoking a now obsolete definition, she is a "memory, a recollection" (*OED*). However, like a souvenir intended to represent an event or place, the Daisy who is reunited with Gatsby after five years is not the real thing, if she ever was. This Daisy is capable of adopting poses, of assuming an attitude of jaded sophistication and then smirking "as if she had asserted her membership in a rather distinguished secret society to which she and Tom belonged" (18). Gatsby is waiting for Daisy to bring meaning to the cardboard world he has created, but Daisy actually negates meaning because she has none of her own to give. In order to supply meaning and value to objects, one must first possess these qualities, and Daisy's only meaning and value comes from without, not from within. The moment when she tries to express whatever admiration or desire she feels for Gatsby and can only come up with his similarity to an advertisement demonstrates the limits of her capacity for awe. Their contrary responses in the same situation are indicative of Gatsby's and Daisy's relationship not only to desire but, more specifically, to the concept of wonder.

Near the end of the novel, Nick observes Tom and Daisy through a

window, "sitting opposite each other at the kitchen table," making plans
after Myrtle Wilson's death (146). United in their positions as untouch-
able objects, their presentation behind glass also highlights their connection to consumer culture. Tom is once again in possession of Daisy,
who is decidedly out of Gatsby's reach. Gatsby, meanwhile, is watching
Daisy's bedroom window, waiting for a signal that will never come. Nick
leaves him there, the sole possessor of all the information available at
this moment: Daisy's responsibility for Myrtle's death, and that this
may not have been an accident; the fact that Daisy has returned to Tom;
Gatsby's ultimate act of devotion. Fitzgerald's novel opens by juxtapos-
ing the wide-eyed naiveté of youth, the Nick who went to the East, with
the slightly jaded narrator who will remain with us until the end of
Gatsby's journey. Not only is Nick our "guide, pathfinder, [and] original
settler" (4) but as the "author" of this narrative he is also the ultimate
collector and curator of this eclectic collection, one in which Gatsby ultimately turns out to be the only item with any real or lasting value.

In many ways, Nick has been preparing for this encounter with Gatsby
his entire life, and he fancies himself the one person truly able to appreciate his special qualities. While Gatsby's provenance may be uncertain,
he remains a unique and fascinating item. More important, he symbol-
izes Nick's experiences in the East, his desires, his failures, and his delu-
sions about others and himself. Setting the novel in the East also puts
both men at the heart of consumer culture in the early twentieth century; additionally, as a "bond man" on Wall Street (10), a term that com-
bines person and object, Nick is learning to become an active player in
the world of capitalism.

Nick's position evokes an early version of the connoisseur, the virtuoso.
Associated with curiosity and collecting, "virtuosity became a 'cultural
ideal' that shaped the sensibility and activities of a self-styled elite in
seventeenth-century England." The virtuoso was also associated with
curiosity, and "thus ownership of a collection of curiosities became an
essential part of a virtuoso's program of self fashioning" (Swann 76).
Nick's "credentials" as a virtuoso in his appreciation of Gatsby, an expertise he achieves in the space of three months, are established in the
first paragraphs of the novel: he has the ability to "reserve all judgments"; he was raised in the Midwest; he has a rather dubious family

history himself (the Carraways are descended from a man who "sent a substitute to the Civil War" to fight for him then started a hardware business, and not from the Dukes of Buccleauch, as they like to claim) (1, 2–3); finally, he is able to navigate between different social worlds, as comfortable with Daisy and Tom as with Gatsby and those at his parties. Just as the virtuoso is defined by the objects he collects, by the act of singularization, so Nick is ultimately defined by Gatsby.

However, our belief in Gatsby must be grounded in our belief in Nick, and this is undermined at several turns. Nick has difficulty reconciling his feelings about Gatsby with his intellectual appraisal, a dichotomy that is evident in his first description: Gatsby "represent[s] everything for which [Nick has] an unaffected scorn," but he also has a "heightened sensitivity to the promises of life"; and although he "disapprove[s] of him from beginning to end," Nick also tells Gatsby he is "worth the whole damn bunch of them put together" (2, 154). Rescuing Gatsby from the miasma of objects, people, and deceit that compose his memories of that summer, Nick also confers upon him an elevated status, a sacredness that Gatsby was never able to achieve on his own. As an object in Nick's collection, Gatsby shares the quality of other collectibles in that he passes from the category of "the profane," which Belk associates with the "mundane, ordinary, and common" and becomes "sacred" or "extraordinary, special, and capable of generating reverence" ("Collectors and Collecting" 320). It is because he undergoes this transformation through the workings of memory and time—Nick confesses that it is only "much later" that the events of this summer achieve meaning for him (56)—that Gatsby can become an object worthy of admiration. Ironically, Nick's narrative about Gatsby, the space he creates to contain this elusive and fascinating figure, is able to achieve what Gatsby cannot: it allows Nick to repeat the past.

Just as the catalogue validated the private collection, making his assemblage public in the form of a narrative validates Nick's existence; Gatsby is "great" and so is Nick by extension.[34] Certainly the owners and displayers of Cabinets of Wonder hoped or expected the wonder to be translated to them as well. One reason for inviting others in to view the collection was to display one's taste and intelligence, to give evidence that one knew what to collect and could afford to do so. Thus, the

Cabinet of Wonder was about its owner as much as it was about the collection it contained.[35] The same is true of Nick Carraway and his relationship to Gatsby, the central item in his compilation. While Nick is disillusioned and even disgusted by the events of the summer and Gatsby's fate, there is also discernible pride in his ability to understand Gatsby as no one else can. He is, of course, the only one with access to certain information, including the full story of Gatsby and Daisy. He is present at every important moment and has a direct connection to the main players. In addition, he manages to sustain belief in his own objectivity and honesty in the face of what seems like the all-consuming self-interest and hypocrisy represented by everyone else (certainly Tom and Daisy, but also the party guests, Jordan, Meyer Wolfsheim, and Myrtle Wilson).

The descriptive term "wonder" or "marvel" was also applied to artists in the period in which Wunderkammern were popular. An artist who was able to create something new and amazing, "who astounded by means of ingenious ideas and supreme technical skills was perceived as a wonder in himself. Indeed, he was often seen as a kind of miracle worker, doing what others could not have done and achieving what seemed to be the impossible" (Kenseth 39).[36] Nick's narrative is a marvel of its kind, particularly in its ability to salvage Gatsby—bootlegger, "roughneck" (48), and counterfeit—from the ruins of memory. His observation as they cross over the Queensboro Bridge could be the motto for his marvelous creation: "'Anything can happen now that we've slid over this bridge . . . anything at all. . . .' Even Gatsby could happen, *without any particular wonder*" (69; my emphasis). Just as he "creates" Gatsby, Nick casts himself as the one best able to appreciate Gatsby and pronounce final judgment: "Gatsby turned out all right at the end" (2). The irony is that Nick becomes the authenticator/owner of Jay Gatsby, who is the creation of the former James Gatz, a man engaged in the American-approved process of self-fashioning.

Nick's tale, for all its attempts at cynicism, is about the potential for wonder that still exists—or, more to the point, the faith that something to evoke wonder is still possible. While he may not agree with Gatsby's methods or even with the object of his wonder, Nick does not dismiss the wonder itself. He does not diminish Gatsby by revoking the viability of the wonder he felt in the presence of the green light or Daisy. Nick's own judgments, however, are consistently tempered by the need for hard evidence, and this is the problem Fitzgerald ultimately poses in *The Great Gatsby:* the modern need to authenticate and authorize is antithetical to a sense of wonder. Wonder is what happens in the absence of evidence.

On his last evening in West Egg—Gatsby is dead and Daisy has disappeared with Tom—Nick lies on Gatsby's beach, describing what amounts to his own recovered sense of wonder, inspired by his encounter with Gatsby. Greenblatt observes that "the marvelous gestures toward the world by registering an overpowering intensity of response. Someone witnesses something amazing, but what most matters takes place not 'out there' or along the receptive surfaces of the body where the self encounters the world, but deep within, at the vital, emotional center of the witness" (16–17). The "something amazing" that Nick has experienced, and which has shaken his world, is Gatsby himself, whose equal Nick knows "it is not likely [he] shall ever find again" (2).

To collect is to attempt to bring order to chaos, to control space and time, and to give meaning to the self. This need was keenly felt in the sixteenth century and again at the turn of the twentieth, when the proliferation of goods and questions about identity and authenticity could be overwhelming. Fitzgerald seems to have known he was writing at a pivotal moment, and although he could not know it was between two world wars and on the brink of the Great Depression, he certainly recognized that the culture of the commodity had spun out of control. In fact, although it was published several years before Larsen's, Fitzgerald's novel is in many ways the culmination of the consumer mentality in this era, making it the most logical text with which to end a study about the intersections of identity, authenticity, and material culture. Collections represent the tension between the past and the present, a tension articulated in the closing passage of the novel: "Gatsby believed in the green light, the orgiastic future that year by year recedes before us. It eluded us then, but that's no matter—tomorrow we will run faster, stretch out our arms farther. . . . And one fine morning——So we beat on, boats against the current, borne back ceaselessly into the past" (182). Unlike the sixteenth-century Cabinet of Wonders, which "became the allegorical mirror reflecting a perfect and completed picture of the world" (Shelton 185), Nick's tale reflects a world of confusion and disappointment, of counterfeits and lost dreams. The new "golden age" may be a myth, but the search for the authentic object of desire, the one that will make everything wonderful, goes on.

Notes

Chapter 1

1. I am following the example of Arjun Appadurai and using the term "commoditization" as opposed to "commodification" to describe the process of an object becoming a commodity. While commodification suggests that something or someone is absorbed into the world of consumer culture, commoditization implies a more active transition, one in which the object or person is turned into a commodity as part of a process.

2. In *The Real Thing*, Miles Orvell explains: "As the body accommodated itself to the new demands of the industrial world, the border between human motion and automatic motion became increasingly blurred" (147). In other words, people ran the risk of becoming like things themselves, whether those things were machines or the products they created.

3. See Peter C. Marzio for a discussion of chromolithography, by which copies of original artworks were made possible. This technique was criticized as "pseudo culture" (1).

4. These trends also suggest efforts to establish an "authentic" version of American identity.

5. An ironic twist on the authenticity of museum objects is the famous Hall of Forgeries at the Victoria and Albert Museum in London. I am indebted to Angela Weisl for this observation.

6. Leach's *Land of Desire* is among several recent studies that analyze the connections between museums and department stores, the temples of consumer culture in this period.

7. Schlereth refers to this device as a stereoscope.

8. Kopytoff's examples are primarily contemporary: the "selling" or trading of

athletes, prostitution, and the sale of female eggs (85), but the processes and reactions he describes are the same.

9. Pearce describes this list as "a group of interlinked standard [European] oppositions of thought and feeling around which, in terms of our instinctive reactions, mental and emotional values and judgments are traditionally determined" (*On Collecting* 286).

10. Henri F. Ellenberger describes this trend as "prevalent in the 1880's" and evident in the work of Dostoyevsky, Ibsen, Nietzsche, and Freud (273).

11. Examples of such studies include Wyllie's *The Self-Made Man in America;* Cawelti's *Apostles of the Self-Made Man;* and Lindberg's *The Confidence Man in American Literature.*

12. According to Kenneth Womack, Sinfield's entrapment model "functions as a barrier to dissidence, as a means for the ideology in power to sustain its oppressive constructions of class, race, gender, and sexuality" (601).

13. These include the Metropolitan in New York, the Detroit Institute of Arts, and Boston's Museum of Fine Arts (Conn 9).

14. Both also contain important scenes set in museums (Kruse 71).

Chapter 2

1. See Pearce, *Museums, Objects, and Collections,* for an extended and illuminating explanation of what happens when viewing objects in a museum or other type of collection (219).

2. Natural history in the eighteenth century was a science that included such areas of study as meteorology, geology, botany, zoology, and ethnology (Regis 5).

3. See Ed Folsom's study of Whitman and photography, *Walt Whitman's Native Representations* as well as Folsom's earlier essay, "'This Heart's Geography's Map': The Photographs of Walt Whitman." See also "Specimen Daze: Whitman's Photobiography" by Sean Meehan; Orvell's chapter on Whitman in *The Real Thing;* and *Walt Whitman's America* by David Reynolds.

4. See Betsy Erkkila, *Whitman the Political Poet,* for an overview of the structure of *Specimen Days.*

5. Museum labeling is an area of interest in its own right, with books such as Andrée Blais's, *Text in the Exhibition Medium* and Beverly Serrell's *Exhibit Labels: An Interpretive Approach* dedicated to this very specific and important element of the museum enterprise. One need only look at the strong responses to two Smithsonian exhibits— "The West as America" in 1991 and "The Last Act: The Atomic Bomb and the End of World War II" (otherwise known as the Enola Gay exhibit) in 1994—to see the effect labels can have on viewers. In both cases, the Smithsonian was harshly criticized for what critics saw as revisionist history. Criticism of the Enola Gay exhibit was so strong that the exhibit was removed in 1995 (although the Enola Gay itself remained on exhibit for several years).

6. This aspect of the period is discussed by several cultural historians, such as Lears in *Fables of Abundance* and Orvell in *The Real Thing*.

7. Whitman thus anticipates William Carlos Williams's famous declaration in *Paterson* (1946), "No ideas but in things," by about fifty years.

8. In his discussion of Whitman's text as "photobiography," Sean Meehan states: "Whitman's metaphors in these memoranda often suggest the visual connotations of the term 'specimen.' Whether reproduced in writing or seen firsthand in hospitals, specimen cases are primarily visual representations, as the etymological *spec* of the word 'specimen' (Lat. *specere*: to look at or behold) would suggest. A part or extract thus gives a visible trace of the whole, and for Whitman, such a notion remains the only way to read the real war that will never get in the books. But this too is Whitman's war: the experience of the 'real war' *in relation to* the experience of reading and remembering it" (484).

9. Reynolds gives a detailed description of the creation of the "Whitman Myth" in *Walt Whitman's America* (451–63).

10. Genealogical research became increasingly popular in the late nineteenth century as a way to validate one's authenticity. Americans traced their ancestors or tried to establish connections to Revolutionary War heroes in order to prove their own "provenance," coats of arms suddenly appeared on carriages, and the nouveau riche found that by "using the appropriate methods," one could purchase rank in Europe, where new wealth was more readily accepted than it was in their own country (Bryce 815).

11. In a note to "Of the Terrible Doubt of Appearances," Blodgett and Bradley call attention to lines 32–33 of the poem "Scented Herbage of My Breast," "in which 'real reality' is contrasted with 'these shifting forms of life.' Here the same idea—that only love confirms reality—is developed into powerful form" (120).

12. This poem is included in "Second Annex: Good-bye My Fancy."

13. In *Reconstituting the American Renaissance: Emerson, Whitman, and the Politics of Representation*, Jay Grossman reconsiders the extent to which Emerson influenced Whitman, arguing that contrary to previous theories, "it does not seem that Whitman shares with either Emerson or the dictates of the transcendentalized literary history derived from him a predilection toward idealized abstraction and 'the Real'" (85).

14. I am here adapting phrases that Baudrillard uses in a different context in his chapter on advertising (*System of Objects*).

15. As Baudrillard explains, "even when a collection transforms itself into a discourse addressed to others, it continues to be first and foremost a discourse addressed to oneself" (*System of Objects* 103).

16. See Baudrillard, *The System of Objects*, for more extensive comments on this connection.

17. In his study of natural historians from John Bartram to William James, Christoph Irmscher claims that "American natural history [went] out with a whimper" (5). Ironically, the natural historian who most resembles Whitman may be P. T. Barnum. In his collections, "[n]atural history [became] completely incidental to the main purpose of

the collection—the collector's self-aggrandizement" (4). Self-aggrandizement is not Whitman's purpose, but the self is central to his project.

18. Pearce describes museums as "interpretative acts intended to create value and significance" (*Museums, Objects, and Collections* 239).

CHAPTER 3

1. The Norton critical edition of *Adventures of Huckleberry Finn* gives the author as Samuel Langhorne Clemens. As a result, while I use the name "Mark Twain" throughout this chapter for the sake of consistency, the novel citations are in reference to the text listed under Samuel Clemens in the Works Cited.

2. Recent scholarship has begun to consider the complex economic relationships that underpin the novel. See David L. Smith, "Huck, Jim, and American Racial Discourse."

3. See *Mark Twain's Letters to His Publishers, 1867–1894*, edited by Hamlin Hill.

4. For example, see Shelley Fisher Fishkin's *Was Huck Black?* and Peter Messent's "The Clash of Language: Bakhtin and *Huckleberry Finn*" in *New Readings of the American Novel: Narrative Theory and Its Application*.

5. According to Appadurai, considering anything that is intended for exchange a commodity "gets us away from the exclusive preoccupation with the 'product,' 'production,' and the original or dominant intention of the 'producer' and permits us to focus on the dynamics of exchange" (9).

6. Carl F. Wieck also discusses the card as representing the knowledge Huck is acquiring, although he is more concerned with the fact that in tearing up the card, "what pap is actually doing his best to teach Huck amounts to nothing other than to stop learning" (151).

7. See Mensch and Mensch, for example.

8. Alan Trachtenberg makes a similar point in "The Form of Freedom in *Huckleberry Finn*," arguing that "[t]he book is finally more persuasive as a document of enslavement, of the variety of imprisonments within verbal styles and fictions than as a testimony to freedom" (356).

9. Orvell observes about trades such as this, "Being on the winning end of such transactions was yet another way of elevating one's status in a democracy, where all were equally vulnerable" (55).

10. In *Searching for Jim: Slavery in Sam Clemens's World*, Terrell Dempsey cites a letter Twain published in the *Hannibal Journal* in 1853 that also uses the word "trash" in a derogatory way, this time to refer to children he sees when in New York City (233).

11. Messent argues that Huck is "absolutely caught within the language and (racist) ideology of that culture which has helped mould him" (224).

12. See David L. Smith's reading of the novel as Twain's attack on racism through his subtle undermining of the concept of "the Negro" (359).

13. I am using Kopytoff's terminology here (69).

14. For a discussion of the function of money in society, see Georg Simmel's *The Philosophy of Money.*

15. P. T. Barnum was, of course, the great manipulator of reality in the late nineteenth century. See Orvell; and David M. Lubin.

16. The con man Waldo Demara, Jr., on whom the film *The Great Impostor* was based, said "Every time I take a new identity, some part of the real me dies" (Schwartz 71).

17. Messent believes that the voice of the "Notice" is one of "forceful (guns at his command) authority, attempting to control the responses of those of inferior status, a potentially undisciplined and undiscriminating audience" (205). However, such preemptive defensiveness is often evidence of just the opposite: insecurity and uncertain authority.

18. See Orvell on the attempt to rise in class status "through the purchase and display of goods," with an emphasis on "appearance" over "substance" (49).

19. Huck's ability to "name" Miss Watson as a stand-in relative is indicative of what Lee Clark Mitchell describes as the "free floating" language of the novel, where people establish new identities "by mere assertion" (88).

20. The early sociologist William Graham Sumner referred to such established standards of behavior as "folkways"; he also argued that the one who "adopts the mores of another group is a still more heinous criminal" than the one who simply dissents (96).

21. "Sincerity" was the means designated in the conduct manuals to combat hypocrisy, part of the culture of sentiment of the nineteenth century (Halttunen xvi).

22. Naming has special significance in this episode, particularly the names Grangerford and Shepherdson. See Victor Doyno for a reading of the two names as Twain's satire of farming versus grazing interests (13). Also, a "grange" was typically associated with a gentleman farmer, which introduces the element of class into the discussion, while the word "ford" is associated with the water that permeates the novel, in this case as a shallow place where one might cross a river (*OED*). (I am indebted to Angela Weisl for this latter observation.)

23. An example of this is print ads in magazines that contain a picture of an item—a handbag or a pair of shoes—but no text, sending the subliminal message that anyone who does not already know the name of this product is not even a potential consumer; such a reader is not of the group that "knows" by virtue of class status.

24. Claudia Durst Johnson addresses this issue in *Understanding* Adventures of Huckleberry Finn.

25. Orvell suggests that "Burton Benedict's observation about world's fairs during this period" might also be applied to "the whole panoply of consumer culture, from the home to the department store—that in such places 'man is totally in control and synthetic nature is preferred to the real thing'" (55).

26. Schwartz argues: "Impersonation, not imposture, is at home with quiet deceit and may breed underground. Both may be impeccably costumed, yet in the final dressing down, imposters want attention and love, and we betray them; impersonators want our money, our secrets, our family line, and they betray us" (73).

27. See Terence Martin's *Parables of Possibility* for more on the American "romance with beginnings and the promise that attends them" (41).

CHAPTER 4

1. This language turns Lily into what Baudrillard calls "a pure object" ("The System of Collecting" 20).

2. See Maureen Howard's "On *The House of Mirth*"; Lillian Robinson's "The Traffic in Women: A Cultural Critique of *The House of Mirth*"; Wai-Chee Dimock's "Debasing Exchange: Edith Wharton's *The House of Mirth*"; Ruth Barnard Yeazell's "The Conspicuous Wasting of Lily Bart"; Thomas Loebel's "Beyond Her Self"; Frances L. Restuccia's "The Name of the Lily: Edith Wharton's Feminism(s)"; and Benjamin Carson's "'That Doubled Vision': Edith Wharton and *The House of Mirth*.

3. My analysis of Lily was inspired in part by Michael Thompson's seminal study *Rubbish Theory,* which articulates very specific ways in which commodities move through the various phases of their existence.

4. Appadurai's five characteristics of luxury goods serve as the basis for my analysis of Lily here: "1) restriction, either by price or by law, to elites; 2) complexity of acquisition, which may or may not be a function of real 'scarcity'; 3) semiotic virtuosity, that is, the capacity to signal fairly complex social messages . . . ; 4) specialized knowledge as a prerequisite for their 'appropriate' consumption, that is, regulation by fashion; and (5) a high degree of linkage of their consumption to body, person, and personality" (38).

5. Although Wharton did not consider the book part of her "literary career" (*Backward Glance* 112), it does share some of the same concerns as *The House of Mirth:* the interest in "harmony and proportion," "simplicity," and "moderation, fitness, relevance" (*Decoration* 192). It is in fact the absence of these things that leads to Lily's destruction.

6. In his analysis of another Wharton story, "The Daunt Diana," Allan Hepburn refers to the narrator, Ringham Finney, as a cicerone who "[aspires] to become a collector" (36).

7. Richard Chase's *The American Novel and Its Tradition* is a pioneering study in terms of the themes of both authenticity and identity in American literature, in particular his chapter on Henry James's *The Portrait of a Lady.* As Chase observes, Gilbert Osmond misrepresents both himself and his reasons for marrying Isabel Archer, who is little more than "another art object" to be added to his "collection," while Isabel "subscribes to the American romance of the self" (132, 131). Chase's description of Isabel might just as easily be applied to Lily: "she sees reality as the romancer sees it . . . [she] is patently romantic in the sense that she has highly imaginative dreams which prove to be beyond the possibility of fulfillment" (129).

8. The notion that the gaze is exclusively male—a concept that originated with a landmark essay by Laura Mulvey titled "Visual Pleasure and Narrative Cinema"—has been contested by such scholars as Lorraine Gamman and Margaret Marshment in their edited collection *The Female Gaze: Women as Viewers of Popular Culture.* For a discus-

sion of Lily's self-construction through the gaze (such as looking at herself in mirrors), see Gary Totten's "The Art and Architecture of the Self: Designing the 'I'-Witness in Edith Wharton's *The House of Mirth*." See also Cynthia Griffin Wolff's "Lily Bart and Masquerade Inscribed in the Female Mode."

9. Restuccia describes Selden as trying throughout the novel "to commodify Lily as an objet d'art (the only way, obtuse playboy that he is, he can enjoy her), and now that she is dead, his reconstruction of Lily—as a 'work'—can ossify" (410). The same is true of Wolff and her observation that the dead Lily has become "the most superb piece in his collection" (*A Feast of Words* 132).

10. In *The System of Objects*, Baudrillard considers the relationship between objects and dreams.

11. William Leach also makes this connection, writing, "Commodities of all kinds were immersed in dreamlike surroundings" (117).

12. According to Margot Norris, "'the argument from design'" is a "pre-Darwinian theory which held that the manifold adjustments of an organism to its environment were evidence of the guiding hand of the Creator" (435). Norris is interested in the biological origins of this expression, but her definition suggests the hand of an artist at work.

13. Lears touches on some of these ideas in his brief discussion of the novel in *Fables of Abundance*, although he does not explain how Lily becomes an artifact.

14. Hepburn's essay is most interesting for his discussion of Wharton's use of the terms "dilettante," "connoisseur," and "collector."

15. See Belk on the "cycle of desire" in collecting (*Collecting in a Consumer Society* 4).

16. Dimock discusses the practice of getting without spending in her essay on the novel, including Selden in her analysis.

17. As Abigail Solomon-Godeau points out, "One of the most conspicuous features of commodity culture is its sexualization of the commodity, its eroticization of objects, which in turn inflects, if not determines, the psychic structures of consumer desire" (113).

18. Saisselin draws parallels between the nineteenth-century world of women, luxury, and the bibelot and "that fascinating and ambiguous zone of the bourgeois style of life and psyche, the demimonde" (53).

19. This phrase is used by Jean-Christophe Agnew in reference to a woman featured in an ad for the perfume "Private Collection": "one sees a figure who is at once collector *and* collectible. Of all the exquisite objects in the room, she is the only self-consuming artifact" (155).

20. In "Unpacking My Library," Walter Benjamin asserts that "for a collector—and I mean a real collector, a collector as he ought to be—ownership is the most intimate relationship one can have to objects. Not that they come alive in him; it is he who lives in them" (67).

21. This is what Thomas Loebel refers to as "the sex/gender economy" in the text (107).

22. The designation of woman-as-commodity applies to another emerging icon of

the early twentieth century, the fashion model. Like the fashion show, the tableau disguises "the commercial nature of the transaction in theatrical illusion" (Evans 280). According to Diana de Marly, "The model girl was beginning to replace the seamstress and the shopgirl in the imagination of the predatory male as the sort of girl who was ripe for seduction but not for marriage" (140).

23. In *For a Critique of the Political Economy of the Sign,* Baudrillard examines the art auction as a "crucible of the interchange of values, where economic value, sign value and symbolic value transfer according to the rules of the game, can be considered as an ideological matrix—one of the shrines of the political economy of the sign" (112).

24. Baudrillard notes that the "absolute singularity" of an object "depends entirely upon the fact that it is *I* who possess it—which, in turn, allows me to recognize myself in it as an absolutely singular being" ("The System of Collecting" 12).

25. I am indebted to Angela Weisl for this observation.

26. Appadurai's expression for the ways in which objects end up in museums—the "traffic in artifacts" (27)—resonates with the term the "traffic in women" that was originally used by Emma Goldman to describe the role of women in marriage.

27. Old New York is figured as an heirloom—a type of collectible—in Sara Elisabeth Quay's "Edith Wharton's Narrative of Inheritance."

28. Despite the title of Yeazell's essay, "The Conspicuous Wasting of Lily Bart," she does not actually consider Lily as waste per se; instead, hers is a Veblenian reading of the novel, emphasizing his theories about a woman's role in the conspicuous display of her husband's wealth.

29. Howard describes *The House of Mirth* as "a novel of concealment and revelation, of what is presumed socially and must be discovered morally and emotionally by both of its principals, and of what remains unknowable to them" (1).

30. Norris addresses this idea to some extent, but her analysis is concerned with the various discourses in the text (art, science) and the ways they reveal their own inability to tell the truth or project reality.

31. The *Social Register* came into existence as a way to authenticate identity, "a convenient listing of one's friend's and potential friends." It first appeared in New York City in 1888, and the premiere edition contained the names of fewer than two thousand families (Baltzell 269). The appearance of the *Social Register* is one more manifestation of the growing need to identify one's neighbors and especially to identify those who do not "belong."

32. In *The World of Goods,* Mary Douglas and Baron Isherwood observe that "female infanticide" is one way societies have traditionally reduced the number of marriageable women and also addressed the problem of having to provide a dowry or other financial settlement. The other way to address the problem is through polygamy, allowing wealthy men to have multiple wives (87).

33. As one of the anonymous reviewers of this manuscript pointed out, "The description of Lily as 'a flower from which every bud had been nipped except the crowning blossom' compares her specifically to the American Beauty rose." There is a distinct possibility that Wharton is alluding to a well-known declaration of John D. Rockefeller:

"The American Beauty rose can be produced in the splendor and fragrance which bring cheer to its beholder only by sacrificing the early buds which grow up around it. This is not an evil tendency in business. It is merely the working out of a law of nature and a law of God" (Hofstadter 31).

CHAPTER 5

1. Brian Carr's "Paranoid Interpretation, Desire's Nonobject, and Nella Larsen's *Passing*" provides a good overview of the readings of homosexuality in *Passing*.

2. I am indebted to one of the reviewers of the original manuscript of this study for reminding me about the ironic connection between passing and the publication history of Larsen's novel. It seems that Knopf, Larsen's publisher, wanted to withhold the black identity of its author. See George Hutchinson's essays on Larsen, including "Nella Larsen and the Veil of Race."

3. See, for example, Veblen's chapter in *The Theory of the Leisure Class* on "Dress as an Expression of the Pecuniary Culture."

4. This is from an Elizabethan Statute of Apparel (*Greenwich, 15 June 1574, 16 Elizabeth I*): "None shall wear in his apparel: Any silk of the color of purple, cloth of gold tissued, nor fur of sables, but only the King, Queen, King's mother, children, brethren, and sisters, uncles and aunts; and except dukes, marquises, and earls, who may wear the same in doublets, jerkins, linings of cloaks, gowns, and hose; and those of the Garter, purple in mantles only" (Secara).

5. Wald claims that passing narratives are "profoundly and inevitably gendered" and that this gendering generally takes the form of "tropes of domesticity and/or homecoming" (16). I would add "fashion" to this in the case of Larsen's novel. Also see Georg Simmel's "The Philosophy of Fashion," which proffers one explanation for women's attraction to fashion, and, unintentionally, a possible connection between constructions of the self, fashion, and race. Lacking power and control, women have traditionally tended toward the socially acceptable, the "'right and proper,'" in order to avoid situations where they would need to defend individualized choices and decisions. For those in such a situation, fashion offers a possible middle ground, because it allows them to experience both "relative individuation and general conspicuousness" in a socially approved arena (240).

6. See Karen Halttunen for a discussion of the success cult in the late nineteenth and early twentieth centuries and its ramifications for what was described as "sincerity" (34).

7. The reformer Ida Tarbell wrote in 1912 that "the folly of woman's dress . . . lies in the pitiful assumption that she can achieve her end by imitation, that she can be the thing she envies if she look like that thing" (Matt 381).

8. This dual awareness, that race is not always identifiable and that it is socially constructed, is repeated in the observation by a Washington historian: "'Passing' apparently became so common in the 1920s that one theater in Washington employed a 'black doorman to spot and bounce intruders whose racial origins were undetectable by whites'" (Gatewood 337).

9. F. James Davis notes: "Concern about people passing as white became so great that even behaving like blacks or willingly associating with them were often treated as more important than any proof of actual black ancestry" (56).

10. See Ginsberg's *Passing and the Fictions of Identity* for some of the ramifications of passing.

11. See Corrine Blackmer on Irene's internalizing of "the separate but equal dictum of *Plessy* as well as the ideology of bourgeois morality, both of which lead to a notable prudishness on her part and an obsessive attention to seemingly miniscule distinctions of caste and class" (100).

12. See *Authentic Blackness* by J. Martin Favor for a discussion of constructions of blackness and social class.

13. Teresa Zackodnik's "Passing Transgressions and Authentic Identity in Jessie Fauset's *Plum Bun* and Nella Larsen's *Passing*" has a discussion of Brian's entrenchment in the black bourgeoisie.

14. Jacquelyn Y. McLendon, in *The Politics of Color in the Fiction of Jessie Fauset and Nella Larsen,* also discusses the use of Clare and Irene as doubles, although she is primarily concerned with Larsen's parodic treatment of "the formulaic tragic-mulatto tale" (7).

15. One example from the conservation movement in the early twentieth century is the "nature fakir" controversy, instigated by books such as *Wild Animals I Have Known* by Ernest Thompson Seton and the stories of Jack London, which anthropomorphized animals in fictional tales, much to the dismay of naturalists such as John Burroughs. Even Teddy Roosevelt weighed in on the matter in an essay that appeared in *Everybody's Magazine* in 1906 in which he coined the term "nature faker" and attacked the popular work of such writers as misleading and false.

CHAPTER 6

1. Scott Donaldson observes that the house "contains a little bit from every period: Restoration salons and Marie Antoinette music rooms, period bedrooms and an Adam study" (208).

2. Adam may refer to a style inspired by Robert Adam, the famous eighteenth-century architect who was part of the classical revival in England. See Matthew J. Bruccoli's *F. Scott Fitzgerald's* The Great Gatsby: *A Literary Reference.*

3. This inability to articulate what one sees and feels in the presence of the marvelous is an inherent characteristic of the experience of wonder (Greenblatt 24).

4. This is a pattern repeated in each text in this study. The counterfeit has a limited shelf life, until the deception is discovered and the consequences must be dealt with.

5. According to Bourdieu, taste is an indicator of class position and an instrument of class dominance, and "one of the most vital stakes in the struggles fought in the field of the dominant class and the field of cultural production" (*Distinction* 11).

6. See Giles Gunn's essay "F. Scott Fitzgerald's *Gatsby* and the Imagination of Wonder," which also picks up on this theme as well as its connection to the early settlers.

7. See Marjorie Swann's *Curiosities and Texts: The Culture of Collecting in Early Modern England;* and Anthony Alan Shelton's "Cabinets of Transgression: Renaissance Collections and the Incorporation of the New World" for the connection between the catalogue and the private collection it records.

8. The ubiquity of objects in *The Great Gatsby* is a feature critics have addressed, usually to make a point about class issues in the novel or Fitzgerald's treatment of capitalism. See Ross Posnock, "'A New World, Material without Being Real': Fitzgerald's Critique of Capitalism in *The Great Gatsby;* Richard Godden, *Fictions of Capital: The American Novel from James to Mailer;* and John Hilgart, "*The Great Gatsby*'s Aesthetics of Non-identity."

9. As Swann explains, "The seventeenth-century vogue for collecting—whether the accumulation of art by aristocrats or the acquisition of curiosities by 'middling sort' individuals—was one aspect of the brave new world of consumer goods that emerged during the Renaissance" (5).

10. Baum, best known for his Oz books, also wrote a popular book on department store window displays, *The Show Window* (Leach 60–61).

11. Hilgart claims that Daisy is a "mere place-holder object," that "Gatsby has not advanced his quest, merely transferred it to the illusion of the commodity—itself incarnated in Daisy's house—and thereafter to its idealized *consumer,* Daisy" (102).

12. Simmel observes: "Objects are not difficult to acquire because they are valuable, but we call those objects valuable that resist our desire to possess them" (*Philosophy of Money* 67).

13. In "Unpacking My Library" Benjamin describes collecting as a "process of renewal," one that allies collectors with children, who experience such "renewal of existence in a hundred unfailing ways." He continues, "To renew the old world—that is the collector's deepest desire" (61).

14. Baudrillard believes, for example, that consumption becomes a reason for living, and that it can never be satisfied (*System of Objects* 204–5). See also Lears's *Fables of Abundance* for a discussion of "the perfectionist project" in advertising.

15. Baudrillard associates the act of collecting with desire and the attempt to transcend the cycle of life and death: "A person who collects is dead, but he literally survives himself through his collection, which (even while he lives) duplicates him infinitely, beyond death, *by integrating death itself into the series, into the cycle*" (*System of Objects* 97).

16. Pearce describes the fetish collection as one "made by people whose imaginations identify with the objects which they desire. Powerful emotions are aroused by the objects which the objects seem to return, stimulating a need to gather more and more of the same kind. . . . The whole process is a deployment of the possessive self, a strategy of desire, and this is part of the reason why this mode of collecting is described as fetishistic" (*Museums, Objects, and Collections* 81). Pearce's example of such a collector is Sigmund Freud, who assembled an astonishing "1,900 pieces of Roman, Greek, Assyrian, Egyptian, and Chinese antiquities" (73), all of which he kept in two rooms where he did most of his work.

17. I am indebted to one of the anonymous reviewers of this manuscript for this observation.

18. While Pearce attempts to sidestep the sexual connotations of the word "fetish," she acknowledges that the term can "help to give us an understanding of the fierce energy which can be directed towards collection-making" (*Museums, Objects, and Collections* 82). Posnock reads Gatsby's displaying of the shirts to Daisy is "a symbolic sexual act" (208).

19. In "The Cultural Biography of Things," Kopytoff writes that objects are considered "sacred" when they are no longer available for commoditization (73).

20. Appadurai defines "tournaments of value" as "complex periodic events that are removed in some culturally well-defined way from the routines of economic life. Participation in them is likely to be both a privilege of those in power and an instrument of status contests between them. The currency of such tournaments is also likely to be set apart through well understood cultural diacritics. Finally, what is at issue in such tournaments is not just status, rank, fame, or reputation of actors, but the disposition of the central tokens of value in the society in question" (21).

21. This attitude toward social climbers is reflected in Gabriel Tarde's *The Laws of Imitation*, published in 1903.

22. Baudrillard addresses this social function of objects in *For a Critique of the Political Economy of the Sign*.

23. As a study by W. Lloyd Warner, Marchia Meeker, and Kenneth Eells indicates: "Something more than a large income is necessary for high social position. Money must be translated into socially approved behavior and possessions, and they in turn must be translated into intimate participation with, and acceptance by, members of a superior class" (195)

24. This is reminiscent of the medieval world of carnival described by Mikhail Bakhtin in *Rabelais and His World*, a world on "the borderline between art and life" (7).

25. Belk credits fairs and expositions with an important role in the process of "legitimizing consumer culture" (*Collecting in a Consumer Society* 12).

26. For example, Clifford contends: "The curiosities of the New World gathered and appreciated in the sixteenth century were not necessarily valued as antiquities, the products of primitive or 'past' civilizations. They frequently occupied a category of the marvelous, of a present 'Golden Age'" (222). The American 1920s represent another such "golden age," at least on the surface.

27. As Baudrillard explains in *The System of Objects*, "The systematic and limitless process of consumption arises from the disappointed demand for totality that underlies the project of life. . . . Consumption is irrepressible, in the last reckoning, because it is founded upon a *lack*" (205).

28. According to Pearce, "Systematic collection depends upon principles of organization, which are perceived to have an external reality beyond the specific material under consideration. . . . [It] works not by the accumulation of samples . . . but by the selection of examples intended to stand for all the others of their kind and to complete a set" (*Museums, Objects, and Collections* 87).

29. Baudrillard describes pets as "an intermediate category between human beings and objects. The pathos-laden presence of a dog, a cat, a tortoise or a canary is a testimonial to a failure of the interhuman relationship and an attendant recourse to a narcissistic domestic universe where subjectivity finds fulfillment in the most quietistic way" (*System of Objects* 89). This intermediate category includes children such as Daisy's daughter, who seems to exist purely as an object for display and status (after all, the ideal American couple cannot be childless), as well as the women who bear them.

30. In "Teddy Bear Patriarchy: Taxidermy in the Garden of Eden, New York City, 1908–1936," Donna Harraway discusses the connection between eugenics and the American Museum of Natural History at the turn of the century. She observes that "the white supremacist author of *The Passing of the Great Race,* Madison Grant," was a museum trustee (57).

31. The novel is filled with sly allusions to the fake or counterfeit, such as the reference to Belasco. As the notes to *Trimalchio,* an earlier version of *Gatsby,* explain, Belasco was a "Broadway dramatist, producer, and director . . . known for the realistic illusions created by his sets" (169).

32. See Baudrillard, *System of Objects,* on this aspect of collecting.

33. While I am not unaware of the irony of a "daisy" serving as a symbol of death, this connection is not without precedent, as the phrase "pushing up daisies" (a metaphor for death) suggests. As one of the anonymous reviewers of this manuscript observed, Fitzgerald apparently named Daisy Buchanan after James's Daisy Miller—a wildflower that blossoms in spring and then dies.

34. According to Stewart, the souvenir "will not function without the supplementary narrative discourse that both attaches to its origins and creates a myth with regard to those origins." This "narrative of origins" is "a narrative of interiority and authenticity. It is not a narrative of the object; it is a narrative of the possessor" (136).

35. Reflecting on the movement from private to public that many collections underwent in Milan in the sixteenth century, Shelton points out: "This transfer to the public gallery of sumptuous private property, paralleling a change in its perception from souvenirs to the 'great world' metaphor, consecrated collecting as an expression of the worthiness of an individual life. Private biography was thereby magnified and projected through public exhibition" (186–87).

36. Kenseth uses the examples of painters such as Michelangelo and Bernini and of Giacomo Torelli, the stage designer, but also those who worked in fields such as architecture, science, and landscape design (39).

Works Cited

Agnew, Jean-Christophe. "A House of Fiction: Domestic Interiors and the Commodity Aesthetic." *Consuming Visions: Accumulation and Display of Goods in America, 1880–1920.* Ed. Simon J. Bronner. New York: Norton, 1989. 133–55.

Aldrich, Nelson W., Jr. *Old Money: The Mythology of America's Upper Class.* New York: Knopf, 1988.

Appadurai, Arjun. "Commodities and the Politics of Value." Introduction. *The Social Life of Things: Commodities in Cultural Perspective.* Ed. Arjun Appadurai. New York: Cambridge UP, 1986. 3–63.

Bakhtin, Mikhail. *Rabelais and His World.* Trans. Hélène Iswolsky. 2nd ed. Bloomington: Indiana UP, 1984.

Baltzell, E. Digby. "*Who's Who in America* and *The Social Register:* Elite and Upper Class Indexes in Metropolitan America." *Class, Status, and Power: Social Stratification in Comparative Perspective.* Ed. Reinhard Bendix and Seymour Martin Lipset. 2nd ed. New York: Free Press, 1966. 266–75.

Baudrillard, Jean. *For a Critique of the Political Economy of the Sign.* Trans. Charles Levin. New York: Telos, 1981.

——. "The System of Collecting." *The Cultures of Collecting.* Ed. John Elsner and Roger Cardinal. Cambridge: Harvard UP, 1994. 7–24.

——. *The System of Objects.* 1968. Trans. James Benedict. London and New York: Verso, 1996.

Belk, Russell W. *Collecting in a Consumer Society.* London and New York: Routledge, 1995.

——. "Collectors and Collecting." *Advances in Consumer Research* 15 (1988): 548–53. Rpt. in *Interpreting Objects and Collections.* Ed. Susan M. Pearce. London and New York: Routledge, 1994. 317–26.

Benjamin, Walter. "On the Mimetic Faculty." *Reflections: Essays, Aphorisms, Autobiographical Writings*. Ed. Peter Demetz. Trans. Edmund Jephcott. New York and London: Harcourt Brace Jovanovich, 1978. 333–36.

——. "Unpacking My Library." *Illuminations*. 1955. New York: Schocken, 1969. 59–67.

——. "The Work of Art in the Age of Mechanical Reproduction." *Illuminations*. 1955. New York: Schocken, 1969. 217–52.

Benstock, Shari, ed. *Case Studies in Contemporary Criticism:* The House of Mirth. Boston and New York: Bedford Books of St. Martin's, 1994.

Bentley, Nancy. *The Ethnography of Manners: Hawthorne, James, Wharton*. Cambridge: Cambridge UP, 1995.

Berman, Marshall. *The Politics of Authenticity: Radical Individualism and the Emergence of Modern Society*. New York: Macmillan, 1970.

Berman, Ronald. *The Great Gatsby and Modern Times*. Urbana and Chicago: U of Illinois P, 1994.

"Bibelot." *Oxford English Dictionary Online*. 2nd ed. 1989. Oxford English Dictionary. Aug. 1, 2003 <http://dictionary.oed.com.ezproxy.shu.edu/>.

Blackham, H. J. "An Introduction to Existentialist Thinking." *Reality, Man, and Existence: Essential Works of Existentialism*. Ed. H. J. Blackham. New York: Bantam, 1965. 1–15.

Blackmer, Corrine. "The Veils of the Law: Race and Sexuality in Nella Larsen's *Passing*." *Race-ing Representation: Voice, History, and Sexuality*. Ed. Kostas Myrsiades and Linda Myrsiades. Lanham: Rowman & Littlefield, 1998. 98–116.

Blais, Andrée, ed. *Text in the Exhibition Medium*. Montreal: Société des musées québécois, 1995.

Blodgett, Harold W., and Sculley Bradley, eds. *Collected Writings of Walt Whitman:* Leaves of Grass, *Comprehensive Reader's Edition*. New York: New York UP, 1965.

Bourdieu, Pierre. *Distinction: A Social Critique of the Judgment of Taste*. Trans. Richard Nice. Cambridge: Harvard UP, 1984.

——. *Language and Symbolic Power*. Trans. Gino Raymond and Matthew Adamson. Cambridge: Harvard UP, 1991.

Bowlby, Rachel. *Just Looking: Consumer Culture in Dreiser, Gissing, and Zola*. New York: Methuen, 1985.

Branch, Michael. "Indexing American Possibilities: The Natural History Writing of Bartram, Wilson, and Audubon." *The Ecocriticism Reader: Landmarks in Literary Ecology*. Ed. Cheryll Glotfelty and Harold Fromm. Athens: U of Georgia P, 1996. 282–302.

Breitwieser, Mitchell. "Jazz Fractures: F. Scott Fitzgerald and Epochal Representation." *American Literary History* 12.3 (2000): 359–81.

Brody, Jennifer DeVere. "Clare Kendry's 'True' Colors: Race and Class Conflict in Nella Larsen's *Passing*." *Callaloo* 15.4 (1992): 1053–65.

Bruccoli, Matthew J. *F. Scott Fitzgerald's* The Great Gatsby: *A Literary Reference*. New York: Carroll & Graff, 2000.

Bryce, James. *The American Commonwealth*. 1893. New York: Macmillan, 1921.

Burns, Sarah. "The Price of Beauty: Art, Commerce, and the Late Nineteenth-Century American Studio Interior." *American Iconology: New Approaches to Nineteenth-Century Art and Literature.* Ed. David C. Miller. New Haven and London: Yale UP, 1993. 209–38.

Butler, Judith. *Bodies That Matter: On the Discursive Limits of "Sex."* New York and London: Routledge, 1993.

Carby, Hazel. *Reconstructing Womanhood: The Emergence of the Afro-American Woman Novelist.* London and New York: Oxford UP, 1987.

Carr, Brian. "Paranoid Interpretation, Desire's Nonobject, and Nella Larsen's *Passing.*" *PMLA* 119.2 (March 2004): 282–95.

Carson, Benjamin. "'That Doubled Vision': Edith Wharton and *The House of Mirth.*" *Women's Studies* 32.6 (September 2003): 695–717.

Cawelti, John G. *Apostles of the Self-Made Man.* Chicago: U of Chicago P, 1965.

Chase, Richard. *The American Novel and Its Tradition.* Baltimore: Johns Hopkins UP, 1957.

Christian, Barbara. *Black Women Novelists: The Development of a Tradition, 1892–1976.* Westport, CT: Greenwood, 1980.

"Cicerone." *Oxford English Dictionary Online.* 2nd ed. 1989. Oxford English Dictionary. July 1, 2004 <http://dictionary.oed.com.ezproxy.shu.edu/>.

Clemens, Samuel Langhorne. *Adventures of Huckleberry Finn.* Ed. Sculley Bradley, Richmond Croom Beatty, E. Hudson Long, and Thomas Cooley. New York: Norton, 1977.

Clifford, James. *The Predicament of Culture: Twentieth-Century Ethnography, Literature, and Art.* Cambridge and London: Harvard UP, 1988.

Conn, Steven. *Museums and American Intellectual Life, 1876–1926.* Chicago and London: U of Chicago P, 1998.

"Correspondence." *Oxford English Dictionary Online.* 2nd ed. 1989. Oxford English Dictionary. Aug. 15, 2004 <http://dictionary.oed.com.ezproxy.shu.edu/>.

"Counterfeit." *Oxford English Dictionary Online.* 2nd ed. 1989. Oxford English Dictionary. Aug. 15, 2004 <http://dictionary.oed.com.ezproxy.shu.edu/>.

Crew, Spencer R., and James E. Sims. "Locating Authenticity: Fragments of a Dialogue." *Exhibiting Cultures: The Poetics and Politics of Museum Display.* Ed. Ivan Korp and Steven D. Lavine. Washington, DC and London: Smithsonian Institution Press, 1991. 159–75.

Cutter, Martha J. "Sliding Significations: Passing as a Narrative and Textual Strategy in Nella Larsen's Fiction." *Passing and the Fictions of Identity.* Ed. Elaine K. Ginsberg. Durham and London: Duke UP, 1996. 75–100.

Davis, F. James. *Who Is Black? One Nation's Definition.* University Park: Pennsylvania State UP, 1991.

de Grazia, Victoria, and Ellen Furlough, eds. *The Sex of Things: Gender and Consumption in Historical Perspective.* Berkeley: U of California P, 1996.

de Marly, Diana. *Worth: Father of Haute Couture.* London: Elm Tree, 1980.

Dempsey, Terrell. *Searching for Jim: Slavery in Sam Clemens's World.* Columbia and London: U of Missouri P, 2003.

Dias, Nelia. "The Visibility of Difference: Nineteenth-Century French Anthropological Collections." *The Politics of Display: Museums, Science, and Culture.* Ed. Sharon Mac-Donald. New York: Routledge, 1998. 36–52.

Dimock, Wai-Chee. "Debasing Exchange: Edith Wharton's *The House of Mirth.*" Benstock 375–90.

Donaldson, Scott. "Possessions in *The Great Gatsby.*" *Southern Review* 37.2 (Spring 2001): 187–210.

Douglas, Mary, and Baron Isherwood. *The World of Goods: Towards an Anthropology of Consumption.* London and New York: Routledge, 1979.

Doyno, Victor. "The Composition of *Adventures of Huckleberry* Finn." Harris 9–17.

Ellenberger, Henri F. *The Discovery of the Unconscious: The History and Evolution of Dynamic Psychiatry.* New York: Basic, 1970.

Erkkila, Betsy. *Whitman the Political Poet.* London and New York: Oxford UP, 1989.

Esch, Deborah, ed. *New Essays on* The House of Mirth. Cambridge: Cambridge UP, 2001.

Evans, Caroline. "The Enchanted Spectacle." *Fashion Theory* 5.3 (Sept. 2001): 271–310.

Fadiman, Clifton. "A Note on 'The Real Thing.'" *The Short Stories of Henry James.* Ed. Clifton Fadiman. New York: Modern Library, 1945. 216–17.

Favor, J. Martin. *Authentic Blackness: The Folk in the New Negro Renaissance.* Durham and London: Duke UP, 1999.

Fishkin, Shelley Fisher. *Was Huck Black? Mark Twain and African American Voices.* London and New York: Oxford UP, 1993.

Fitzgerald, F. Scott. *The Great Gatsby.* New York: Charles Scribner's Sons, 1953.

———. *Trimalchio: An Early Version of* The Great Gatsby. Cambridge: Cambridge UP, 2000.

Folsom, Ed. "'This Heart's Geography's Map': The Photographs of Walt Whitman." *Walt Whitman Quarterly Review* 4 (Fall–Winter 1896–87): 1–76.

———. *Walt Whitman's Native Representations.* Cambridge: Cambridge UP, 1997.

"Ford." *Oxford English Dictionary Online.* 2nd ed. 1989. Oxford English Dictionary. July 1, 2003 <http://dictionary.oed.com.ezproxy.shu.edu/>.

Forty, Adrian. *Objects of Desire.* New York: Pantheon, 1986.

Frazier, E. Franklin. *Black Bourgeoisie.* New York: Free Press, 1957.

Furnas, J. C. *Americans: A Social History of the United States, 1587–1914.* New York: G. P. Putnam's Sons, 1969.

Gamman, Lorraine, and Margaret Marshment, eds. Introduction. *The Female Gaze: Women as Viewers of Popular Culture.* Seattle: Real Comet, 1989. 1–7.

Gatewood, Willard B. *Aristocrats of Color: The Black Elite, 1880–1920.* Bloomington and Indianapolis: Indiana UP, 1990.

Ginsberg, Elaine K. "The Politics of Passing." Introduction. *Passing and the Fictions of Identity.* Ed. Elaine K. Ginsberg. Durham and London: Duke UP, 1996. 1–18.

Godden, Richard. *Fictions of Capital: The American Novel from James to Mailer.* New York: Cambridge UP, 1990.

"Grange." *Oxford English Dictionary Online.* 2nd ed. 1989. Oxford English Dictionary. July 1, 2003 <http://dictionary.oed.com.ezproxy.shu.edu/>.

Greenblatt, Stephen. *Marvelous Possessions: The Wonder of the New World*. Chicago: U of Chicago P, 1991.

Grossman, Jay. *Reconstituting the American Renaissance: Emerson, Whitman, and the Politics of Representation*. Durham and London: Duke UP, 2003.

Gunn, Giles. "F. Scott Fitzgerald's *Gatsby* and the Imagination of Wonder." *Journal of the American Academy of Religion* 41 (1973): 171–83.

Hallock, Thomas. "'On the Borders of a New World': Ecology, Frontier Plots, and Imperial Elegy in William Bartram's *Travels*." *South-Atlantic-Review* 66.4 (Fall 2001): 109–33.

Halttunen, Karen. *Confidence Men and Painted Women: A Study of Middle-Class Cultures in America, 1830–1870*. New Haven: Yale UP, 1986.

Harraway, Donna. "Teddy Bear Patriarchy: Taxidermy in the Garden of Eden, New York City, 1908–1936." *Social Text* 11 (Winter 1984–85): 20–64. Rpt. in *Primate Visions: Gender, Race and Nature in the World of Modern Science*. London and New York: Routledge: 1989. 26–58.

Harris, Susan K., ed. *Adventures of Huckleberry Finn: Complete Text with Introduction, Historical Contexts, and Critical Essays*. Boston and New York: Houghton Mifflin, 2000.

Hepburn, Allan. "A Passion for Things: Cicerones, Collectors, and Taste in Edith Wharton's Fiction." *American Quarterly* 54.4 (Winter 1998): 25–52.

Hilgart, John. "*The Great Gatsby*'s Aesthetics of Non-identity." *Arizona Quarterly* 59.1 (Spring 2003): 87–116.

Hill, Hamlin. *Mark Twain's Letters to His Publishers, 1867–1894*. Berkeley and Los Angeles: U of California P, 1975.

Hofstadter, Richard. *Social Darwinism in American Thought, 1860–1915*. Philadelphia: U of Pennsylvania P, 1945.

Hollander, Ann. *Seeing through Clothes*. New York: Avon, 1975.

Howard, Maureen. "On *The House of Mirth*." *Raritan* 15.3 (Winter 1996): 1–22.

Hull, Gloria, et al., eds. *All the Women Are White, All the Blacks Are Men, but Some of Us Are Brave: Black Women's Studies*. Old Westbury, NY: Feminist P, 1982.

Hutchinson, George. "Nella Larsen and the Veil of Race." *American Literary History* 9 (1997): 329–49.

Irmscher, Christoph. *The Poetics of Natural History: From John Bartram to William James*. New Brunswick, NJ and London: Rutgers UP, 1999.

James, Henry. "The Real Thing." *Collected Stories*. Ed. John Bayley. Vol. 2. New York and Toronto: Everyman's Library/Alfred A. Knopf, 1999. 39–65.

Johnson, Claudia Durst. *Understanding* Adventures of Huckleberry Finn. Westport: Greenwood, 1996.

Johnson, Paul. *A History of the American People*. New York: HarperCollins, 1997.

Jones, Mark, "Why Fakes?" Introduction. *Fake? The Art of Deception*. Ed. Mark Jones, with Paul Craddock and Nicolas Barker. Berkeley and Los Angeles: U of California P, 1990. 11–22.

Kaplan, Amy. *The Social Construction of American Realism*. Urbana and Chicago: U of Illinois P, 1988.

Kaplan, Justin, ed. *Walt Whitman: Complete Poetry and Collected Prose*. New York: Library of America, 1982.

Keenan, William J. F., ed. "*Sartor Resartus* Restored: Dress Studies in Carlylean Perspective." Introduction. *Dressed to Impress: Looking the Part*. London and New York: Berg, 2001. 1–49.

Kenseth, Joy, ed. "The Age of the Marvelous: An Introduction." *The Age of the Marvelous*. Hanover NH: Hood Museum of Art/Dartmouth College, 1991. 25–59.

Kopytoff, Igor. "The Cultural Biography of Things: Commoditization as Process." *The Social Life of Things: Commodities in Cultural Perspective*. Ed. Arjun Appadurai. New York: Cambridge UP, 1986. 64–91.

Kravitz, Bennett. "Reinventing the World and Reinventing the Self in *Huck Finn*." *Papers on Language and Literature* 40.1 (Winter 2004): 3–27.

Kruse, Horst. "The Museum Motif in English and American Fiction of the Nineteenth Century." *Amerikastudien/American-Studies* 31.1 (1986): 71–79.

Larsen, Nella. *Passing: An Intimation of Things Distant. The Collected Fiction of Nella Larsen*. Ed. Charles R. Larson. New York: Doubleday, 1992. 163–275.

Leach, William. *Land of Desire: Merchants, Power, and the Rise of a New American Culture*. New York: Vintage, 1993.

Lears, Jackson. *Fables of Abundance: A Cultural History of Advertising in America*. New York: Basic, 1994.

Lindberg, Gary. *The Confidence Man in American Literature*. London and New York: Oxford UP, 1982.

Loebel, Thomas. "Beyond Her Self." Esch 107–32.

Lubin, David M. "A Manly Art: American *Trompe l'oeil* and the Manufacture of Masculinity." *The Material Culture of Gender: The Gender of Material Culture*. Ed. Katharine Martinez and Kenneth L. Ames. Hanover and London: UP of New England, 1997. 365–91.

Lurie, Alison. *The Language of Clothes*. New York: Vintage, 1983.

Martin, Terence. *Parables of Possibility: The American Need for Beginnings*. New York: Columbia UP, 1995.

Marzio, Peter C. *The Democratic Art: Pictures for a Nineteenth-Century America*. Boston: David R. Godine, 1979.

Matt, Susan J. "Frocks, Finery, and Feelings: Rural and Urban Women's Envy, 1890–1930." *An Emotional History of the United States*. Ed. Peter N. Stearns and Jen Lewis. New York: New York UP, 1998. 377–95.

McDowell, Deborah. Introduction. Quicksand *and* Passing. New Brunswick, NJ: Rutgers UP, 1986.

McLendon, Jacquelyn Y. *The Politics of Color in the Fiction of Jessie Fauset and Nella Larsen*. Charlottesville: UP of Virginia, 1995.

Meehan, Sean. "Specimen Daze: Whitman's Photobiography." *Biography* 22.4 (Fall 1999): 477–516.

"Memento." *Oxford English Dictionary Online*. 2nd. ed. 1989. Oxford English Dictionary. Aug. 1, 2004 <http://dictionary.oed.com.ezproxy.shu.edu/>.

Mensch, Elaine, and Harry Mensch. *Black, White, and Huckleberry Finn: Reimagining the American Dream*. Tuscaloosa and London: U of Alabama P, 2000.

Messent, Peter. *New Readings of the American Novel: Narrative Theory and Its Application*. New York: St. Martin's, 1990.

Michaels, Walter Benn. *The Gold Standard and the Logic of Naturalism: American Literature at the Turn of the Century*. Berkeley and Los Angeles: U of California P, 1987.

Mitchell, Lee Clark. "'Nobody but Our Gang Warn't Around': The Authority of Language in *Huckleberry Finn*. *New Essays on* Adventures of Huckleberry Finn. Ed. Louis J. Budd. Cambridge: Cambridge UP, 1985. 83–106.

Monteiro, George. "Carraway's Complaint." *Journal of Modern Literature* 24.1 (Fall 2000): 161–71.

Mulvey, Laura. "Visual Pleasure and Narrative Cinema." *Contemporary Film Theory*. Ed. Antony Easthope. London: Longman, 1993. 111–24.

Nadel, Alan. *Invisible Criticism: Ralph Ellison and the American Canon*. Iowa City: U of Iowa P, 1988.

Norris, Margot. "Death by Speculation: Deconstructing *The House of Mirth*." Benstock 431–46.

Orvell, Miles. *The Real Thing: Imitation and Authenticity in American Culture, 1880–1940*. Chapel Hill: U of North Carolina P, 1989.

Pearce, Susan M. *Collecting in Contemporary Practice*. London and New Delhi: Sage, 1998.

———. *Museums, Objects, and Collections: A Cultural Study*. Washington, DC: Smithsonian Institution Press, 1992.

———. *On Collecting: An Investigation into Collecting in the European Tradition*. New York and London: Routledge, 1995.

Peiss, Kathy. "Making Up, Making Over: Cosmetics, Consumer Culture, and Women's Identity." de Grazia and Furlough 311–36.

Pomian, Krzysztof. *Collectors and Curiosities: Paris and Venice, 1500–1800*. Trans. Elizabeth Wiles-Portier. Cambridge, UK: Polity, 1990.

Posnock, Ross. "'A New World, Material without Being Real': Fitzgerald's Critique of Capitalism in *The Great Gatsby*. *Critical Essays on F. Scott Fitzgerald's* The Great Gatsby. Ed. Scott Donaldson. Boston: GK Hall, 1984. 201–13.

Quay, Sara Elisabeth. "Edith Wharton's Narrative of Inheritance." *American Literary Realism* 29.3 (1997): 26–48.

Regis, Pamela. *Describing Early America: Bartram, Jefferson, Crevecoeur, and the Rhetoric of Natural History*. DeKalb: Northern Illinois UP, 1992.

Restuccia, Frances L. "The Name of the Lily: Edith Wharton's Feminism(s)." Benstock 404–18.

Reynolds, David. *Walt Whitman's America: A Cultural Biography*. New York: Alfred A. Knopf, 1995.

Robinson, Lillian. "The Traffic in Women: A Cultural Critique of *The House of Mirth*." Benstock 340–58.

Saisselin, Rémy G. *The Bourgeois and the Bibelot*. New Brunswick, NJ: Rutgers UP, 1984.

Sattelmeyer, Robert. "Steamboats, Cocaine, and Paper Money: Mark Twain Rewriting Himself." *Constructing Mark Twain; New Directions in Scholarship.* Ed. Laura E. Skandera Trombley and Michael J. Kiskis. Columbia and London: U of Missouri P, 2001. 87–100.

Schlereth, Thomas J. *Victorian America: Transformations in Everyday Life, 1876–1915.* New York: HarperPerennial, 1991.

Schwartz, Hillel. *The Culture of the Copy.* New York: Zone, 1996.

Secara, Maggie. "Who Wears What I: Enforcing Statutes of Apparel" [Greenwich, June 15, 1574, 16 Elizabeth I]. *Elizabethan Sumptuary Laws.* Aug. 13, 2004 <http://renaissance. dm.net/sumptuary/who-wears-what.html>.

Serrell, Beverly. *Exhibit Labels: An Interpretive Approach.* Walnut Creek, CA: AltaMira, 1996.

Shelton, Anthony Alan. "Cabinets of Transgression: Renaissance Collections and the Incorporation of the New World." *The Cultures of Collecting.* Ed. John Elsner and Roger Cardinal. Cambridge: Harvard UP, 1994. 177–203.

Simmel, Georg. "The Philosophy of Fashion." Trans. M. Ritter and D. Frisby. *Simmel on Culture.* Ed. D. Frisby and M. Featherstone. London and New Delhi: Sage, 1997. 192–203. Rpt. in *The Consumption Reader.* Ed. David B. Clarke, Marcus A. Doel, and Kate M. L. Housiaux. London and New York: Routledge, 2003. 238–45.

———. *The Philosophy of Money.* Trans. Tom Bottomore and David Frisby. London, Henley; Boston: Routledge and Kegan Paul, 1978.

Sinfield, Alan. "Art as Cultural Production." *Literary Theories: A Reader and Guide.* Ed. Julian Wolfreys. Washington Square: New York UP, 1999. 626–45.

Singh, Amritjit. *The Novels of the Harlem Renaissance.* State College: Pennsylvania State UP, 1976.

Smith, David L. "Huck, Jim, and American Racial Discourse." Harris 356–69.

Solomon-Godeau, Abigail. "The Other Side of Venus: The Visual Economy of Feminine Display." de Grazia and Furlough 113–50.

"Specimen." *Oxford English Dictionary Online.* 2nd ed. 1989. Oxford English Dictionary. Aug. 1, 2003 <http://dictionary.oed.com.ezproxy.shu.edu/>.

Stewart, Susan. *On Longing: Narratives of the Miniature, the Gigantic, the Souvenir, the Collection.* Baltimore and London: Johns Hopkins UP, 1984.

Sumner, William Graham. *Folkways.* 1907.

Swann, Marjorie. *Curiosities and Texts: The Culture of Collecting in Early Modern England.* Philadelphia: U of Pennsylvania P, 2001.

Tarde, Gabriel. *The Laws of Imitation.* Trans. E. C. Parsons. New York: Henry Holt, 1903.

Tate, Claudia. "Nella Larsen's *Passing:* A Problem of Interpretation." *Black American Literature Forum* 14.4 (1980): 142–46.

Taussig, Michael. *Mimesis and Alterity: A Particular History of the Senses.* New York and London: Routledge, 1993.

Taylor, Charles. *The Ethics of Authenticity.* Cambridge and London: Harvard UP, 1991.

Thompson, Michael. *Rubbish Theory: The Creation and Destruction of Value.* London and New York: Oxford UP, 1979.

Totten, Gary. "The Art and Architecture of the Self: Designing the 'I'-Witness in Edith Wharton's *The House of Mirth. College Literature* 27.3 (Fall 2000): 71–87.

Trachtenberg. Alan. "The Form of Freedom in *Huckleberry Finn.*" Harris 345–56.

———. *The Incorporation of America.* New York: Hill & Wang, 1982.

Trilling, Lionel. *Sincerity and Authenticity.* Cambridge: Harvard UP, 1972.

Twain, Mark. *Life on the Mississippi.* 1883. New York: P. F. Collier, 1917.

Veblen, Thorstein. *The Theory of the Leisure Class.* New York: Mentor, 1953.

Wald, Gayle. *Crossing the Line: Racial Passing in Twentieth-Century U.S. Literature and Culture.* Durham and London: Duke UP, 2000.

Wall, Cheryl. "Passing for What? Aspects of Identity in Nella Larsen's Novels." *Black American Literature Forum* 20.1–2 (1986): 97–111.

Wallach, Alan. "On the Problem of Forming a National Art Collection in the United States: William Wilson Corcoran's Failed National Gallery." *The Formation of National Collections of Art and Archaeology.* Ed. Gwendolyn Wright. Washington, DC: National Gallery of Art, 1996. 113–25.

Walsh, Kevin. *The Representation of the Past: Museums and Heritage in the Post-modern World.* London and New York: Routledge, 1992.

Warner, W. Lloyd, Marchia Meeker, and Kenneth Eells. "Social Class in America." *Social Stratification: Class, Race, and Gender in Sociological Perspective.* Ed. David B. Grusky. Boulder: Westview, 1994. 190–96.

Washington, Mary Helen. *Invented Lives: Narratives of Black Women, 1860–1960.* New York: Anchor-Doubleday, 1987.

Wharton, Edith. *A Backward Glance.* New York: D. Appleton-Century, 1934.

———. *The House of Mirth. Edith Wharton: Novels.* Ed. R. W. B. Lewis. New York: Library of America, 1985. 3–347.

Wharton, Edith, and Ogden Codman, Jr. *The Decoration of Houses.* 1897. *The Revised and Expanded American Classical Edition.* New York and London: Norton, 1997.

Whitman, Walt. *The Correspondence.* Ed. Edwin Haviland Miller. Vol. 3. New York: New York UP, 1964.

———. *Leaves of Grass.* New York: Modern Library, 1980.

———. *Memoranda.* J. Kaplan 1276–1301.

———. "Of the Terrible Doubt of Appearances." J. Kaplan 274–75.

———. *Prose Works.* Ed. Floyd Stovall. Vol. 1. New York: New York UP, 1963.

———. "Shakspere-Bacon's Cipher." "Second Annex: Good-bye My Fancy." J. Kaplan 643.

———. "Song of the Exposition." Kaplan 341–50.

———. *Specimen Days and Collect.* Kaplan 689–927.

Wieck, Carl F. *Refiguring* Huckleberry Finn. Athens: U of Georgia P, 2000.

Wolff, Cythia Griffin. *A Feast of Words: The Triumph of Edith Wharton.* London and New York: Oxford UP, 1977.

———. "Lily Bart and Masquerade Inscribed in the Female Mode." *Wretched Exotic: Essays on Edith Wharton in Europe.* Ed. Katherine Joslin and Alan Price. New York: Peter Lang, 1993. 259–94.

Womack, Kenneth. "Theorising Culture, Reading Ourselves." Introduction. *Literary*

Theories: A Reader and Guide. Ed. Julian Wolfreys. Washington Square, NY: New York UP, 1999. 593–603.

Wyllie, Irvin G. *The Self-Made Man in America: The Myth of Rags to Riches.* New York: Free Press, 1954.

Yeazell, Ruth Barnard. "The Conspicuous Wasting of Lily Bart." Esch 15–41.

Youmans, Mary Mabel. "The Other Side of Harlem: The Middle-Class Novel and the New Negro Renaissance." Dissertation-Abstracts-International. Ann Arbor, MI, 1977.

Zackodnik, Teresa. "Passing Transgressions and Authentic Identity in Jessie Fauset's *Plum Bun* and Nella Larsen's *Passing.*" *Literature and Racial Ambiguity.* Ed. Teresa Hubel and Neil Brooks. Amsterdam and New York: Rodopi, 2002. 45–69.

Index